D1556991

TERRIBLE TRAIL:

THE MEEK CUTOFF, 1845

PLATE I: Stephen H.L. Meek, trapper and mountain man,
as he appeared in later years.

TERRIBLE TRAIL:

THE MEEK CUTOFF, 1845

By
KEITH CLARK
and
LOWELL TILLER

ILLUSTRATED WITH PHOTOGRAPHS
AND MAPS

MAVERICK PUBLICATIONS, INC.

— *A Maverick Publication* —

ISBN 0-89288-233-6

Library of Congress Cataloging-in-Publication Data

Clark, Keith, 1925-
        Terrible trail :   the Meek Cutoff, 1845 / by Keith
Clark and Lowell Tiller.
            p.   cm.
        Includes bibliographical references and index.
        ISBN 0-89288-233-6   : $14.95
            1. Oregon----History----To 1859.   2. Meek, Stephen
Hall, 1805-1889. 3. Overland journeys to the Pacific.
I. Tiller, Lowell, 1925- .   II. Title.
F880.C57   1966
979.5' 03----dc20   93-16761
                                                                  CIP

Maverick Publications, Inc.
P.O. Box 5007
Bend, Oregon 97708

To
Leah Collins Menefee,
in memoriam

AUTHORS' NOTES

O N THE following pages the authors have submitted for reader interest and edification the results of time and research, not only on the part of the authors but also of many, many people who volunteered information, answered letters, copied family material, directed to other sources, and generally confirmed the authors' belief in humanity.

The contents of this book represent not only our interest but the interest and information of people across the state, and across the nation. We take this opportunity to thank them all, and to hope that our efforts are acceptable. We have taken the utmost pains with authenticity. Where we did not find an answer, or where we guessed, we indicated that such was the case.

The reader may question the amount of quotation encompassed within these pages, but there are, we believe, good reasons for its inclusion. It has seemed necessary to give more than one account in places where documentation by an acceptable source did not exist.

Furthermore we felt that the words of those who experienced or witnessed the happenings chronicled here held more color and more validity than our own. They said it better.

This 1993 edition, on the 150th anniversary of the Oregon trail, contains the original text. Some first edition errors have been corrected, some photographs changed or deleted; some additional roster information sent by descendants in the years since 1966 has been included. Acknowledgements made in 1966 continue with one or two small changes.

ACKNOWLEDGMENTS

WERE it not for the efforts of interested people, this work would never have been written. Librarians, homesteaders, descendants, historians—all helped.

In determining the route, the contributions of these persons were vital: Gene Clark, of Pasadena, California; Del Ninshaw, Bert Houston, Bend, Oregon; Mrs. Leah Collins Menefee, Eugene, Oregon; Charles Porfily, Redmond, Oregon; Robert Porfily, Prineville, Oregon; Cecil and Velda McKenzie, Prineville, Oregon; Cleon and Wanda Clark, formerly of Prineville, now of Redmond, Oregon; "Buck" Hankins, John Day, Oregon; Ken Kessler, Vale, Oregon; George Tackman, Prineville, Oregon; Tom Joyce, Beulah, Oregon.

We are grateful to Miss Priscilla Knuth and Tom Vaughan of the Oregon Historical Society, who helped us in every way possible. Mrs. Margaret Keillor, David Duniway, and Mrs. Mary Thompson of the Oregon State Library responded to every request for information; Mrs. Harriet Moore of the Oregon State University library and Dr. Martin Schmitt and staff of the Oregon Room at the University of Oregon were of great assistance. Also we thank the personnel of various county courthouses, historical societies, and libraries.

Carrying on the task of ordering and obtaining material on interlibrary loans were Mrs. Elizabeth Ward and Mrs. Al Peden, librarians for the city of Redmond, and James Baker and Don Lowry, former librarians of Redmond Union High School. Here, too, we must thank the Deschutes County Library at Bend, Oregon.

In the collection of personal data regarding the pioneers, very special thanks go to Mrs. Donna Wojcik, of Portland, and to Mrs. Menefee, of Eugene. Mrs. Mercedes Paul, of Tigard, Oregon; James R. Ellis, of Portland; Mr. and Mrs. Dell Brunell, of Coos River; Mrs. John Bowman of Whidbey Island, Washington; and Mrs. Sylvan Mullin, of Medford, Oregon, contributed to our cause.

A list of helpful descendants is in the Bibliography of this book. Much of the information submitted was not available in the libraries and we thank them for sharing it with us—Bible records, reminiscences, letters.

For the photographs here we credit Lambert Florin, of Portland; Mrs. Prince Staats, of Bend; the Bureau of Land Management; Malheur Wildlife Refuge; Oregon State Highway Commission; Stanley Clark, of Redmond; Child's Photographers; Priscilla Knuth, of Portland; Don Moody, Bend; Web Loy, Bend; and The Oregon Historical Society. The Territorial Documents are from the Archives, Oregon State Library.

And to all who responded to our appeal placed in various newspapers—whether the information was or was not used— we extend our gratitude. Many of those letters contained leads for further information.

FOREWORD

THOSE of us who are denizens of the interior of the state of Oregon (and east to the Snake River) absorb at some time in our growing up stories of the Oregon Trail emigrants, of lost trains, of gold nuggets. Perhaps because the country here is largely unchanged by the passage of a century, the stories seem more real to us than they may to residents of the great Willamette Valley. For whatever reason, the tales are romantic and enjoyable and mysterious.

Because man is curious, and the authors are no exception, we have, on the following pages, attempted to wipe away some of the mystery connected with Stephen Meek's Cutoff party of 1845, with two exceptions a small, commonplace incident in a time of many similar adventures connected with the great migrations of the middle nineteenth century.

The two exceptions make the story of the Cutoff notable:

(1) Meek's party got lost, wandered for a time, used up supplies, suffered sickness and deaths beyond the average.

(2) A portion of the group found gold nuggets, the discovery of which gave rise to the legend of the Blue Bucket Mine. That legend gave a name and starting point to consequences which rippled out through Oregon's subsequent history in the 1850's and 1860's, until the origin was submerged in complications like the eastern Oregon and Idaho gold rushes, and the growth of cattle ranching in eastern Oregon.

Because of the gold stories, the Meek route through Oregon was searched and prospected, and traced, in part. The passage of years, however, and the coming of many wheels to eastern Oregon confused and dimmed the route of the first lost train. Its memory remained, half legend, in sections along the way.

A careful reconstruction of pieces and tags, and a close scrutiny of terrain and water conditions have made it possible to reconstruct the Meek route almost entirely. In determining the route of these unfortunates of the Cutoff seven general factors have been helpful:

(1) Terrain and contemporary description.

(2) Mileage records given by Jesse Harritt, Samuel Parker, and James Field, emigrants of 1845. (Oxteams traveled, on the average, two to three miles per hour, depending upon weight of the load, terrain, and condition of the animals. Two miles per hour as a rough rule of thumb in computing the distances of a day's travel has proved surprisingly accurate. Ten to twelve miles was the daily average.)

(3) Some knowledge of the country between Vale and The Dalles.

(4) In part, information about the route of the 1853 Elliott party, most generously supplied by Leah Collins Menefee, of Eugene.[1]

(5) Knowledge of wagon travel by other pioneer groups which clarified the limitations of wagons and oxen. Those old prairie schooners, Conestoga or not, were admirable in many ways. Strong and sturdy, they allowed repair for most damages. However, they were forced to go comparatively straight uphill and down, or they would tip. Furthermore, they were difficult to work through rocky canyons and defiles, so that it became standard practice to "take to the ridges and points"

---

1   Mrs. Menefee's research on the 1853 Elliott party proved invaluable to us. Her kindness and her aid are deeply appreciated.

with the wagons, not descending to valleys or following ravines unless absolutely necessary. Hence wagon trails are, usually, considerably apart from Indian or trapper trails along streams. This latter fact has some bearing on Meek's difficulty in getting his people through.

(6) Lieutenant Dixon's maps of the expedition of Captain H. D. Wallen (1859) and of Major Enoch Steen (1860), together with maps drawn by Louis Scholl, a contemporary, which have been shared by Miss Priscilla Knuth, Oregon Historical Society.

(7) Knowledge by natives of local portions of country and of old legends of the trains, which, while considerably hazy and intertwined, still linger on in various sections of eastern Oregon and contain a slender thread of truth.

Who was responsible for the Cutoff? While history names various people, certainly the guide is a central figure.

Stephen H. L. Meek was a Virginian, born in Washington County, in 1805.[2] He was an older brother of Joseph Meek of Oregon fame, and one of fourteen children. At twenty he came to St. Louis where he worked for William Sublette in a fur warehouse "rumming" beaver hides. His older brother Hiram had a store and gristmill at Lexington, Missouri, and in 1829, Stephen worked for him. But finding the life of a store clerk too tame, in 1830[3] he went with Sublette and Robert Campbell to the fur rendezvous at Green River.

The life of a mountain man and the fur trade engaged his subsequent attention until the fur trade evaporated, together with the beaver hat. In 1833 he was with Bonneville's party (Walker), traveling through the Sierra. In 1834, again with Bonneville, he trapped John Day, Malheur, Owyhee, and

2 *Oregonian*, April 30, 1885, p. 2. (Taken largely from Meek's *Autobiography* which gives the same date.)
3 Fred Lockley, "Impressions and Observations of the Journal Man," *Oregon Journal* April 16, 1927.

Powder rivers. He spent the winter of 1835 at Fort Vancouver and as a Hudson's Bay Company employee he went to California in the spring of 1836 with Tom McKay. About the time his brother Joe settled in Oregon he bought the first lot in Oregon City from Dr. McLoughlin, shortly to lose it in litigation with the Reverend A. F. Waller, Methodist missionary, later in charge of the mission at The Dalles.

In the spring of 1840 McGoffin Brothers hired him as wagon master in charge of a train of supplies being sent to Santa Fe from St. Louis. He wintered at Chihuahua where, in 1841, he joined a party of Americans, led by James Kirk (or Kirker), hired to fight Apaches by the Mexican governor of Chihuahua.

In March, 1842, Meek was in Independence, Missouri, "hired to pilot seventeen families to Oregon."[4] This was the train headed by Elijah White, and included such well-known Oregon pioneers as Medorem Crawford, F. X. Matthieu, and Lansford Hastings. The trip was made without particular incident and the train arrived safely in Oregon.

Still restless and footloose, Stephen guided a party of dissatisfied emigrants from the Willamette Valley to Sutter's Fort in 1843. Then he embarked on a 'round the world ocean voyage which terminated at Guayaquil, Ecuador, where he almost died of yellow fever. Finally reaching New York in July, 1844, he traveled on to his old home in Virginia before going again to Missouri.

In his autobiography, Meek says:

> . . . I got letters of recommendation from Fitzpatrick, Wm. Sublette and Rob. Campbell, which secured me the position as guide to the immense emigrant train of 480 wag-

---

4 *Oregonian*, April 30, 1885. Some discrepancy exists here. The Fred Lockley account has Meek joining the party on the South Platte. Carey's *History of Oregon* and Meek's *Autobiography* both indicate Meek's presence at Independence.

ons then preparing to go to Oregon. We started on the 11th of May, 1845, on which day I first saw Elizabeth Schoonover, whom I married a week later.[5]

In the early spring of 1845, emigrants, by diverse paths, came through Independence and St. Joseph, Missouri, to the places of rendezvous on the prairie where the great trains could organize their departure to the west. Some were going to California, but the majority were "for Oregon" and the promise of free land.[6] There were families from Kentucky and Virginia, from Illinois and Iowa, from Tennessee and Ohio and Missouri. Some of those present had considerable impact on the later course of Oregon history; others in these busy groups were to find death, tragedy, and suffering in the course of their long journey and were to be recorded in history as the

---

5 Records from Meek descendants state that Elizabeth Schoonover was a Canadian girl, born May 16, 1828. Joel Palmer's entry for May 17: "In the evening after we had encamped [on Little Vermilion Creek] and taken our supper, a wedding was attended to with peculiar interest." "Joel Palmer's Journal" in Thwaites' *Early Western Travels, 1748-1846* (Cleveland: The Arthur H. Clark Company, 1906), Vol. XXX.
    John Ewing Howell, "Diary of an Emigrant of 1845," *Washington Historical Quarterly*, Vol. I (1906-7), May 18 entry: "Pilot [married] to a Miss Emigrant."
6 Senator Lewis F. Linn's Oregon bill (which granted each settler 640 acres of land) was argued in the U.S. Senate in the winter of 1842-43 and passed in February but failed in the House. It was the basis of much frontier interest in Oregon. In 1843 the provisional Oregon government had passed land laws allowing for individual claims of 640 acres per married man and 320 acres per single man, provided each had reached the age of twenty-one. While this early law was abrogated by Congressional action, its features were incorporated in the Donation Land Law of 1850. It would appear that the emigrants of 1845 were motivated in part by existing land law in Oregon and in part the confidence of the pioneer in his own ability to take land and hold it.

"Lost Wagon Train of 1845," the "Blue Bucket Train," or "Meek's Party."

TABLE OF CONTENTS

LIST OF ILLUSTRATIONS

Maps

TERRIBLE TRAIL:
THE MEEK CUTOFF, 1845

Chapter I

THE WAGONS ROLL

THE stir and bustle of the frontier which normally surrounded Independence and St. Joseph, Missouri, was considerably increased in the spring of 1845 by the arrival within their environs of large numbers of emigrants determined to make the perilous crossing to Oregon. All through the winter, meetings had been held with this same air of excitement by those who had the Oregon fever. William A. Goulder[7] remarks in his *Reminiscences* that this was an "epidemic," not only prevalent in Missouri but also in the adjoining states.

At St. Joseph the man who conducted many of these meetings was "Uncle Fred" Waymire; he came with his overcoat pockets stuffed with letters and papers from Oregon. Letters from Peter H. Burnett, who had gone to Oregon in 1843, were particularly influential and of extreme interest at these gatherings.

---

7 W. A. Goulder, who wrote his *Reminiscences* in later years, was a young, single man infected with the "Oregon Fever" in St. Joseph in the spring of 1845. His book, now rare, is one of the most readable accounts it has been our good fortune to discover. Goulder was a Virginian of the old school, who combined the instincts of a gentleman with insight and humor. W. A. Goulder, *Reminiscences of a Pioneer* (Boise, Idaho: Timothy Regan, 1909), p. 111.

Some emigrants from neighboring states had arrived during the winter, eager to set out on the long trail, but patience had to prevail, for the spring grass must grow and the rivers and creeks must subside to allow passage with a minimum of trouble.

Trains in after years would organize in much the same manner and the excitement would run as high, but the combined membership of this year was to form the largest group yet readying for the journey and, incidentally, to swell the population of the Oregon country to six thousand people, just double.

Between the latter part of April and the last of May, 1845, various companies left the Missouri country for the territory west of the Rockies.

From Independence, Samuel Hancock, with forty wagons,[8] was one of the first to leave. The Stephens-Palmer-Barlow Company then departed Independence on May 6, encompassing about one hundred wagons—a large, unwieldy group, as they were soon to learn. Accounts mention a Captain Brown with thirty-eight wagons passed on the road from Independence, and it is said that Lawrence Hall left with a company of thirty wagons from that point.

St. Joseph, too, was the scene of many departures that year. One of the larger groups leaving in early May called itself "The Savannah Oregon Emigrating Society," but it was soon to be known as the "Tetherow Train," for Solomon

---

8   *Narrative of Samuel Hancock* (New York: Robert M. McBride & Company, 1927), p. 2. While Samuel Hancock, in his *Narrative*, makes no mention of his leadership of a train, Sam Tetherow in "The McNemees and the Tetherows with the Migration of 1845," *Oregon Historical Quarterly*, XXV (December, 1924), 359, credits Hancock with forty wagons. In the same article, however, a Samuel Hancock is listed as a member of the St. Joseph company, leaving Missouri about the same time, as a cattle driver, single, in charge of no wagons.

Tetherow, an old frontiersman, was to captain the main body the full distance. He would shoulder the responsibilities for families totaling sixty-six wagons. Factions split from his group along the way, but replacements kept his total fairly constant. Small groups which left Tetherow were captained by H. M. Knighton, Nicholas Ownbey, Wayman St. Clair, and H. D. Martin.

One of the most colorful individualists leaving St. Joe was Samuel Parker, with forty-eight wagons. Never hesitant, Samuel would steadily forge ahead in the weeks to come, to find himself near the point of the entire migration at Fort Boise in the Oregon Territory. At Independence Rock, his command would split and John Stewart would lead twenty wagons.

The William McDonald and Levin English parties made their exodus from St. Joseph early in May. Although a "Captain Smith" receives mention by various emigrants, more is not presently known about him.

Probably the last group to depart from St. Joseph for the year was that captained by Abner Hackleman. With a membership of fifty-two wagons, it left about May 24, titled "The New London Emigration Company for Oregon."

One other large group, about sixty-four wagons, took leave from the northern point on the Missouri River, led by W. G. T'Vault for a short period.[9] Disagreements of various

----

9   *St. Joseph Gazette*, May 2, 1845, I, No. 2, 2:
Oregon Meeting
At a general meeting of the Oregon Emigration held at Mr. Waymeir's [sic] Encampment opposite St. Joseph in Buchanan Co. The meeting was organized by calling John M. Forest to the chair and appointing James Allen, secretary; whereupon Col. Tvault, Chairman of the Committee appointed to draft and report laws for the government of the company during their march, made his report, which was adopted with but few dissenting voices.
Whereupon the Company proceeded to organize by electing their officers when it was declared by the Chairman that William G. Tvault of Kosciusko Co., Indiana, was elected Captain of said

natures soon split the organization into several smaller groups, among which were the John Herren family, the James B. Riggs Company, the John Waymire group, and the James McNary Train.

A story in the *St. Joseph Gazette,* concerning the T'Vault organization, reflected the typical enthusiasm of the departing companies:

The Oregon Emigrants

On the 29th inst. a part of the Company of Oregon Emigrants, who have been for some time encamped four miles below St. Joseph on the opposite side of the river, started from that place on their journey. On the next day the remainder of those there encamped went on and joined their companions at a distance of ten miles. In a few days these will be joined by many others from above at Wolf river, and about twenty-five miles from this place, whence they will make a real and final start over the almost boundless prairie and the lofty mountains to their future homes. Wm. G. Tvault, Esq., is the elected Captain of the Company with whom we had some conversation and thereby gained the following information. It is estimated that the company, when made up and organized fully, will consist of above one thousand persons, one hundred wagons and about two thousand cattle. It was ascertained by examination that each family had a full supply of provisions, and the whole wealth of the company is near

---

company. John Waymire was elected Lieutenant; James Allen, John Martin, William Frazer, and Alexander Smith, Sergeants; Nathan [Nahum] King, superintendent of driving cattle and John M. Forest, Arnold Fuller, Philip Harris, Nathan King and John Heron [Herren], a Committee of Safety, and Rowland Chambers, Sheriff; and Frederick Waymire, Clerk. The Company then employed Mr. Clark as their pilot.

On motion of Capt. Tvault, Monday the 28th of April, 1845, was appointed the day when the Emigration will take up their line of march.

N.B. The Company did not leave on the 28th of April, owing to the death of Mrs. Fuller, wife of Arnold Fuller. Mrs. Fuller was from Lafayette Co., Mo.

one hundred and thirty thousand dollars. We visited their camping ground on the morning of the day when they started, and accompanied them a short distance, most of the families were comfortably prepared for traveling, and believed themselves as comfortable as if in a dwelling house. All seemed full of resolutions, and we were surprised to see such cheerfulness, with the women as well as the men. They were then leaving all this probably forever, and yet scarce a tear was shed. We saw no manifestations of anxious grief and vain repining. Each seemed to have a part to act and full determination to do his part.[10]

And while these laudable American characteristics were evident among the emigrants, there was strong indication of another equally American characteristic: every company was composed of strong-willed, vociferous pioneers who were not slow to criticize those who held positions of leadership.

And so they started, some from St. Joseph and some from Independence.[11] The larger groups hired temporary guides to lead them to the place on the prairie where they could organize in earnest. Stephen Meek, an interested member of the company which included Palmer's, Stephens', and Barlow's groups, was much in evidence.

Joel Palmer's *Journal* says that on May 13, 1845, having two days before caught the large emigrating company, they stopped on the banks of Big Soldier Creek

. . . for the purpose of organizing the company by an election of officers; the officers *then* acting having been elected to serve only until the company should reach this place. It was decided when at Independence that *here* there should be a thorough and complete organization. . . . the excitement was intense. The most important officers to be elected were the pilot and [the] captain of the company. There were two candidates for the office of pilot, —one a Mr.

10 *Gazette*, p. 2.
11 The main groups. Other towns, such as Weston, also witnessed departures.

Adams, from Independence, —and the other, a Mr. Meek from the same place . . . Mr. Meek, an old mountaineer, had spent several years as a trader and trapper, among the mountains, and had once been through to Fort Vancouver, he proposed to pilot us through for two hundred and fifty dollars, *thirty* of which were to be paid in advance and the balance when we arrived at Fort Vancouver.[12]

Mr. Adams,[13] according to Palmer, "had once been as far west as Laramie," "had engaged a Spaniard, who had traveled over the whole route, to accompany him, and moreover had been conspicuously instrumental in producing the 'Oregon fever.'"

Whether Stephen Meek was elected because of his lower bid (Adams wanted five hundred dollars) or his experience, makes little difference now. A physician of Independence, Presley Welch, was elected captain.

The results of the election were not satisfactorily unanimous and on May 19 Palmer relates that the large company split into three, each electing its own officers, though retaining Welch and Meek in their respective positions. These smaller groups became known as Stephens' Company, Palmer's Company, and the Barlow Company.[14]

---

12 The sum of $179 pilotage actually was collected, of which $113 was paid at the time of Meek's election. See Oregon Provisional & Territorial Government Papers, No. 613, Archives, Oregon State Library.

13 Captain T. M. Adams "had been elected Captain of the whole immigration, the duties of which office he had discharged to the best of his abilities had crossed and camped the principal part of them on the other side of the Kansas where they proceeded to a new organization, and elected Stephen Meek pilot of the immigration. Captain Adams for private reasons threw up his command and returned." *St. Louis Weekly Reveille*, Thursday morning, May 29, 1845.

14 It should be fully understood that at this point Meek's services as guide were initiated, and only for these three companies. Other groups had other arrangements.

For some time this arrangement worked; Meek and Welch traveled ahead with a different company each day, the other two waiting their turns to lead. But eventually chafing against the ignominious and dusty positions in the rear, the other companies decided to travel at their own gait and consequently were spread out on each side, for some distance traveling abreast. William Barlow describes the situation in his "Reminiscences of Seventy Years":

> So we rolled on until we struck the North Platte River at Ash Hollow, where, according to arrangements at the start, we were all to go into camp and let the big chief, Captain Welch, take the lead. But there were four or five companies ahead of us, the Barlow company; but when we got there there were no companies to be seen; so from that time on each company was an independent company of its own, and the "Devil take the hindmost," was the saying.[15]

Others had similar experiences, organizing and reorganizing until few of the original companies remained together at the end of the journey. Almost in the beginning T'Vault lost command of his large group from St. Joseph. As the rigors of the trail began to be felt, the company rebelled and split into fragments. James Field's account in his journal, relating the dissolution of T'Vault's leadership through May, 1845, closely parallels Barlow's comment. So much shifting took place that it is difficult to determine leadership and position of the various wagon groups on the long trail across the continent. Many smaller units were formed from the original unwieldy aggregation.

The nature of the journey soon demonstrated the advantages of traveling in smaller groups, strung out over fifty to one hundred miles. A small company could move more

---

15 William A. Barlow, "Reminiscences of Seventy Years," *OHQ*, XIII (September, 1912), 255.

rapidly, find better camp spots, and supply its immediate needs for grass and water more easily than a larger one.

Joel Palmer, Samuel Parker,[16] Jesse Harritt[17] (McNary Company), Samuel Hancock, James Field[18] (Riggs Company)—whose contemporary accounts contribute much— mention many times passing and being passed by other companies along the routes. For instance, Palmer wrote on June 5:

> Yesterday we traveled about twelve miles, passing Captain Stephens, with his advance company. To-day we traveled about the same distance, suffering Stephens' company to pass us. At noon they were delayed by the breaking of an axletree of one of their wagons, and we again passed them, greatly to their offence. They refused to accede to our terms, and we determined to act on our own responsibility. We therefore dissolved our connection with the other companies, and thenceforward acted independently of them.

It would not be accurate to say that the 1845 plains crossing from the Missouri to the Snake River at Fort Boise was uneventful. The diaries and narratives of 1845 emigrants are full of descriptions of adventure and misadventure. Buffalo herds, Indian scares, stampedes, and, above all, the extreme arduousness of the journey leave a contemporary reader filled with amazement at those people. The trail wore them thin. But most of the companies were singularly free from the Indian attacks of later years, although both Parker and Hancock mention several incidents. Cattle thievery was usual and night guards were stationed at all camps with orders to shoot at the first sign or sound of marauders.

---

16 Diary of Samuel Parker, 1845. Copy on file at Oregon Historical Society; original diary in possession of Parker descendants.
17 Diary of Jesse Harritt, 1845, *Oregon Pioneer Association Transactions, 1910-11*, Portland, Oregon.
18 Diary of James Field "Crossing the Plains," printed in the *Willamette Farmer*, Portland, April-June, 1879.

They met a slender stream of traffic headed east. Goulder noted a meeting with a group of 1844 emigrants beyond the Big Sandy, who were returning from the Willamette Valley to "the states"

> for the purpose of bringing out their families and friends the following year. . . . About the first question they asked us was "Who is President of the United States?" We gave the privilege of answering this question to our leading Democrat, who proudly replied, "James K. Polk of Tennessee." "Is it Poke or Polk; who is he anyhow?" None of us knew enough about the man with the strangely-sounding name, but we were all agreed that the happy individual who bore it must be a very great man, since the Democrats had chosen him for President and he had beaten Henry Clay.[19]

Between Laramie and Fort Hall the Stephens' Company, with whom Stephen Meek and his wife Elizabeth were then traveling, merged with the McDonald Party.

At Fort Hall there were new changes in the trains' organization. Just beyond the fort the California Trail forked to the south: fifty wagons took that branch.[20] Some said in later years that Meek attempted to persuade a portion of the trains to accompany him to California on this route; there is little reason to believe this statement.

For reasons which are not now apparent, Meek's services terminated at Fort Hall. Either the companies were dissatisfied with his piloting, the original agreement had been to lead them this far, or the original group was so splintered that a pilot's services were hopeless. It is of interest to note that in 1846 Meek sued Presley Welch for $130 of the pilotage fee

---

19 Goulder, *op. cit.,* p.116.
20 Palmer, *Journal*, entry for August 8: "About fifteen wagons had been fitted out, expressly for California; and, joined by the thirty-five aforementioned, completed a train of fifty wagons. . . ." In Thwaites' *Early Western Travels, 1748-1846* (Cleveland: The Arthur H. Clark Company, 1906), Vol. XXX.

and was awarded $66.[21] The fact that he was not paid in full may signify that he left the companies on his own initiative.

Whatever the cause, Meek found himself unemployed. He rode ahead with his wife and young Nathan Olney, talking to advance companies as he passed. He had a new idea. If he could convince sufficient numbers of the pioneers to follow him, he could open a new, shorter route to the Willamette Valley. Others of the mountain brotherhood were acting as guides; he had already brought a train by the regular route in 1842. A shorter, less hazardous way than that through the Columbia Gorge was a much-needed and much-discussed object. When Stephen Meek proposed his route in the early fall of 1845, neither the Barlow Road nor Applegate's Trail was in existence.[22]

With Meek's firsthand knowledge of the Malheur River country and with what he had heard from other trappers of the land to the west, he was confident such a route could be found. He, Elizabeth, and Nathan Olney rode on to Fort Boise.

Behind them the battered and dusty wagons jolted through the dry sage plain, following a dim track to the edge of the Snake River. There, in the distance, rose the sunbaked adobe walls of Old Fort Boise.

Built by the Hudson's Bay Company in 1834 and located on an island at the Boise River's confluence with the great Snake, the post was a trading point of minor importance in this wild, unsettled territory. Yet it was a welcome sight to the emigrants after the long road from Fort Hall.

Arrival at Fort Boise signified that the emigrants were nearing the end of their long trek. Although still ahead lay the

---

21 See Oregon Provisional & Territorial Government Papers, Nos. 581, 613, 529. Meek was awarded sixty-six dollars more by jury decision, January 12, 1846, at Oregon City.

22 The Barlow Road, which grew out of the pressures of the 1845 emigration, was not a reality until 1846. The Applegate Trail, a long, difficult detour to the south, was first used by a train in 1846.

tortuous passage over the Blue Mountains, and the long road down the Columbia River, at the end lay the great Willamette Valley and their future.

Chapter II

FORT BOISE

T HE journey to this point, long and difficult,
was now behind. Fort Boise offered a chance for fleeting rest,
some provisions, some fresh fruit or fish from the Indians.
Most of all it afforded fresh information about the road ahead.

For some of the emigrants their coincident arrival was a
piece of bad fortune: at Fort Boise the factors which contributed to the ensuing tragedy were introduced. Samuel Hancock, traveling with the foremost group, wrote:

> Continuing our travels peacefully for three or four days
> we reached Fort Boise, where we had to recross Snake River;
> and here we encamped and remained a day. During this time
> a man whose name was Steven S. Meeks (Meek) came along
> with a company of Parkers (packers)[23] for Oregon; he said he
> had traveled the country between this point and Oregon many
> times and was quite familiar with the route; and that he would
> pilot us a near way that would save us a number of days'
> travel, provided that we would pay him for this service five
> dollars for each wagon in our train. We consulted with the
> Manager at Fort Boise, in relation to this and he informed us
> that Mr. Meeks had passed the Fort three times to his knowl-

---

23 The parenthesized "packers" is apparently the interpretation of
Arthur D. Howden Smith, who edited the *Narrative of Samuel
Hancock* in 1926. Quite probably Mr. Smith did not know of
Samuel Parker. Hancock's original statement is correct.

edge, and also that he knew that there was a pack trail, through the country that Mr. Meeks designed going, so the most of us decided to follow him; . . .[24]

Goulder, traveling with Captain Nicholas Ownbey,[25] recalled the events in these words:

On reaching old Fort Boise, late in the afternoon of a bright day in September [August], 1845, our company went into camp on the right bank of the Snake River, just below the fort. The Hudson Bay Company's agent at that place was Mr. Payette, after whom the Payette River had been named.[26] Besides the agent and his people, there were several hundred Indians in the bottom near the place where we were encamped for the night. Stephen Meek, a brother of the somewhat renowned Joseph L. Meek, had overtaken us as we were journeying down the Boise Valley. Meek was accompanied by his young wife, whom he had married somewhere on the road, and also by a young man, Nathan Olney, who afterwards became prominent in the history of Oregon. From Fort Boise westward, the route heretofore taken by the immigrants was the old Hudson Bay route by the way of Burnt River and the Grande Rounde Valley, and across the Blue Mountains, to the waters of the Umatilla River. It had been made known to us that the Walla Walla and Cayuse Indians, who then inhabited the country west of the Blue Mountains, the region through which the abovenamed route lay, were somewhat disposed to be unfriendly to the whites, and that they had threatened to make themselves troublesome to immigrants passing through the country. At Fort Boise, Meek told us that we could avoid all trouble and danger by taking a route over which he could guide us from Fort Boise to The Dalles of the Columbia. With

24 Hancock, *op. cit., pp. 26-27.*
25 At this point, Goulder is apparently far in advance of the main migration. See his work, p. 117, "July 15th." Ownbey's (variously spelled) small group of seven wagons was swifter. Goulder errs about the month.
26 Goulder is in error about the factor. Hudson's Bay Company records show Francois Payette at Fort Boise in 1844, in Canada 1845.

the assistance of Olney, Meek made a rude map of the country, showing a route up the Malheur River and across low intervening ridges to the Des Chutes, and thence to the Dalles. This route, he said, would give the Cayuse and Walla Walla country a wide berth and enable us to avoid all contact with the supposedly hostile Indians.[27]

James Field relates the same rumor of Indian trouble in his entry for August 13 and, more completely, on August 24:

> The story of the murder of the two Frenchmen by the Walla Wallas is pronounced a humbug by the people of the fort. They say that the Walla Wallas entertain a hostile feeling toward us, and will probably try to injure us as we pass through their territory, but their numbers or their equipment would not render them dangerous to such sized companies as we are in at present. Still, the nature of the country is such that if they took advantage of it they could damage us considerably.[28]

Ironically, one of the factors encouraging the cutoff venture might have been the "better safe than sorry" philosophy. Then, too, the difficulty of passage through the portion of the Blue Mountains which lay ahead on the trail was well known. The travelers had dreaded it all the way across the plains, for Peter Burnett and others had been blunt about its condition.

---

27 Goulder, pp. 124-25. It would appear Olney had been through some of the country before: "A younger brother, Nathan, in 1843, when he was only twenty years old, had made the long journey overland to The Dalles in Oregon Territory." See "Cyrus Olney, Associate Justice of Oregon Territory Supreme Court," Sidney Teiser, *OHQ* LXIV (December, 1963), 311; see also A. J. Splawn, *Kamiakin, Last Hero of the Yakimas* (Portland, Oregon; Binfords and Mort, 1944), for later biography on Olney.

28 The hostility of the Walla Wallas was not all humbug. Sarah J. Cummins' account of the Lemmon-Walden party details the great uneasiness with which their train traveled through Walla Walla country in 1845. The Whitman Massacre occurred only two years later.

After passage through the Blues, pioneers still faced arduous travel down the Columbia, fording the mouths of rivers like the John Day and Deschutes, constructing rafts at The Dalles, and rafting down to the Willamette, encountering difficult portages. So perhaps a new route would offer an easier alternative.

Apparently there was talk about the advisability of such a cutoff at Fort Hall, for Joel Palmer's entry for September 30 mentions it. But most impressive was Meek's self-confidence. He had "seen the elephant," knew the country, had trapped with Bonneville, rubbed elbows with men whose names were known on the frontier. There was reason to believe he could do what he said he could. Doubters went to the factor at Fort Boise who, as Hancock relates, reassured them of Meek's experience, though perhaps expressing doubt about the practicality of the route.

The decisions weighed heavily. Selection of either trail meant separation from relatives and friends; family ties were too complicated. For a married daughter to insist upon traveling with her parents could mean that her husband must separate from his.

The McDonald Party settled its decision in a most unusual way, as evidenced in a colorfully-spelled letter written by a young member of the company:

> . . . on the Malheur river we stoped for several days here we come to Meeks cutoff   the company did a great deal of parlying as to whether we could go this cutoff we were here to [two] days, before the decision was made some had concluded to go the cutoff but some could not decide so this part of the company settled the question by chusing two strong men to take hold of Pliny Garrison and pull in the two directions and they pulled him on to the old road   everything being in readiness they started Several of different companies come up and went this cutoff   Mr. Twilerger[29] left our train

---

29   James Terwilliger.

and went with them   Steve Meeks and his wife had come into
our company on the north Platte   they rode on horses back
he professed to know all about this route. . . .[30]

From the beginning there were those who had misgivings
about following Meek. Among them was H. D. Martin who
included this comment in a letter written home in 1846:

. . . there we crossed the Snake River the second time and
a fine gentleman by the name of Stephen Meek encouraged
the company to take a new route with him for pilot. I was
much opposed to it but the company would go and I went
also. . . .[31]

Samuel Parker wrote tersely:

tuck what is caled the meeks Cut of . . . [and a later
addition to this entry] . . . A Bad cut of fore all that tuck it[32]

Jesse Harritt, not being in an administrative position, only
chronicled the turning of the McNary group onto the untried
route. His diary makes no mention of the serious discussions
which preceded the decision.

William Barlow, whose earlier experience with Meek
apparently led to enmity, held to the regular route. In after
years he wrote:

We had hired Steve Meek, brother of Joe Meek, to pilot
the emigrants clear through to The Dalles, for one dollar a
wagon and board. He said he knew every trail and camping
ground from Fort Laramie to Vancouver, west of the Cascade
mountains. But he proved himself to be a reckless humbug
from start to finish. All he had in view was to get the money
and a white woman for a wife before he got through. He got
the wife and part of the money. He and his company then went
on and made a stand at the mouth of the Malheur river, which

30   Ellen Garrison Carlin, Vertical File, Oregon Historical Society.
31   *St. Joseph Gazette*, July 10, 1846.
32   August 24 entry.

empties into the Snake River, where, he said, he could make a cut-off that would take them to The Dalles before we could get to the Grande Ronde Valley. This route, he said would give them plenty of wood, water and grass all the way, and there would be no Blue Mountain to cross, which he described as almost impassable.[33]

Crossing the Snake for the last time, the wagons continued west. As soon as they left the green border of the river they encountered chokingly dusty expanses. Field, writing on the twenty-fifth, comments:

> ... Since crossing to this side of the Snake River again the road has been fearfully dusty. In fact, a person who has never traveled these wormwood barrens can form no idea as to what depth dust may be cut up in them by the passing of a few wagons. To a person walking in the road it is frequently more than shoe deep, and if the wind happens to blow length-wise of the road, it raises such a fog that you cannot see the next wagon in front.

A grim reminder that it was a difficult stretch exists today where the Henderson grave marks the burial of an emigrant who died of thirst August 9, 1852, only a few yards from the Malheur water. The present green fields of the Malheur Valley offer sharp contrast. In 1845 the hot springs near the Malheur flow were a welcome relief from the hot dusty road.

When the trains paused at the hot springs to reorganize and to take a deep breath, leadership fell on the shoulders of those who had proven their worth. While women washed clothing in the springs and prepared food for the days ahead, the final groupings were made. The Parker, McNary, and Riggs companies had merged some miles east of Fort Boise (Field, August 15). At the fort on the twenty-fourth, James B. Riggs was elected to captain these three groups: forty wagons.

---

33 Barlow, "Reminiscences of Seventy Years," *OHQ*, XIII (September, 1912), 254.

First to swing onto the new trail was Ownbey's Company, which included Hancock and Goulder, with Meek as guide. Next came the Riggs combination, then a collection of wagons containing the King, Chambers, Norton, and Fuller families. Its leadership is not certain; perhaps Alexander Liggett was captain. Other groups following but not necessarily in this order, were John Stewart's, H. D. Martin's, and Solomon Tetherow's. There may have been others; Wayman St. Clair is reported to have led the last company on the Cutoff.[34]

The number of wagons attributed to the split at the hot springs has been calculated by various sources as 100 to 300, although most sources agree that about 200 families were involved, between 1,000 and 1,500 people. These wagons, more or less together, left the old emigrant trail at the hot springs in Vale, turned west up Malheur River and Bully Creek, and disappeared from the knowledge of the other emigrants until early in October when the first tattered remnants staggered into The Dalles.

The other 1845 emigrants kept to the usual Oregon Trail route, traveling north toward Burnt River: the English group, the wagons of the Samuel Barlow, McDonald, and Knighton parties, and later companies including Joel Palmer, Abner Hackleman, and Captain Brown.

It seems appropriate here to discuss the part played by Dr. Elijah White in the ensuing misfortunes. Bancroft (and later historians) have pointed an accusing finger at White as an opportunist who should bear much of the blame:

> . . . at the Hot Springs near Fort Boise a portion of the endless caravan, one of the Independence companies, was met by White. . . . From the fact that this company was the

---

34 Lewis A. McArthur, "Mary's River," *Oregon Geographic Names,* Portland, Oregon, Oregon Historical Society, 1952 edition, p. 389. McArthur states that St. Clair and John Lloyd were alternate captains of the last group to take the Cutoff.

one to try his projected route to the heart of the Willamette Valley, it appears that White was responsible for the disasters that followed, though the guide, Stephen H. L. Meek, who probably followed White's advice, and was ambitious to distinguish himself also, incurred all the blame. . . .[35]

Our research does not bear this out. While it is a matter of record that Meek knew Dr. White as a leader of the emigration of 1842, we find no record which would indicate correspondence between the two. White is credited with convincing the emigrants that Stephen Meek's Cutoff was entirely feasible, but chronology would indicate otherwise. Samuel Parker took the Cutoff August 24; James Field, who gives the twenty-fifth as starting date for the Riggs party, says that Ownbey is traveling ahead. On September 3, the King family (in the third group) was already at Castle Rock on the North Fork of the Malheur for it was here on this day that a member of that train, Sarah King Chambers, died.

White's party, on its way back to the States to deliver a petition to the Congress of the United States, did not arrive near Fort Boise until the third of September. Dr. White had left the Willamette Valley the fifteenth of August, reaching Walla Walla Mission on the twenty-sixth. On the first of September he records his meeting with eight hundred emigrants in the Grande Ronde country, headed by Barlow, Knighton, and McDonald. Wagons, he noted, numbered eighty-seven.[36]

Joel Palmer offers additional testimony:

... Mr. Meek, who had been engaged as our pilot but had previously went in advance of the companies who had em-

---

35 H. H. Bancroft, *History of Oregon*, I, chap. XIX (San Francisco: History Company, 1886), 512.

36 *Ten Years in Oregon—Travels and Adventures of Dr. E. White and Lady*, compiled by Miss A. J. Allen (Ithaca, New York: Mack, Andrus, & Co., Printers, 1848), p. 282.

ployed him, and who had after reaching Fort Hall, fitted up a party to pilot through to Oregon, informed the emigrants that he could, by taking up this stream to near its source, and then striking across the plains, so as to intersect the old road near to the mouth of Deschutes or Falls river, save about one hundred and fifty miles travel; also that he was perfectly familiar with the country through which the proposed route lay, as he had traveled it; that no difficulty or danger attended its travel. He succeeded in inducing about two hundred families to pursue this route; they accordingly directed their course to the left, up this creek, about ten days previous to our arrival at the forks.[37]

The passage from Palmer has Meek's party turning off the main road "about ten days previous" to Palmer's arrival at the forks at Vale, on September 3. This statement agrees with the departure date of Parker, Harritt, and Field, who kept day-by-day diaries. Therefore, since White obviously did not travel by the Cutoff himself, it was a physical impossibility for him to have influenced any one of these groups to try the new route. Palmer's group did not attempt the Cutoff, even though he records meeting Dr. White on September 3, at the junction of the Meek road. Dr. White corroborates this meeting in his own writings.

In a biographical sketch of Colonel James Taylor, who was traveling in company with Palmer, the statement is made, "On this side of the Rockies they met Doctor White and party en route for the East, who delivered a speech to the emigrants, concluding with the advice to keep on the old route down Snake river. . . ."[38]

White's *Ten Years in Oregon* does mention encountering, near the falls of the Snake River, the "St. Joseph's Party, who

37 Palmer, *Journal*, entry for September 3. In Thwaites' *Early Western Travels, 1748-1846* (Cleveland: The Arthur H. Clark Company, 1906), Vol. XXX.
38 Elwood Evans, *History of the Pacific Northwest* (Portland, Oregon: North Pacific History Co., 1889), II, 598-99.

had lagged considerably behind the rest of the emigration due to their refusal to travel on the Sabbath." This is the "New London Emigration Company for Oregon" from St. Joseph, captained by Abner Hackleman. Dr. White speaks of meeting a Mr. Fisher in this train, the same Reverend Ezra Fisher who wrote a letter from the Salmon Falls, September 12, 1845, to "Br. Hill in the East," in which he expresses happiness in meeting Dr. White, "the Indian agent for Oregon, on his way to your city and Washington."[39] The Fisher correspondence and William Findley's diary of 1845[40] record the details of travel of this leisurely group of fifty-two wagons. Both started from the Nemaha Agency (twenty-five miles west of St. Joseph) on May 24, considerably later than the advance trains. Findley records September 25 as the day of arrival at Fort Boise; no mention is made of the Meek Cutoff. Since that date was a month later than the Cutoff departure of the other groups, it is highly unlikely that another split took place at the forks at Vale.

The hardy souls who swung west up the Malheur following Meek's leadership included some who kept diaries or journals of their travel. Three were available to the authors— the accounts of Samuel Parker, Jesse Harritt, and James Field. Neither Parker nor Harritt is specific enough in his daily entries to continually demonstrate where his company was at all points. Field, however, is very detailed in his commentary and in combination with Parker and Harritt reveals much of the route.

Other evidence about the route is provided by a later attempt to follow it: eight years after Meek's ill-fated effort to establish a shortcut by a "middle route" to the Willamette

---

39 "Correspondence of the Rev. Ezra Fisher," *OHQ*, XVI (December, 1915), 411.
40 Coe Collection, Yale University Library. Copy kindly loaned by Mrs. Donna Wojcik, Portland, Oregon.

Valley, Elijah Elliott guided an even larger group by the Malheur. Although Elliott was ultimately successful, arriving at Eugene late in the fall, the hardships of the 1853 emigrants were quite similar to those of the 1845 people. In fact, the story of each train is so similar that the legends and stories written about them are badly confused. Even their trails have been confused. Thus 1853 Elliott cutoff accounts are valuable for the portion of the route first encountered by the 1845 emigrants since the Elliott group followed the dim tracks of the Meek party. Especially illuminating are the diaries of Andrew and James McClure. Andrew was an observer of the caliber of James Field and his descriptions of terrain and topographical features leave little doubt about this portion of the route.

Chapter III

UP THE MALHEUR

AFTER the decision to follow the new route the wagons started up the Malheur on August 25, 1845. From the evidence contributed by Andrew McClure's 1853 account,[41] the course of the Cutoff west from Vale lay three miles to the left of the river. This would put the wagons on the bench north of the valley. Parker, in his 1845 entry,[42] says that they were in the hills all day and came to the river at night. Harritt says "tolerable" road.[43] They encountered Bully Creek about six miles from their start but they followed up the benchland between the Malheur plain and the creek. Some ten miles east of Harper the wagons were forced by terrain to turn southwest, back to the Malheur. Field's August 26 entry reads:

---

41 Limited edition, mimeographed by the Lane County Pioneer-Historical Society (Eugene, Oregon, 1959). The work includes the diaries of Andrew S. and James F. McClure.
42 Diary of Samuel Parker, 1845, copy on file at the Oregon Historical Society; original diary in possession of Parker descendants.
43 Diary of Jesse Harritt, 1845, *Oregon Pioneer Association Transactions, 1910-11*, Portland, Oregon. In most of Harritt's entries spelling and punctuation from the original diary were retained.

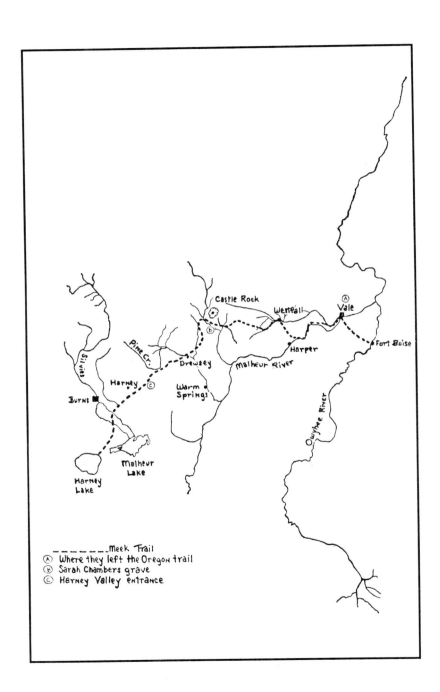

Castle Rock

Westfall

Vale Ⓐ

Pine Cr.

Harper

Drewsey

Malheur River

Fort Boise

Silvies R.

Harney

Ⓒ

Warm Springs

Owyhee River

Burns

Malheur Lake

Harney Lake

— — — — — Meek Trail
Ⓐ Where they left the Oregon trail
Ⓑ Sarah Chambers grave
Ⓒ Harney Valley entrance

UP THE MALHEUR

> Went about ten miles, still keeping up Malheur, crossing and re-crossing it twice, and camping upon it. We were obliged to take to the bluffs to get across several narrow bends of the river, and we there found some as hard road as any we had yet traveled. Indeed, I begin to think wagons can go anywhere.

The terrain gets progressively rougher the farther west one travels and both the '45 and '53 trains were forced into the bed of the Malheur for a distance, about five miles east of Little Valley. Andrew McClure's entry for September 2, 1853, is given, in part, below:

> Travelled four miles up the river and crossed it four times. The road is very rocky and the river bottom composed of large stones, which make it bad fording; water shallow not exceeding two feet deep.

At Harper the valley widens again and two choices were apparently offered the emigrants—to go northwest toward the present site of Westfall or to continue west up the Malheur. Scouting must have shown them the eventual impossibility of the latter route for they swung north to strike Bully Creek again in the Westfall Valley.

Harritt wrote:

> August 27 (1845). Commenced winding our way through the blue mountains   at noon we left this pleasant stream to the left turning gradually to the north west   travleed over a tolerable bad road   reached the head of a small sinking rivulet affording excelent water and timber   cotton wood willow and aulder   the latter being the principal part of which there is some of the largest I ever saw measureing from 12 to 14 inches in diametore   12 ms (miles)

On the same day Field entered in his journal:

> Went about 18 miles today. The road, although leading across the bluffs which in a country in which mountains are a rarity would pass for pretty good sized ones, was tolerably fair, but there is an abundance of small, sharp stones in it, black and hard as iron, and very wearing on the feet of the

cattle. We camped upon Carter's fork, from its appearance a branch of Burnt River.

This valley is comparatively narrow and is formed from the junction of Bully, Cottonwood, and Indian creeks. None of the avenues is good for wagon travel but the Cottonwood drainage is most feasible. Up Cottonwood they went, over progressively rougher, stonier bottom until, about a mile past the present Lawrence ranch, they pulled out of the canyon and headed northwest toward Indian Creek. From here to Buckaroo Springs the country offers little choice of easy travel. To both north and south are tremendous canyons and high ridges, the Malheur Mountains.

All accounts mention the stony ground. Samuel Hancock's description is vivid:

> Sometimes for the distance of many miles the entire surface of the Country was covered with a medium sized stone or boulder, just large enough to make it difficult to travel over them; the only way the teams behind could distinguish the route was by the bruised and broken boulders, occasioned by the wheels of the front wagons passing over them and the blood from the feet of our poor animals that suffered almost beyond endurance. . . .[44]

Field, in his entry for August 29, notes these same stones:

> The mountains are covered with small, black, hard, nine-cornered stones, about the size of those used to macadamize a road, and our cattle cringe at every step.

They began to lose stock. Field comments on the thirtieth that three or four oxen lay down and "gave out" every day.

Samuel Parker, though succinct, is equally clear about the difficulties of terrain:

---

44 *Narrative of Samuel Hancock* (New York: Robert M. McBride & Company, 1927), pp. 27-28.

August 27 Bad Road went 12 (miles)

August 29 Verry bad Road Broak 3 wagens this day 5 (miles)

August 30 Rock all day pore grass more swaring then you ever heard 11 (miles)

Field, Parker, and Harritt, in 1845, all found water in this higher country, but not enough for their livestock. The wagons crossed the Bendire Range to the top of Immigrant Hill, south and east of Castle Rock, and traveled painfully down the west slope to Warm Springs Creek above the Munkres' ranch. The scars of their descent were still visible on the west side of Immigrant Hill in June, 1960. Harritt, in his entry for August 30, mentions a "warm spring bursting from the side of a lofty mountain—a little above blood heat." It is still there on upper Warm Springs Creek, about a mile and a half above the Munkres' ranch.

Now the train had reached the present Agency Valley where there were good grass and plenty of water. Although it seems they would have delayed here for several days to rest the stock and recuperate, neither Harritt, nor Parker, nor Field indicates doing so; their next day's entries list travel mileage.

The terrain is remarkable here—high rocky ridges; rounded tops; level, willow-bordered fingers which poke into the recesses wherever a stream has worn its way. The grass at this place was good, the water sweet. Castle Rock, standing as a sentinel to the north and then to the east as the train moved along, remained long in the memories of the passengers.

The wagons traveled around the shoulder of Castle Rock, called by Harritt and Field "Fremont's Peak,"[45] to the North

---

45 Though Fremont's exploration in October, 1843, did not approach this far west, here, no doubt, he observed Castle Rock, for it is a landmark of considerable magnitude. Why Harritt and Field refer to it by this tag is another unsolved mystery although a Herren account (Bancroft Pacific Series Microfilm, Reel No. 3) relates the

Fork of the Malheur. From here they made their way by extremely rocky and difficult passage up the Malheur for about five miles. Field comments on the "first rate camping," even though the road grew progressively worse.

The quality of the road deserves further consideration for it has been the contention of some gold seekers that the train turned south here and followed the North Fork downstream. Indeed, the travel would be better for a way. Another route which would seem to offer fewest difficulties would have been southwest toward Drewsey where the old stage road was located later, taking off just north of the present Beulah Dam. But McClure is most explicit:

> Wednesday, Sept. 7 (1853)—The mountains before us look to be impracticable for wagons, but Meeks and Elliot have both ascended and *"what man has done man can do."* [46]
> Thursday, Sept. 8 (1853)—From camp the road again led *up the bluff on the right east bank* of the river.[47] This road nears the mountain peak on the left. The river on our left running through rock canyons. Some distance onward the trail turns to the left, passing down a ravine and over some very rough points. We came to the river and grazed.

In the same entry, he states that "the crossing is about S. 80 degrees W. from the mountain peak with a rock top."[48] Parker wrote in 1845:

> Aug. 31 went up the creek 5

---

discovery of gold nuggets on a stream which is probably the North Fork of Malheur River—"Among the speculations indulged in was one supposing that some of Fremont's company had lost these bits of metal when he camped on the same spot one year before, as they found his old camping spot and used the half-burned brands to kindle their fire." The assumption may have resulted in naming the rock.

46   Authors' italics.
47   Authors' italics.
48   Castle Rock, north of Beulah Reservoir, Malheur County, Oregon.

> Sept. 1   the worst Road you ever seen   5 wagons broak. . . .

And Harritt, September 2:

> made an erly start over bad road for 2 (?) ms   broake one axletree which detained us about 2 hours   balance of the road tolerable good. . . .[49]

Of interest here is a letter received from Cecil E. Fletcher, of Independence, Oregon:

> During the latter part of 1920, I was on a survey party in the "Castle Rock" section. Our camp site on the Little Malheur was the location of an old camp site of the wagon train. We found pieces of the felloes, spokes, utensils, etc., where they had made repairs. Property at that time was part of the Pacific Coast land and livestock (old Miller and Lux) "Monkey Wrench" ranch. This creek is now called the "North Fork" of the Malheur.[50]

About where they first reached the North Fork is the only known, marked grave of the lost '45 emigration, that of Sarah Chambers, the young wife of Rowland Chambers and daughter of Nahum King, who later settled Kings Valley and lent his name to much of that local area. The marker is of native stone, painstakingly scratched "S. Chambers, Sept. 3, 1845." None of the diarists mentions her death, and it would appear they knew nothing of it.[51] It is worthy of more than passing notice for it indicates that at this point the wagon companies were becoming more and more separated—a fact which has bearing on future determination of the route. On the third of

---

49   This entry is one of the rare times when Harritt, apparently irrepressibly optimistic, records any difficulty!
50   Letter in authors' file.
51   Through the interest of Mr. Eugene Clark, of Pasadena, California, Mr. Ken Kessler, of Vale, Oregon, and others, the stone marking her grave has been mounted in concrete. There is, at present, an historical marker placed by Oregon-California Trails Association.

September Parker, Harritt (McNary party), and Field (Riggs Company) are about two days in advance of the King-Chambers families who were once led by T'Vault.

At the compass direction given by McClure the west side of the North Fork of the Malheur slopes gently but rockily to the north and east. With great labor it was possible to cross and gain the top of the ridge, traveling in a southwest direction. Crossing the top of the ridge, they dropped down into upper Cottonwood Creek, moving down it for a mile and one half (perhaps more for Parker). They were obliged to regain the top of the ridge because the creek bed became too rocky and they turned up a ravine to the east in order to do so. It is very rough travel, as Field shows in his journal:

> Sept. 2—Traveled about 15 miles today, in a direction but little west of south, camping upon a small branch of the Malheur which puts into the South Fork. About four miles of our road this morning rather exceeded anything we have passed over yet for rock, they being both large and sharp, lying in a narrow ravine where there was no shunning them. We got through, however, with only one broken axletree and two wagon-tongues, together with some other little fixings, which was really a favorable come-off.

Continuing down the ridge they descended to the head of Drewsey Valley where travel in the bottomland afforded better going. They camped (at a springs) near the site of the present Altnow ranch before continuing down the valley toward the Middle Fork of the Malheur which they encountered just west of the present town of Drewsey.

It has been argued by later researchers and those seeking the Blue Bucket that the train now made a long detour to the South Fork of the Malheur, eventually to reach Harney Valley by way of the Crane Creek entrance. While Harritt's diary says specifically "the South Fork of the Malheur" there are evidences that he was mistaken. For one thing, his mileages will not allow such a detour.

Parker, who is quite evidently traveling the same route, crosses to "the headwaters of the digger's lakes" two or three days later. These, of course, being Malheur and Harney lakes, he could not possibly have gone to the South Fork.

McClure (1853) also mentions the South branch of the Malheur, but he says, "I suppose it is." His mileage will not support the premise, either. From Cottonwood Creek, west of the North Fork of the Malheur to the South Fork, as the crow flies, it is close to forty miles. Parker, from the North Fork, travels seventeen miles; Harritt, from the North Fork, travels twenty-two miles; McClure, from the North Fork, travels eighteen miles.

There can be little question that the trains traveled the route hitherto described to this point. How, then, account for the confusion? Since Harritt calls the Middle Fork the South Fork and since he had not been in the country before, he must have received his information from Meek. Although the writers can uncover no evidence that Meek had ever traveled this way before (his trapping experience being limited to Harney Valley and east, by way of the Owyhee, to the Snake River), we extend here a theory: the Middle Fork runs in a generally southeastern direction from its head to join the North Fork. Meek, believing he was farther south than he really was, applied to it the name of the more southerly stream—the "South Fork." Therefore, that is what the '45 emigrants called it. This is the most logical assumption in view of the evidence, not only from the diaries, but also from accounts of later searchers for the lost gold, who followed the still visible tracks across the route here described.

Field's diary entry for September 3 throws a curious sidelight on the geographic discussion:

> . . . It is now pretty evident that Meek, the pilot who is leading the company this route instead of the old one, does not intend to fall down to the Columbia via the John Day river at all as he told them on leaving Fort Boise, for we are evidently now through the Blue Mountains, and still making a southwest course. It is now said that Meek's intention is to take us over onto the head of the Willamette if he can find a place along the Cascades which will admit of the passage of

wagons through, and if not we go down the Deschutes River to the Columbia.

Four miles northwest of Drewsey, the trains turned southwest, crossing branches of Stinking Water Creek, and gradually ascending the Stinking Water Mountains. For a time their direction was almost due south. Such is the steepness of the country that their descent into Pine Creek necessitated taking advantage of every bit of flat terrain, and switching back and forth. They came through a break in the cap rock which crowns the Stinking Water ridges on the east of Pine Creek and the scars of their tortuous passage became the basis for a later freight road. At the bottom they encamped among the springs in a "hollow."[52]

McClure describes the crossing of the Malheur and the arrival at the place of encampment in these words:

> From the crossing of this stream the trail takes a southwesterly course and, passing around a point again, turns to the west and winding over stony ground in ravines and on ridges, it descends a hill and passes down a smooth valley to a very steep hill, which we descended and came into the valley of several small branches. Encamped on the second. . . .

Harritt wrote:

> September 4. Made an advance of 11 miles and encamped in a deep hollow out of which proceeded a number of fine springs, affording us as good water as ever run, with a few small willows.

Parker merely says in his diary, "to a spring," but Field identifies the branch as a fork of the Malheur:

---

52 Diary of Samuel Parker, September 4, 1845; Diary of Jesse Harritt, September 4, 1845; Diary of Andrew McClure, September 10, 1853.

Sept. 4—Went about 18 miles, the latter part of the road being rough and rocky. Camped upon the head of a small branch of the South fork of Malheur. The mountains where we first struck them were naked and perfectly destitute of timber. Near Fremont's Peak we began to see some timber upon them, and since passing that point the hills have all had more or less timber upon them, it being generally low cedar, and on reaching the top of the last hill before descending into the hollow, tall pines appear to crown the hill-tops before us.

Today those springs are almost gone. Wet patches in early summer show where the water was but overgrazing, stream diversion, and settlement have all changed the water flow. Cows have a tendency to trample a spring to the point of its eventual disappearance. The tall pines to the west are still there.

The wagon line, the next day, followed the scouts in an ascent almost as difficult, winding through rock flats and across points to reach pine timber at the head of Big Rock Creek. Whether the descent into Harney Valley was by way of Big Rock Creek or East Cow Creek the writers are unable to determine. The mileage will fit either exit. A later stage road led down the ridge above East Cow Creek, and it is our opinion that this was the probable route to the flat expanses of Harney Valley. There are corroborative statements. C. A. Sweek, retracing the route of the lost train in 1881, says:

The emigrants left visible evidence as to their trail for, in 1881, when I followed their trail, I would frequently see on the bunchgrass hills deep ruts where the wheels were locked going down into Harney valley—on Cow Creek.[53]

Grover Jameson, of Burns, in a letter to the writers dated June 23, 1960, says in part:

My deceased wife's grandmother was a small girl of seven and was on this train, and from other sources I learned

53 Fred Lockley, *Oregon Journal,* November 13, 1924.

that upon entering the valley in the vicinity of Cow Creek, the train divided at this point and the main train came on to the vicinity of Burns, thence south westerly toward Wagontire Mountain.[54]

Final corroboration is contained in the testimony of the late Dr. R. C. Clark, of the University of Oregon, during his appearance before the United States Supreme Court, October Term, 1932. In part, it is quoted below:

Since my appearance as a witness in the case I have discovered two diaries, then unknown to me, written by men who visited the lakes region in 1845 and in 1853.

The first of these diaries was written by Jesse Harritt, who crossed the plains in 1845, and is a day-by-day record of distances traveled, streams crossed, and incidents of the trip. The entries are for the most part brief but from it the route of travel may be traced with approximate accuracy. Harritt's wagon train reached the crossing of the Malheur River by the Oregon Trail (the route most usually followed by the emigrants to Oregon) on August 24, 1845. Here he and others, some two hundred wagons, were persuaded to follow Stephen Meek by a route directly westward for the purpose of reaching the Willamette Valley by a shorter road.

On August 25, 1845, the Meek party after crossing the Malheur River left the Oregon Trail and traveled up that stream a little south of west 13 miles and the next day followed it for 10 miles. On the 27th, leaving the Malheur to the left and turning gradually to the northwest, they traveled 12 miles to the head of a small sinking rivulet. The next day, five miles southwest to a small stream and on the 29th, 12 miles over the mountain to a spring. The route can best be followed on the Dixon map . . . which shows the road surveyed by Wallen in 1859. The distance traveled these five days, 52 miles, corresponds with striking exactness to distances and directions indicated on the Wallen survey on the Dixon map from the Malheur crossing to Ice Spring shown on that map. In like manner, the distances and descriptions of the Harritt diary show that his party followed the Wallen road

---

54   Letter in writers' file.

to reach Harney Valley. After leaving the spring on the 30th they traveled ten miles "over huge mountains to a beautiful little branch." The next two days they made 10 miles up a stream, the north fork of the Malheur, a route identical with that shown on the Wallen map. On Sept. 2 they traveled 12 miles to camp on "a small rivulet" and the next day seven miles to what Harritt calls the "South Fork of the Malheur." The distance shown on the Dixon map from the North Fork of the Malheur to the main stream is approximately nineteen miles as given by Harritt. Without doubt Harritt had reached the main stream rather than its South Fork as he supposed.

. . . diary entries clearly show that they traveled through Harney Valley to reach the present Silvies River, the Crooked River of the diary. The second stream crossed on Sept. 8 was the west branch of Silvies River and the lake reached on that day was Harney Lake.

Another immigrant party reached the Harney Basin in 1853 by the same route followed by Meek. I have lately discovered a diary of this immigration that was kept by A. S. McClure one of a party of some 1,500 people who branched off from the usual trail at the Malheur in 1853 to reach the Willamette Valley by travelling directly westward.

I have compared the McClure and Harritt diaries, have traced the distances and directions followed for each day, streams mentioned as crossed in the McClure diary with the Wallen route traced on the Dixon map and am convinced that the route of the party of 1853 into Harney Valley followed almost exactly that of Meek in 1845 and the one surveyed by Wallen in 1859.

The party of 1853 was led by Elijah Elliott and will be referred to as the "Elliott Party." McClure's diary indicates that the wagon tracks made by the Meek party in 1845 could still be seen and that the route of that party as far as Harney Valley was followed.

The writers spent considerable time through two hot and dusty summers tracing this section of the route, interviewing people, absorbing atmosphere, only to arrive at the same conclusion. It was anticlimactic to read Dr. Clark's account, but his statement was heartening confirmation.

To all intents the wagons were through the "Blue Mountains" and the road ahead looked promising.

Chapter IV
INTO THE DESERT

AFTER the stony, exhausting passage through the Malheur Mountains, to descend the broad avenue of Cow Creek bottom to the flatland of Harney Valley was a great relief. In Harritt's words, the valley floor road was "butiful and level." There were water, abundant grass, and a profusion of wildlife. In the southern distance shimmered a large lake, framed on the west by an immense mesa. Beyond, to the southeast, were the snowcapped heights of the yet-un-named Steens Mountain. To the north and west lay the timbered ridges which surround the valley.

On the northeastern edge of this plain, Meek wanted to drive south. Field describes Meek's plan on September 11:

> It was his intention to follow down Crooked river to the Deschutes and down it to the old road, but when he came to the marshy lake spoken of last Sunday, the company refused to follow him if he made the circuit necessary to get around it upon Crooked river again so he struck off in a westerly direction in order to get upon the main Deschutes river. He well knew that there was a scarcity of grass and water across here and so informed them, but it was nearer and they would have him go it, and now blame him for coming the route they obliged him to.

This was written at Wagontire some days later, and everyone's hindsight was better than prophecy, but Meek quite evidently did not take the emigrants into his confidence; did

38

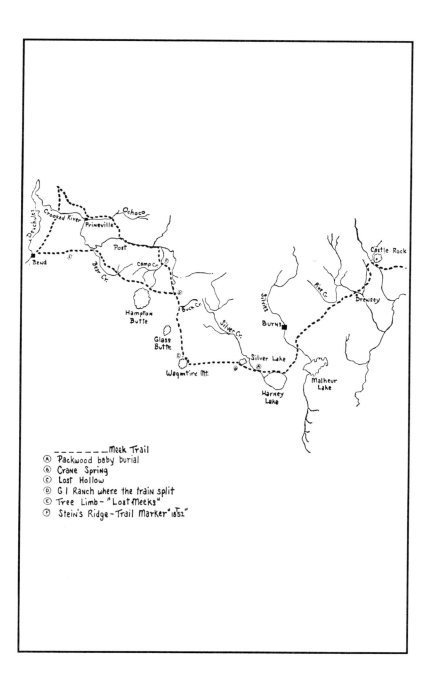

_ _ _ _ _ _ _Meek Trail
Ⓐ Packwood baby burial
Ⓑ Crane Spring
Ⓒ Lost Hollow
Ⓓ G I Ranch where the train split
Ⓔ Tree Limb – "Lost Meeks"
Ⓕ Stein's Ridge – Trail Marker "1852"

not inform them of his real uncertainty; was, understandably, reluctant to admit if he were lost.

Meek's mental map of the country played him a trick here and shortened the distance from the Silvies to Crooked River. It seems probable he was already farther south than he knew. It is doubtful, too, that he had traversed this route in an east-west direction. His original entry into Harney Valley, with Bonneville, seems to have been by way of the John Day River Valley south to the Silvies country. Apparently Elijah Elliott's information was no better for, in 1853, he led elements of his party south of Malheur Lake.

Again, the best contemporary account of the confusion existing in the minds of the emigrants is contained in Field's entries for September 3, 5, and 6. The September 3 entry previously quoted in Chapter Three hints at Meek's intention as: "to take us over onto the head of the Willamette." On September 5 Field says:

> Went 15 miles, camping upon Lake fork of John Day's river. I was mistaken about our being through the Blue Mountains. Although we were through the main range, yet the road for the past few days has led across low mountains which, having their steepest descent toward the west, did not appear high until we ascended them. The map of the country we had with us also indicated that we had passed the head of the John Day River, as the Malheur was made to head much further south than the John Day, and yet we have held a southwest course from the Malheur, and we are now upon the head forks of the John Day River.

The September 6 entry needs little explanation, except that the travelers were camping on the Silvies instead of Crooked River and, consequently, were not in the Deschutes watershed:

> Went about 14 miles today, camping upon another fork of Crooked River instead of John Day as stated yesterday, and we are in fact upon the waters of the Deschutes River, and steering direct toward the Cascade Mountains in order to attempt a passage through them. The tale of our going down

the John Day river was a mere tale of Meek's in order to get us upon this route and then take us wherever he pleased. But if he now fails to take us across the Cascades his head will not be worth a chew of tobacco to him, if what some of our men say prove true. He is with Owensby's company which is one day's travel ahead of ours, and we make their camps every evening, where we find a note buried at the foot of a stake, stating the distance to the next camp, and the names of the streams.

Apparently contributing to the pioneer confusion was the map to which Field refers. It may have been similar to the Mitchell map of 1846, which does not jibe with the geography. It obviously did not jibe with the map in Meek's mind.

The train did move southwest to the northern margin of Harney Lake and from there west into the desert reaches. But whether from pressures by the company, personal design, or disorientation with the geography the result was the same.

The mileage indicated by Harritt on September 5, 6, and 7 (forty-two miles), would take the party from the camp in the "hollow" to the northern edge of Harney Lake, skirting the east side of Wright's Point. An entry from Harritt's diary for September 7 reads:

> road butiful and level   travleed 16 ms   crossed one small stream and encamped on the Northeren margin of a large lake had an abundance of fine grass   no wood except sage

From the diary of Samuel Parker:

> Sept. 7 struck the lakes   Bad water   22
> Sept. 8 Went down the lakes some 5 miles then over the hills to A small creek   one child beried here

The death impressed Field. His entry for September 9 is more detailed about the incident:

> Last evening a child of E. Packwood, of Illinois, which had been ill a few days died suddenly. At present there are a good many sick about the camp, the majority of them complaining of fever. The child was buried in the dry wormwood [a variety of sage] barrens, and as we left the camp the wagons

41

filed over the grave, thus leaving no trace of its situation. The reason for our doing this was that the Indians in this part of the country are very fond of clothing, giving almost anything they possess in order to obtain it, and fearing that they might disturb the grave after we left, we took the precaution of leaving a beaten road across it. I cannot say that they would do anything to a grave, were they to find one, for we have passed several made by the emigrants at various times, and none of them appeared to have been disturbed. Went six miles, camping near a spring which sinks near where it rises.[55]

Today the line of march across the valley seems difficult because of the marshy areas, the Silvies River, the sloughs, but in a drought year it must have been more passable, though Goulder mentions the miry conditions. And the year 1845 was dry. Tree-ring growth studies conducted by the United States Forest Service indicate a considerable drouth from 1839 to 1854.[56] Water was a real problem to the emigrants from the

---

55 Harritt also notes the infant's death (September 8) and burial (September 9). The baby was Elkanah Packwood, son of Elisha and Paulina Packwood who were with the McNarys. Elkanah was born in Platte County, Missouri, December 24, 1843. Location of the grave has been lost. Information taken from the Packwood family Bible.

56 Letter from Paul Keen, USFS consultant, author of "Climatic Cycles in Eastern Oregon as Indicated by Tree Rings," *Monthly Weather Review,* Vol. 65 (May, 1937): ". . . the period from 1839 to 1854 was exceedingly dry in all of Eastern Oregon. This is confirmed by the fact that Goose Lake dried up at the time of the emigrant trains and their wagon track across the bed of the lake didn't show up again until the recent drought in 1917-1937 when in 1926 the lake dried up again. These weather cycles are broad in scope, and while there is some local variation, we have found them to occur all over Eastern Oregon's Great Basin area so you can assume the same general characteristics from the Snake to the Deschutes. Then, too, 1845 was the wettest year in this dry period but was not above normal so we can be sure that conditions were similar to the 1917-1937 period when the springs dried up that were not known to have been affected before. It was a period when

time they left Harney Valley, but the drouth may have aided their progress through portions of the valley.

The wagons moved slowly toward the western end of Harney Valley. Harritt's entry for September 9 gives a travel of six miles to a spring where they encamped with "no wood and but a little grass." A computation of the mileage from the camp on Harney Lake to the present Crane Spring on the western shore of little Silver Lake tallies remarkably close to that given by Harritt, Parker, and Field. Indeed, there is no other spring in a generally western direction that will fit the mileage so well.

Solomon Tetherow, in a letter written to the *Oregon Spectator*, March 18, 1847, says they left "a large rush marsh which this writer pleases to designate as Silver Lake." Tetherow at this point was several days behind Meek and the main party, traveling on their track.

Increasing lack of confidence in the guide introduced a complicating factor. Hancock wrote later:

> A great deal of dissatisfaction was expressed in our company towards our guide, Mr. Meeks, and it was whispered that two gentlemen having about three hundred head of cattle between them had contracted privately with our guide to pilot the train into the Upper Willamette country for the extra sum of one hundred dollars, each, and the company to be kept ignorant of this arrangement, which it was thought had induced Mr. Meeks to depart from the route with which he was acquainted.[57]

Again in later years, W. A. Goulder related:

> It had been becoming more and more evident to us that Meek had no more knowledge of the country through which

---

water was a real problem to the emigrants."

57 *The Narrative of Samuel Hancock,* edited by Arthur D. Howden Smith (New York: Robert M. McBride & Company, 1927), p. 28.

we were passing than we had ourselves, and that, like us, he was seeing it for the first time.[58]

The water at Silver Lake was to be their last for twenty-five miles and there was an increase in murmurings against Meek who began to show doubt and uncertainty about water ahead and grass for the animals.

Jesse Harritt's entry for September 10 points out the train's next move:

> Made a late start   travleed a west cours over a tolerable levle road tho verry stony in places   found no grass nor water for 25 ms   at one oclock this morning we gradually decended a long slope   found a good spring affording an abundance of water and grass with a feiw willows

Of this move Hancock says:

> . . . after journeying along in the most wretched way imaginable, both ourselves and stock destitute of water, we were about to despair when we came to two small springs, where we encamped, though there was very little grass; but we had water and were loth to leave it. . . .[59]

Twenty-five miles west of little Silver Lake looms the large, rocky mass of Wagontire Mountain. There are natural springs; not many and of no great copiousness, but still, water. The main source of water was the present Foster Spring; on the northwest side was the Lost Creek Spring.

It should be emphasized at this point that the train up to and including September 10 had not stopped or hesitated noticeably for any great length of time. Following Meek's scouting there was no apparent hesitation about the twenty-five-mile journey west into the desert to Wagontire. This seems significant in view of the subsequent delay of from five

---

58   William A. Goulder, *Reminiscences of a Pioneer,* (Boise, Idaho: Timothy Regan, 1909), p. 126.

59   Hancock, *op. cit.,* pp. 28-29.

to seven days which was to follow the trains' arrival at Wagontire Mountain. Until this crucial point Meek had successfully led them ever westward, finding water and grass at the end of each day's travel. At Wagontire the pattern was broken and the ordeal began. Meek was the center of a growing mass of human anger, suspicion, and fear. Field writes:

> September 11. . . . It seems there was misunderstanding between us and Meek when we left Snake River respecting the route he intended taking. We understood him that on leaving the Malheur river he intended striking over to the John Day river and down it to the old road. When we found ourselves on the branches of the Deschutes river it rather surprised us, and as we had a report in camp a few days before that he was going to pilot Owensby across the Cascade Mountains to the Willamette settlements, we supposed he was taking a straight shoot for them. It seems that he calls the Deschutes river the John Jay [sic], which he says is the name by which it is known to the mountain traders, and the similarity in the sound of the two names made us mistake the one for the other. . . .[60]

Jesse Harritt made the following entries (after arriving at Wagontire) during the next four days:

> Sept. 12 Made a small move of 5 ms an encamped on a small branch found tolerable grass and ceder timber in abundence.

> Sept. 13 made a start travleed 3 ms Met the men who had accompanyed the pilot in serch of water found none we returned to our old encampment and stoped for the night

> Sept. 14 laid stil all day waiting the return of the pilot He returned late in the evening found no water

---

60 It is apparent that the harried mountaineer found invention equal to the occasion.

Sept. 15 dispatched a company of men with their pack horses loded with water and prision [provisions] in serch of water.

Compounding their difficulties were Meek's continued uncertainty and the arrival of more wagons from the east. As Hancock put it:

> Our company increased at these springs and thirty wagons of our immediate company that had gone forward the day before, came back alarmed at the prospect before them, to find that other trains from the Atlantic side learning of the course we had taken, from the manager at Fort Boise, had followed us here having experienced the same difficulties that we had encountered, so that our company now numbered in wagons, one hundred and fifty.[61]

Harritt's entry for September 13 and Hancock's enumeration of thirty wagons going forward only to return are further evidence of the importance of Wagontire Mountain as the rock against which the tide of immigration broke. Those wagons attempted a portion of the arid wastes west of the mountain, only to be met by a returning pilot (Meek) with the report of no water found. It was a serious setback. Soberly, Field wrote on September 13:

> Started this morning in expectation of a long drive across the plain before us, but when about four miles from camp met Meek's wife in company with a friend, returning with the news that they had found no water as yet and requesting all who were at the spring to remain there until he found a camp and returned or sent word back for them to come on. Nothing remained for us to do but drive back to the camp we had just left, where we found Tethero's company also, so if misery loves company here is enough of it, for this small camping spot is nearly eaten out by our own large stock of cattle, and to add to all this there are some in the company nearly out of provisions.

---

61 Hancock, *op. cit.,* p. 29.

Reluctant to accept the wall of aridity which confined them, increasing numbers of mounted men searched the country to the west. According to Hancock, "the number of men on horseback constantly exploring the mountains in quest of water now numbered one hundred, fully impressed with the anxiety with which they were regarded by their fellow travelers; yet these explorations were continued seven days unsuccessfully." Parker's entry for September 11 is further testimony:

> went to Another spring 5 laid heare 4 days and some five days Codent find now [no] water frome 10 to 20 to 30 men out hunting water some come into camp and codent speek. . . .

The probing to the west proving fruitless, the search turned a new direction. Field's September 14 entry reads:

> Last evening the portion of Owensby's company which were out upon the plains returned with their cattle and water kegs, having left their wagons out upon the plain seven miles from here and no water had then been found within 30 miles of them. Today Meek ordered them to return to this place and sent an order for us to remain at this place until tomorrow morning, then to let 10 or 12 men accompany him with spades and dig for water at a place he thinks it can be found, in the dry bed of a creek. This evening Owensby returned with his wagons, teams, cattle and all, having enough of lying out upon the plain upon uncertainties. Meek came in after dark and said that from the top of a mountain a short distance from here he had discovered a cut in the side of a mountain apparently 15 miles distant where from the bright green appearance of the willows and grass there could be no doubt of our finding water and requesting that some horsemen might accompany him to search the mountain sides still further; he thought there would be no danger in some wagons starting tomorrow.

Hardships which had become commonplace began to take their toll in deterioration in the situation of the people and the stock. Fatigue and lack of food, together with worry and indecision, were sapping away the pioneer strength. Although some families were still stocked with provisions, others through mischance or miscalculation were running low. John Martin later remarked of these individuals, "They almost starved to death, being for five days without food, and they put salt on grass and ate that."[62] Lost Spring "hollow" is today a desolate, gloomy spot.

"Mountain fever," a debilitating result of fatigue and poor food, continued to strike the very young and the very old. Field first mentions it in his entry for September 9.[63]

Betsy (Mrs. Daniel) Bayley wrote in 1849:

> We camped at a spring which we gave the name of "The Lost Hollow" because there was very little water there. We had men out in every direction in search of water. They traveled 40 or 50 miles in search of water but found none. You cannot imagine how we all felt. Go back, we could not and we knew not what was before us. Our provisions were failing us. There was sorrow and dismay depicted on every countenance. We were like mariners lost at sea and in this mountainous wilderness we had to remain for five days. At last we concluded to take a Northwesterly direction. . . . The mountains looked like volcanoes and the appearance that one day there had been an awful thundering of volcanoes and a burning world. The valleys were all covered with a white crust and looked like a salaratus. Some of the company used it to raise their bread. After we got in the right direction, people began to get sick.[64]

---

62 "John Martin," *Portrait and Biographical Record of Willamette Valley* (Chicago: Chapman Publishing Co., 1903), p. 230.

63 There seems to be considerable difference of opinion about this mysterious disease. Evidently it was not cholera. There is a possibility it was some form of anthrax, but no medical proof of this is, of course, available. Characterized by high fever and extreme weakness, it claimed the weakest for victims. See Larsell's *Doctor in Oregon* (Portland, Oregon: Binfords & Mort, 1947), pp. 167, 168, which also contains (pp. 139-43) Tetherows' pioneer remedies.

64 Betsy Bayley letter, Vertical File, Oregon Historical Society.

As desperation grew so did the animosity of many toward Meek. Before the miserable pocket at Wagontire erupted into violence something had to be done. To Samuel Hancock's mind,

> . . . the excitement was intense, and famine seemed inevitable. The feelings of our company towards the guide were of that unmistakable character to justify me in telling him his life was in danger; his reply was "I have known it for several days, but what can I do? I have brought you here, and will take you off, if you will go." He then asked if our teams would follow: I told him that I thought a portion of this large train might be induced to follow, regarding, I must confess, the contingency of remaining here, or following this guide in whom none of us had the slightest confidence, as equally desperate. Many of us thought that at all events, the company had better separate as nothing was being accomplished by remaining together except greater distress; so we admonished the guide to secrete himself in one of our wagons and remain there; during this time inquiries were made after him by parties, who wished him to go with them in search of water, which was of no sort of use as the entire country had been explored; they were told that he had gone, and started; about thirty wagons of our immediate company now commenced preparations for leaving, filling beef hides and everything that would contain water; we left the encampment about two o'clock in the day, feeling rather sad at leaving the others, with so much uncertainty of ever meeting them again. A good many of our company were sick, not only of heart, but body also, occasioned from scarcity of the proper kind of food; in fact we had been compelled to kill stock that we were desirous to save and bring to Oregon if it were possible to get there; there being no game of any kind; however, these cattle would have died if we had not killed them as they were gradually sinking from the fatigue and privations they had had to endure.[65]

---

65   Hancock, *op. cit.,* pp. 30-31.

Chapter V

NORTH TO SAFETY

THE High Desert north of Wagontire is no Sahara. There is little loose, blowing sand. It is a barren, rocky plain formed by volcanoes and erosion. For Hancock's party and those that followed, the water shortage was only one difficulty. But the people were moving again and with the departure of these wagons the ordeal of Wagontire began to draw to a close. Field's diary entry for September 15 witnesses their passing:

> This afternoon about three o'clock 21 of Tethero's together with six or seven of Owensby's company made a start for the spot spoken of yesterday, which lies northeasterly from here, Meek accompanying them. A company of eight or ten wagons passed through the hollow we were encamped in, and started out into the plains by moonlight in the evening. They were a company we had never seen before and they said they were the last to leave the states for Oregon this year, starting some two or three weeks behind us. Their loose stock were nearly all working steers, they having enough apparently to change teams every day.

Midmorning the next day word raced through the dusty encampment: water had been found! good water, in quantity—but twenty-five miles away to the north. The people were not slow to organize, considering their state. As companies mobilized, others followed. Field says:

Sept. 16—Capt. Riggs accompanied by the two Wilcoxes started yesterday to search for water at a place they had seen the day before, and which the description given by Meek of the spot he expected to find water at, applied to precisely. They returned this morning reporting it the same with plenty of water and grass. We made preparation for starting immediately, but could not get ready until late in the afternoon, as our cattle were so scattered. We had a clear, full moon to light us on our toilsome way, which lay across a mountain to the northward, and after traveling about 20 miles we reached the long-sought spot at daybreak.

Parker records his departure from the springs at Wagontire on the sixteenth in brief fashion, giving 3:00 P.M. for the time. On the same day Harritt reports:

The hunters returned this morning at 9 oclock found water in 25 ms in a fiew minits the compny's ware in parade for their oxen made a general collection of stock betwin 4 oclock and sundown about 80 waggons left the branch for the next encampment travleed all night at day brake we reached the place of encampment at a small mountain stream winding its way through a level vally found no wood except sage which grew in abundence near its margin having come 25 ms we stoped to take some refreshment and rest our teames.

The "eight or ten" wagons noted by Field in his September 15 entry were probably the Cornelius party, as the following account would indicate:

At length, at a place called Last Hollow, a council was held, and amid various opinions to go south, north, to continue west, to go back the way they came, or to stay where they were, fearing to leave the water, it was decided by the Cornelius party to go north to the Columbia. Followed by a few other wagons, they set out one evening, taking their course towards the North Star, and at ten o'clock the next day found water and grass in abundance, and sending word back

51

to those still at Last Hollow, were soon joined by the train.[66]

On September 17 Parker, Harritt, Field, and probably the majority of the wagons were at Buck Creek water from which they traveled to the South Fork of Crooked River, for Parker's count totals 198 wagons:

> September 16. left at 3 pm oclock. traveled all nite came to water at sunrise   30 miles   Missis Butts now Betor [no better]   198 wagons in company   2,299 loose cattle   oxen 811 head   all thes cattle to git water and 1051 Gotes also consume a heap of water.

As Field remarked, the spot answered Meek's description of the place he had expected to find when the wagons under his guidance left Wagontire on the fifteenth.

And what of Hancock and "Owensby's seven wagons and 21 of Tethero's"? Hancock, and he is generally accurate here for the experience left its mark on his memory, says his party traveled slowly two and one-half days and two nights finding water just before sunset. Since he left September 15, it is probable he joined the rest of the wagons at the South Fork of Crooked River late in the day of the seventeenth. His account, given below, tallies with the Bayley story, also given:

> It was now about five months since we took our departure from the Atlantic States and there was considerable sickness in our company. Notwithstanding this we traveled all the afternoon and night succeeding our departure from the rest of the emigration, and turned our cattle out to feed upon all they could get, and to obtain the dew that had fallen the night before; after this we started again and traveled all day; towards evening we gave our oxen a little of the water we had brought from the Springs [at Wagontire Mountain], then continued traveling all night, allowing our animals to graze and avail themselves of the dew; as we did the day before and

---

66 Elwood Evans, *History of the Pacific Northwest* (2 vols.; Portland, Oregon: North Pacific History Co., 1889), I, 279. "T.R. Cornelius" biography.

then started on the third day's drive from the Springs, first giving our teams a little water to enable them to proceed. Just before sunset of this day we heard a number of shots fired in the direction we were going and afterwards the firing was renewed much nearer to us; looking forward we discovered a man coming at full speed on horseback—our guide had found water![67]

It is recorded by Goulder that when the wagons traveled at night advance elements, usually mounted men, made piles of sagebrush which they fired. The beacons guided the weary teams through the unfamiliar territory till dawn.

Notice the similarity of the Bayley narrative to Hancock's description:

> At one time they struck the border of what was known as the Great American Desert. They traveled two nights and three hot days with no water except what they had in their casks. The poor animals suffered. The Bayley family would occasionally dampen the parched tongues of their animals with a little water. In the afternoon of the third day, the wearied animals began to show more courage. They quickened their pace till it was almost a trot; they smelled water. Finally the men had to unhitch the oxen, when there was a general stampede to water. The animals would rush in all over—leaving only their heads out.[68]

Evidently this wandering party—Hancock, Ownbey, some of the Tetherows—struck to the north, too far west to find water at Buck Creek, not far enough to strike Camp

---

67 *The Narrative of Samuel Hancock,* edited by Arthur D. Howden Smith (New York: Robert M. McBride & Company, 1927) p. 31. The guide, of course, is Meek.

68 Myron A. Munson, *The Munson Record* (New Haven, Conn.: Tuttle, Morehouse & Taylor Press), p. 506. (Privately printed.) The depth of water necessary for animals to bathe could only have been where the giant springs of Crooked River's South Fork formed pools.

Creek. Solomon Tetherow's letter indicates that an Indian finally guided them to Crooked River:

> The truth is four days after leaving a large rush marsh which this writer pleases to designate "Silver Lake" and two days after taking a northerly direction, an Indian came to us, pointed out the course to Mr. Perkins house (The Dalles) to which he said it was 5 days journey, and so far from refusing to follow the advise of the Indian, at my request he was employed by Mr. Meek to pilot us to Crooked river, which he did for a blanket.[69]

The jubilation of the pioneers at the discovery of water was never to be forgotten by young Samuel Hancock. Many years later he wrote:

> It is impossible to describe the joy with which this news was received; some were so overcome that they could not give utterance to their feelings of joy, while tears of gratitude streamed down their cheeks, others gave vent to their delight in loud exultations; the women and children clapping their hands and giving other demonstrations that they too were enraptured by the announcement of plenty of water. In fact the poor animals seemed to have an appreciation of it too for it is said in scarcity an animal can smell food or water at a great distance; at any rate they traveled along apparently more cheerfully.[70]

When the excitement had subsided and all the parched throats had been soothed with fresh, cool water, there may have been some softening of feelings toward Meek, but this

---

69 Solomon Tetherow, letter to *Oregon Spectator,* Oregon City, March 18, 1847, p. 3, col. 2; ". . . near the center of this alkali-impregnated sage brush plain, the south fork of Crooked river rises boldly, but quietly out of the earth and creeps off northward with no tree nor bush to betray the presence for several miles."—"Crook County," in *History of Central Oregon* (Spokane, Washington: Western Historical Publishing Co., 1905), p. 737.
70 Hancock, *op. cit.,* p. 32.

was not the case with all the emigrants. Having moved from Buck Creek to the South Fork, Field's entry for Thursday, September 18, reflects the attitude of the company:

> This creek has no brush upon its banks, which was the reason for it being overlooked when they searched the country for water. It is evident that Meek's knowledge of the country has rather failed him here, since it is actually a shorter drive from the spring we left on the 10th inst. to the head of the branch we camped upon yesterday than it is from the 10th to the 11th, and apparently a better road. Had we taken that road we would be advanced now at least 80 miles on our journey, besides being saved the trying suspense of remaining in a miserable encampment several days, with no prospect of water ahead for 40 or 50 miles.

Field implies that the whole episode at Wagontire might have been avoided had the trains swung north from Crane Spring, through the valley of Silver Creek to the water at Buck Creek and the South Fork of Crooked River. He is quite correct. However, here again is hindsight in operation. In view of Meek's westward course (for whatever reason) there is little basis to suppose any other outcome.

McNary, Parker, Hancock, Riggs and others totaling at least one hundred wagons—and apparently including those best provisioned—traveled northwest from the grass and water of the headwaters of the South Fork of Crooked River as soon as possible. Terrain forced them almost due north. Passing Cold Springs and descending the steep slope of Stein's Ridge into the Camp Creek Valley, they crossed Camp Creek, turned past the old Bennett place into the series of benches and draws which form the east side of Maury Mountains. Remnants of the track are still to be seen from the top of Stein's Ridge,[71] faintly curling through the sagebrush.

---

71 On this ridge the writers found old wagon tracks scarring the slope down into Camp Creek. Ancient juniper stumps line the rim; decayed upper trunks still showing axe marks are scattered along

Their route carried them on a collision course for Crooked River Valley about three quarters of a mile west from where Camp Creek enters it. Here on the south slope of the bench near the present Pine Creek Cemetery, the old scars of descent are still quite visible from the Paulina road, in the faint green of spring grass or in the shadows of light snow.[72] Here they found water and feed and an apparent route west along the river. The "crookedness" of Crooked River was quite evident—the diary of Harritt mentions crossing and recrossing. In Stewart Canyon the wagons were forced into the bed of the river itself. Harritt states, September 20:

> Continued down the creek   Passed through several narrow evenus where the mountains closed in on both sides where we ware compelled to follow down the channel of the [creek] for several hundred yards in water up to our waggon beds   Continued to follow its meanders crossing its channel a number of times   after an advance of 13 ms we encamped found grass and willows.[73]

the lower portion of the descent where their usefulness as "drags" ended. On the rim, deeply scratched in a soft slab of rock was a "T" and the date "1852." No one presently in the country knows the story behind the stone which is in the Oregon Historical Society's museum in Portland. A cairn on the rim marks the location. The only record of travel that year which we have been able to find is that of the "Road Viewers" who left Eugene City in 1852 to search out a route for the Elliott party. However, the old tracks were located and traveled upon by several parties in search of the Blue Bucket from 1851 to 1861. In 1860 Major Steen passed this way on his wagon road exploration.

72 Mary Glenn Butler, "Crook County Stage Station," *Central Oregonian* (Prineville, Oregon), July 30, 1959, quoted from a booklet, *Eastern Oregon Historic Landmarks,* State Society Daughters of the American Revolution.

73 Harritt refers to Crooked River as the "Sandy." (September 17, 19, entries) Curiously, he calls the Silvies River "Crooked River" in his September 6 entry. This is further indicative of the confusion existing in the train at this date and understandable considering maps in 1845 and what sparse information Stephen Meek gave.

Field writes, on September 20:

> Went about 8 miles, encamping upon the same stream mentioned yesterday, down which we followed all day, frequently crossing, it, and at one narrow pass we were obliged to follow the bed of the river for nearly a fourth of a mile.[74]

They continued down the river, from time to time cutting across the lower points of the bluffs. Tall pine trees were very much in evidence on the hills bordering both sides of the stream.

Parker's mileage and entries indicate that he stayed ahead of Harritt and the McNary group. Field, with Riggs, is behind Harritt. Hancock, and Goulder, with Ownbey, also follow.

Scouting ahead showed them more difficulty in the canyon. North was the direction—they would "cut the bend." So they made a startling climb out of Crooked River at the opening through which Wickiup Creek flows.[75] It is a very

---

For additional detail on Crooked River see McArthur, 1952 edition, pp. 163-64.

74 See Andrew McClure's "Diary of a Mining Expedition, 1858" (on file with the Oregon Historical Society, entry for Friday, September 3, 1858: "This cañon is about four hundred yards long and the hill on the south side rises to the height of four hundred feet. Width, I suppose, from a passing view, to be one hundred feet at the narrowest place."

75 Eldred M. Breese, Prineville, Oregon, letter: ". . . Another way was down Crooked River (by various routes) to the mouth of Wickiup Creek and turn up Wickiup. Not very far up they turned left and went along the South of Pilot Butte [not to be confused with Pilot Butte at Bend, Oregon] and came out on Combs Flat and turned north, not going down into Gravy Gulch. Go north until they came to a draw that goes down to the Keystone Ranch.

"The reason they could not go down Crooked River the way the road goes today, and up past Eagle Rock, was that there was a large rock ledge that jutted out into Crooked River about two miles down the river from the Riverside Ranch. When the river was dry they did go down the bed of the river. The rock was blasted and a

steep ascent "through thick ceder timber; at two o'clock P.M. we gained the top, the scene of the country became butiful and level . . ." (Harritt, September 22).

Parker, first up on top, said of the exhausting climb on September 21: "Some of the Company dident git up till after dark went 4 miles to a small spring . . . swareing without end comeing in all nite."

Field's entry for September 22 paints a vivid, primitive picture:

> Went about 7 miles, keeping still down along the river, which has to be crossed every mile or two and sometimes two or three times to the mile. Camped at the foot of a tremendous hill, which it is necessary to ascend, and which when we first came in sight of appeared to be strung with wagons from the bottom to the top, several companies being engaged in the ascent at the same time.

And the 23rd:

> Went about 20 miles, striking away from the river and camping upon a small branch of it. Had a long hard pull in the morning to ascend the mountain spoken of yesterday, but once up we felt amply repaid the trouble of climbing by the prospect which lay before us. There were the Cascade mountains stretching along the western horizon, apparently not more than 40 miles distant, forming a dark outline varied by an occasional snow peak, which would rise lofty and spire-like, as if it were a monument to departed greatness.

Appearances in central Oregon's dry atmosphere are deceiving. The distance to the summits of the snow peaks is about sixty miles. Nevertheless, some days the Cascade Range seems much nearer. The volcanic silhouettes, softened by mantles of glacier, form an impressive skyline. Reading south to north they are Mount Bachelor, Broken Top, South

---

rock grade put through and travel was along the present route. . . ." May 28, 1962, author's files.

Sister, Middle Sister, North Sister, Mount Washington, Three-Fingered Jack and Mount Jefferson. Far to the north on clear days is the ghostlike form of Mount Hood.

The trains were on top, out of Crooked River, on Combs Flat with travel generally good for a while. From here they made their way north, descending to a juncture with Ochoco Creek, which flows from the east to merge with Crooked River near the site of the Ochoco Grade School in Prineville. According to Harritt, they encamped on September 22, the stream having an abundance of grass, water, and timber.

How far down Ochoco Creek they traveled is not certain. The country allows three possibilities: (1) Angling across the Prineville Valley in a westerly direction they may have crossed Grizzly Mountain on its northeast side. This was the route taken by the military commands of Captain H. D. Wallen and Major Enoch Steen in their later journeys (1859-1860) from The Dalles to the east. Before this it was also the route of Peter Skene Ogden in 1825, and subsequently that of other trappers. (2) Continuing down Ochoco Creek to its junction with Crooked River, west of the present city of Prineville, they may have been lured by the opening of the river valley to the west. Turning north through the Lone Pine Gap, they would have reached the broad plains which border the east side of the Deschutes River. (3) From the junction of Ochoco Creek and Crooked River they may have followed the course of the present highway to Madras, crossing west of the Grizzly Mountain.

Of the three possibilities of travel the third seems most likely, but the mileage will approximate each theory and the reader is invited to take his choice.

On these plains on September 23 the wagons of Parker and McNary camped at a spring, which, from mileage alone, the writers believe is near the present Rim Rock Spring, just south of the old stage road crossing Willow Creek. Rim Rock is about five hundred yards east of the Prineville-Madras highway at the Grizzly turnoff. Neither Parker nor Harritt gives much description. Harritt says, ". . . Travleed 12 miles; stoped at nine o'clock at a spring; found good grass; no wood except a little sage."

Parker, in his usual succinct style, is revealingly pathetic: "To a Spring   18 [miles]   Beried 4 persons heare."

Field, at this point, himself became a victim of the disease which ravaged the group. He made no more daily entries; only confusedly conscious in spots, he remembered bits and patches of the subsequent journey to The Dalles. His last entry on September 24 reads: "Went about 15 miles, camping at a spring in the midst of the plains without a single landmark to tell its situation."

On September 24 both Parker and Harritt left the spring. Harritt records easy traveling through the level plain for fourteen miles where they stopped to make a dry camp approximately at the site of Madras. Apparently Willow Creek was dry. The next day they traveled six miles north and stopped, unsure of their next move. Though Harritt states they are camped "on Chutes or Fall River" it is in a very general sense, for they are several miles from it on the rim of the gigantic Deschutes Canyon. Parker, on September 24, lists mileage for the next three days as sixty-five; a fact which has troubled the writers' reconstruction a great deal. Samuel Parker logically could not go sixty-five miles anywhere, in any direction, and still be with the rest of the wagons on the twenty-sixth day of September, as he indicates. Nor would he have forced his tiring, sick company to such a terrible pace.

What he did has finally become apparent—he scouted, for his train, for the McNary group, the Riggs party, and for other elements comprising this division of the wagons. Traveling ahead on horseback, he scouted the Agency Plains rim for possible descent to water. Locating an avenue into the Gateway valley, he found the water at Sagebrush Spring, examined the travel through Lyle Gap, and returned to where the wagons awaited him. Harritt's notation of only six miles traveled on the twenty-fifth is significant in view of this: The short mileage is not usual, especially at an unwatered camp-site. In addition, the terrain was flat—travel presented no difficulty. On the Agency Plains northwest of Madras the wagons unexpectedly were halted by the deep barrier of the Deschutes Canyon which falls many hundred feet. They could not travel on as long as they were uncertain where to go; and until the scout (Parker) returned, this uncertainty continued.

On the following day the wagons turned northeast to the only open direction and encamped at Sagebrush Spring "in company with about 200 wagons."[76]

---

76 Diary of Jesse Harritt, September 26, 1845, *Oregon Pioneer Association Transactions, 1910-11,* Portland, Oregon.

Chapter VI
THE TRAIN DIVIDES

Fᴿᴼᴹ the springs on the South Fork of Crooked River that portion of the train which contained Tetherow's group did not go with Parker, McNary, Riggs and the others. A split took place, and these people with their wagons headed in a general northwest direction.

At this point in the reconstruction of events a split also took place between the authors' viewpoints. One of the authors maintains that Meek went with Tetherow from Wagontire (as Field related) to the South Fork and then continued on the western fork of the train's divided route. He points out that the travel north was rough and difficult, that Meek would have been more likely to swing northwest around the west side of Maury Mountains, along Bear Creek, and that Tetherow did, in fact, do this, both directed this way by the Indian.

The other author, equally obstinate, maintains that since Hancock quite obviously has Meek with him when he leaves Wagontire, and has Meek with him at the later crossing of the Deschutes River—*ergo* he has had Meek with him all along! (Hancock, very probably following Parker, McNary, *et al.*, in his narrative does not mention Meek's departure during this time.) There is a strange hybrid stubbornness associated with equine desert dwellers which is obvious in this dispute. The argument was still going on up to publication. Frankly, neither of us knows where Meek is at this particular point.

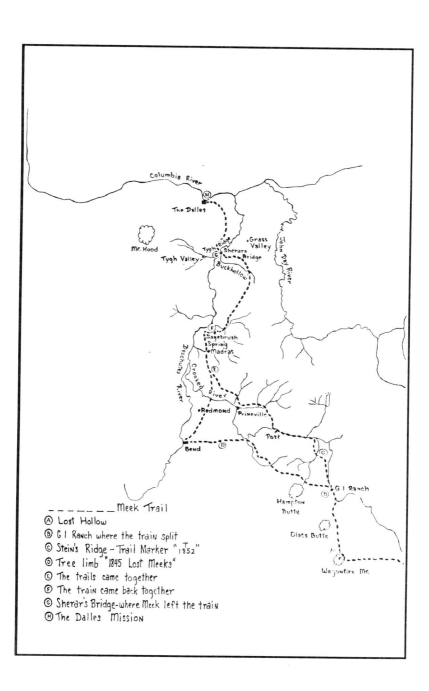

Columbia River

The Dalles

Mt. Hood

Tygh River
Tygh Valley
Sherars
Bridge
Grass
Valley
John Day River
Buckhollow

Sagebrush
Spring
Madras

Deschutes River
Crooked River

Redmond
Prineville
Post

Bend

Hampton
Butte

Glass Butte

G I Ranch

Wagontire Mt.

_ _ _ _ _ _ Meek Trail
Ⓐ Lost Hollow
Ⓑ G I Ranch where the train split
Ⓒ Stein's Ridge – Trail Marker "1852"
Ⓓ Tree limb "1845 Lost Meeks"
Ⓔ The trails came together
Ⓕ The train came back together
Ⓖ Sherar's Bridge-where Meek left the train
Ⓗ The Dalles Mission

Why the wagons separated, the writers have not been able to discover. Perhaps dissatisfaction with Meek caused one group to secede; they may have been further influenced by the logic that a smaller train had more chance of survival with limited water and grass; perhaps they were separated by terrain. Finding water and grass, they felt no need to rejoin the rest.

A further reason may have been the personalities involved. Sam Parker's diary is that of a "driver" who traveled steadily north from the South Fork of Crooked River to The Dalles. Less stubborn leaders were more hesitant in their movement, for the stakes were high.

Somewhere on its route between the head of the South Fork of Crooked River and Bear Creek it became urgently evident that the Tetherow group which split from Parker and McNary was not going to be able to arrive at The Dalles without help. Food was getting very short; some were shaking the last flour from sacks; some were reduced to a partial diet of dried grasshoppers and berries, delicacies they obtained from the Indians.[77]

W. H. Herren wrote a letter to the editor of the *Oregonian*, March 7, 1922, in which he stated:

> When they reached the summit of the mountains they camped on a meadow, and while there some Warm Springs Indians came to their camp. One of the Indians could speak a little English. He told them that if some of them would go with him to a high ridge near by they could see down into the Deschutes and Crooked River valleys. He showed them some buttes that lay south of Prineville and said that they would find water there, but no water between there and the Deschutes. He also showed them what is now called Pilot butte, and told them if they would steer straight for that butte they would find a place in the bend of the river where a man could cross it, go down on the west side, through by way of

---

77 Fred Lockley, *Oregon Journal*, February 27, 1922.

HISTORIC
OREGON TRAIL
MALHEUR CROSSING

NEAR THIS SPOT WAS THE
CROSSING OF THE MALHEUR
BY THE OLD OREGON TRAIL.
HERE PASSED THE ILL-FATED
WHITMAN PARTY IN 1836, THE
WEARY TRAVELERS OF THE
GREAT MIGRATION IN 1843
AND IN THAT YEAR CAPTAIN
FREMONT IN HIS EXPLORA-
TIONS. THE NEARBY HOT
SPRINGS OFFERED A RESTING
PLACE WHERE BATHS COULD
BE TAKEN AND CLOTHING
WASHED.

Courtesy Oregon State Highway Department.

PLATE II: Marker at Vale, Oregon. Here the Meek
wagons separated from the main body.

Courtesy U.S. Dept. of the Interior, Bureau of Land Management.

PLATE III: Castle Rock, Malheur County, Oregon—called "Fremont's Peak" by the emigrants.

PLATE IV: Sarah King Chambers' grave, a few miles above the present Beulah Reservoir. This is the only known marked grave left by the 1845 train.

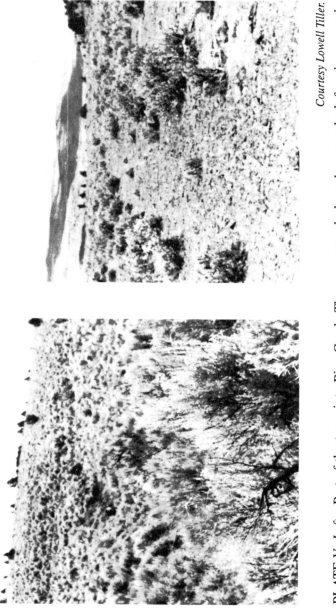

PLATE V: *Left*—Part of the trace into Pine Creek. The wagon tracks have been washed, forming a rut six feet deep in places. *Right*—The trace leading to the very steep descent into Pine Creek. The trace can still be seen thirty-five miles northeast of Burns. This portion of the trail was subsequently used by the military, by the lost Elliott wagon train of 1853, and by early-day freighters.

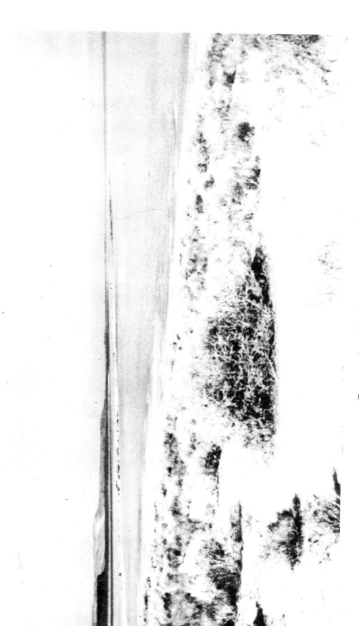

Courtesy David B. Marshall, Malheur National Wildlife Refuge, Burns, Oregon.

PLATE VI: Harney Lake, "A lake of miserable stagnant water."

Courtesy Oregon State Highway Commission.

PLATE VII: Wagontire Mountain—an expanse of sage. With an elevation of 6,504 feet, it is seen here from U.S. Highway 395 near Wagontire, Oregon.

Courtesy Don Moody.

PLATE VIII: Lost Hollow as it appears today. Lost Creek
can be seen flowing through the center of the meadow. In
this little bowl families and animals competed for water
and space, mid-September, 1845.

PLATE IX: Here the Tetherow Train descended into Bear Creek, opposite the old Dunham Ranch.

Courtesy Portland General Electric.

PLATE X: Crooked River, northwest of Redmond, Oregon.
This immense chasm barred further progress westward.

Courtesy Oregon State Highway Commission.

PLATE XI: Towering over ten thousand feet, the Three Sisters form the background for this view of Smith Rock, northeast of Redmond. The "bluffs of the followers of Meek," with the Cascades on the west.

Courtesy Oregon State Highway Commission.

PLATE XII: The Crooked River near Smith Rock. These wind-sculpted buttresses are colorfully picturesque.

Courtesy Portland General Electric.

PLATE XIII: Crooked River, showing the confluence of the Deschutes and much of the area now covered by the pool from Round Butte Dam. Approximately ten miles north of this point, the pioneers realized the need to turn back northeast.

Courtesy Priscilla Knuth.

PLATE XIV: Stewart Canyon, looking east. Here the wagons of the pioneers jolted down the stream bed.

Courtesy Stan Clark.

PLATE XV: Sixty miles southeast of Prineville, the old trace on Stein's Ridge leading to the Camp Creek Crossing.

PLATE XVI: Very old juniper stumps on Stein's Ridge. The trees were cut for drag logs and used in the descent to Camp Creek.

Courtesy C. L. Clark.

PLATE XVII: On the very edge of Stein's Ridge, a small cairn held this rock, scratched "T 1852." Will Tandy, one of the road viewers in 1852, was known to have been here. Perhaps it was he who carved the stone.

the Metolius and Tygh valley and that they would eventually reach The Dalles.

So men were sent ahead with packhorses to The Dalles. The party included a member of the Tetherow families (perhaps Sol's son, eighteen-year-old Amos), William T. (Billy) Vaughan, Felix Dorris, John Hampton, and, according to Center descendants, Samuel Center. Peterson descendants have stated that Asa Peterson went ahead for supplies at The Dalles and it is possible that he was of this party. The names of all are not known. Estimates range from six to ten men in number.[78] They crossed the Deschutes where Tumalo stands today and took a well-established Indian trail to The Dalles.

This ancient trail to which the party was, no doubt, directed by the Indians, was a link between the Columbia and Klamath and Shasta areas, a migratory path to the trading and fishing spots. On the west side of the Deschutes, at Tumalo, the trail led north to Fly Creek, a tributary of the Metolius, then on to Box Canyon Creek and Tenino Creek, just east of the juncture with Shi-ti-ke Creek. At this point, the magnificent, snowcapped Mount Jefferson towers to the west, a proud member of the rugged Cascade Range.

The way led to Dry Creek, thence to Hot Springs at Warm Springs River where it took a northwesterly course, crossing Quartz Creek near the highest point of its bend in the north

---

78 See Joel Palmer, *Journal of Travels Over the Rocky Mountains* in Thwaites' *Early Western Travels, 1748-1846,* Vol. XXX, entry for September 30 (ten men); "Discovery of Blue Bucket Mine Real," *The Oregonian,* April 27, 1919, sec. 2, p. 6, col. 1 (seven men), statement by George Millican; William Walter, "Reminiscences of an Old 45'er," (six men) obtained from descendants, Mrs. Mabel B. Blum, White Salmon, Washington, and Mr. and Mrs. Lee Mantz, Waitsburg, Washington; "The Trials and Tribulations of the Powells and Centers in 1845 While Crossing the Plains from Illinois to Oregon," (ten men) provided by Powell-Center descendant, Mrs. Arthur G. Elkins, Portland, Oregon.

and Nena Creek just before it bends to the north. Skirting the Mutton Mountains which are west of the Deschutes River, the trail turned gradually east to Wapinitia, north to Tygh Valley, over Tygh Ridge north to Fifteen Mile Creek and The Dalles at the Columbia.[79] Fremont followed the trail in 1843, and the route closely parallels that of the Abbot Pacific Railroad Survey party of 1855.

Joel Palmer, following the Oregon Trail with his party in 1845, arrived in The Dalles September 29. His journal records the arrival of the relief party from the western group of Meek Cutoff travelers on "the day previous to our arrival," which would be the twenty-eighth. He further states that the men had ridden for ten days which would make their departure from Crooked River on or about September 18. This is two days after Parker's departure from the South Fork springs, one day after Harritt's, and about the estimated date of Hancock's departure.

It had been thought that the ride to The Dalles would take two days; the men took with them a scanty supply of provisions. Upon their arrival at the mission, they were so weak from hunger and their limbs so rigid from riding the great distance, it was necessary to assist them to dismount. The only food procured other than the packed provisions was a rabbit and a fish supplied by an Indian, whom they had met on the way.

The wagons which sent them out could not, and did not, wait at the South Fork oasis. Following generally on the trail of the horsemen and scouting ahead they moved toward Bear Creek.

---

79 Map compiled by Ralph M. Shane and Ruby D. Leno, Warm Springs Indian Reservation, Warm Springs, Oregon, J. W. Elliott, Supt., April, 1949. Copy in possession of Mrs. Carl Galloway, Redmond, Oregon. See Ralph M. Shane, "Early Explorations Through Warm Springs Reservation Area," *OHQ*, LI (December, 1950), 273-309.

W. A. Goulder's comment, while applicable to the Cutoff as a whole, seems appropriate here:

> We had entered upon this new and untrodden route at a time when our oxen were already worn down and footsore by the long trip, thus far, across the plains, and when we were all tired and several of the company sick from exposure, privation, and fatigue. The new route was a trackless waste, covered, for the most part, by immense fields of sage-brush that grew tall, strong, and dense. Through these sage-fields we were obliged to force the oxen, the teams taking turns, day about, in breaking their way through the sage. It often consumed a good deal of time in the morning in compelling the oxen to begin their daily task of breaking road. Added to this, was the scarcity of water in many parts of the route, which caused much suffering, especially to the women and children. This was followed by daily increasing cases of sickness. The suffering ones, who could no longer walk or ride on horseback, had to find places in the wagons, thus adding painfully to all the other discomforts of the journey, and taxing greatly the already-overtasked strength of the poor oxen.[80]

Tetherow, with a portion of the group which included the Herrens, Durbins, and Gesners, cut northeast of Hampton Buttes, crossed the northern edge of Pringle Flats and dropped down into Bear Creek about where Ant Creek drains.

The original survey of Township 19 South, Range 19 East, surveyed in 1876 by Alonzo Gesner, and T20S R20E, also surveyed by Gesner, show a route labeled "Meeks Immigrant Road." Gesner, who at three years of age accompanied his parents on the Cutoff, quite probably knew what the tracks were through family discussions in later years.[81]

---

80 Goulder, *Reminiscences of a Pioneer* (Boise, Idaho: Timothy Regan, 1909), p. 126.
81 Reuben Gesner and wife Mary (Bailey) Gesner settled in Marion County. Alonzo was Indian agent at Warm Springs Agency 1883-84, in addition to positions as surveyor in diverse localities.

From here we have no record of the progress of this portion of the train. According to terrain they would have crossed Bear Creek and continued north to the west of the present Bill McCormack ranch, headed for Taylor Butte. There is some confirmation.

On the Dunham ranch, east of Taylor Butte and on the east side of Bear Creek, are old ruts where wagons came down the hill. Local legend has it that in early days there were wagon parts, dishes, and other mementoes scattered along the hillside. From the look of the descent it is likely several wagons overturned. Ascending from this spot, following a draw west and south of Taylor Butte, the emigrants struck easy travel but another dry stretch.[82]

---

82 "There was one place where a little ridge ran down into the main draw that the immigrant road followed. It had been leveled and in order to have adequate width a juniper tree was cut off at road level. This stump showed great age." Information from Carl Johnson, Bureau of Reclamation, Vale, Oregon.

In the *Oregonian* March 26, 1916, p. 8, appeared the following news story: "Old Gold Mine Sought—(Baker, Oregon)—Relocation of the Blue Bucket Mine, known in Oregon legend as the richest gold prospect in the Northwest is expected by J. W. Buckley and K. C. Harpan of this city who believe they have discovered the location sought in vain by prospectors for more than 60 years. According to tradition, the diggins rich in virgin gold are in the Prineville country and were worked in 1849 by a party of immigrants who, after a short stay were driven out by Indians. All efforts to relocate the gold deposits have been in vain. The place found by Mr. Buckley and Mr. Harpan, Mr. Buckley says tallies with the description furnished by the legend. According to the story, a woman of the party died and was buried before the immigrants left. The Baker men found a rude head stone bearing the inscription 'Mary E.—1849.' Further fixing the date were two old linch pin wagons . . ." Old residents in the Post country remember the two; point to Sheep Rock as their area of search. It is interesting to note that a *Mary E.* Harris appears on the 1845 death list compiled by Hiram Smith, 1845 emigrant. See our chap. IX, footnote 118.

Their guides were the Three Sisters and, later, Pilot Butte, near what is now the city of Bend. Original surveys of the Alfalfa area show old tracks going almost due west toward Pilot Butte; the then-dim trace is labeled "Old Emigrant Road." Later it became the "old Bear Creek Road."

There is a grave by the old road where the Central Oregon Irrigation canal crosses about a half mile south of the old Alfalfa store. A nearby juniper was blazed and deeply-burned letters inscribed on the west side of the tree. Unfortunately, time and the action of wind and sand have all but obliterated the legend. It has been impossible to determine the exact date of the grave, other than it is "very old." W. D. Staats, one of the earliest pioneers of the central Oregon area, dated the grave "1845 or 1846" in an *Oregonian* article, April 25, 1926. He further said he had seen the marker for the first time forty-six years before and that it was "old" then. The inscription read in part, "Sacred to the Memory of JE—IE." Probably a child's grave, it is about twelve miles from the crossing at Bear Creek and it seems reasonable to assume the dusty, sage-covered flat was a dry camp for the wagons.[83]

A letter from Clyde Roberts, Union, Oregon, places the line of march near the old Frank Houston ranch: ". . . I have personally known the people of the younger generation that was in the train of 1845. Those two springs I spoke about in my map lay side by side at the old Houston homestead. One was warm enough to wash dishes in, the other was ice cold. The tree with the iron bar was cut down the last time I was in there. The woman died at the creek when they camped after she gave birth to the baby. The baby was buried at the edge of the Butte which is 60 miles east of Bend."

83 The writers are indebted for information about this grave to the late Prince Staats, of Bend, to Arthur Horsell, of Powell Butte, to the Peter Hohnstein family of Alfalfa.

A letter from Roy Rannells, Riddle, Oregon, was further help: "4-18-1962. Aubry Perry of Bend, Oregon, sent me the paper clipping of your Blue Bucket story. In 1905 my father spent some time on the wagon trail hunting for the Blue Bucket. As to the grave in the Alfalfa district, she was in Sol Tetherow's Train."

Northwest of the grave, in T16S, R13E, stands a giant juniper. *The Bend Bulletin*, April 27, 1949, carried a story of its discovery by two Bend residents, Fred Carter and R. R. Edwards, each of whom found the tree independent of the other, while cutting wood. The tree was kindly shown to the writers by Mr. Carter in 1960. Carved deeply into the aged, gray wood of a huge limb was the date "1845" and a word which we believe to be "lost" and a clearly legible "Meeks." Between "lost" and "Meeks" is carved what appears to be a surveyor's arrow of direction—pointing west toward The Sisters.

How the inscription came to be on the tree is a mystery. The writers offer two theories: It may have been carved by a member of the six-man (or more) rescue party, mentioned earlier in this chapter, on its way to The Dalles, as a marker to the following wagons, for the great juniper was not then hidden by the curtain of younger trees which presently surrounds it. The other theory, equally plausible, is that the limb was carved by some member of the wagon company on its way north from camp on the Deschutes. Sighting north toward Crooked River from Bend places the marked limb roughly on the southern end of a line with Smith Rock on the north. Here, once again, terrain is a limiting factor in the course of the train.[84]

There were two graves. The other one was in the C.O.I. Ditch rightaway and was dug up. The tree bore the name Alise 1848. Leelan Covert cut open the healed in bark and the scribing was as plain as it was in the beginning. Mr. Perry, Aubry Perry's father, was rightaway superintendent and I was on the Survey location under Tom Langdon. There is a redhead buried somewhere between this grave and the narrows of Harney lake. One of Sol Tetherow's ox yokes was found east of Wagontire Mountain. He was the wagon master . . . When Ed Rannells first settled in Crook County the iron stained rocks were plain where they crossed Bear Creek near the old Dunavan [Dunham] Ranch."

84   Of interest here is an excerpt from an account printed in the *Bend*

At the present site of the city of Bend, it would have been possible to cross the Deschutes. Whether this western split did so is improbable, for the terrain across the river to the west and north is eventually such as to render wagon travel impossible.

But the natural meadows bordering the river were a welcome site to the dusty travelers. The luxuriant grass brought strength to the animals and the clear cold water refreshed the pioneers. There was no time to spare here; regardless of the beauty of the tall pines the train then began a northern course along the Deschutes, bearing east to avoid the beginnings of the Crooked River Gorge.

A later stage and freight road from Bend to Madras follows this route closely. It is well-planned, skirting the rock flats and winding around the lava outcroppings. North of the present Bend airport it goes, then northeast toward the gap at Lone Pine. The route enters the Crooked River Valley through a short draw now thickly covered with juniper, about one-fourth mile southwest of the old stage station of O'Neil.

From the east side of Tetherow Butte, near Redmond, the gap at Lone Pine and the great outcroppings of Smith Rock are visible. A route east allowed them to avoid most of the rough, rocky ridges, and to bypass both the Crooked River Canyon and the Gray Buttes.

Bulletin, July 3, 1912, "History of Bend's Development Has Many Interesting Features," by J. M. Lawrence: "At Fort Boise they fell in with Stephen H. Meek, uncle of an esteemed citizen, Frank Nichols, who piloted them by a new route straight across the country to Bend. Their experiences were so terrible, however, that there were threats of summary action against Meek, who deemed it prudent to depart from the Bend camp alone at night for The Dalles. Bend and Farewell Bend got their names at that time, according to Frank Nichols." The limb is presently in the Deschutes Historical Center in Bend, Oregon.

TERRIBLE TRAIL: THE MEEK CUTOFF, 1845

An interesting corroboration is offered in Andrew McClure's diary of a mining expedition in 1858. A party of twenty-seven men left Eugene City, August 20, 1858, for the central Oregon region, traveling east up the South Fork of the Willamette River toward Diamond Peak. At least one man who had been with Meek in 1845 was in the party. The purpose of the expedition was, of course, the rediscovery of the famed Blue Bucket gold. North of present Redmond, the party moved to examine the great cliffs of Smith Rock, then unnamed. McClure speaks of them as the "noted bluffs of the followers of Meek." (Field, Parker, and Harritt make no mention of these outcroppings. Their route lay farther east so that the rocks were not visible to them.)

On Wednesday, September 15, 1858, after fruitless searches which had led the party up Crooked River, into Camp Creek, and south to the present G. I. Ranch (South Fork of Crooked River), back-tracking the Meek trail, McClure wrote: "Twenty-seventh day. [at junction of Ochoco Creek and Crooked River] Started [north], and soon striking Meek's trail, tried to follow it. Followed to the summit of a divide which it crosses north east of Rocky Bluff."[85]

"Rocky Bluff" is the present Smith Rock. McClure was traveling northwest and it is interesting to note that the McClure party of 1858 soon lost Meek's trail, even then—only thirteen years later. It is no wonder that subsequent searchers for the Blue Bucket nuggets found great difficulty in tracing the old ruts.

On the plains south of Madras the 1845 party had easy travel for some miles and somewhere on this wide area they sighted the other group, for Harritt in his entry for September

---

85 The divide is that crossed today by the highway to Madras from Prineville. McClure Diary, Vertical File, Oregon Historical Society.

26, records camping at "a good spring in company with about 200 wagons."

One of the Herrens reported later, "We all came together again before we reached the Dalles."[86]

This spring is, beyond question, Sagebrush Spring; it is the only one in the area which fits the direction of travel, and the mileage to the next point. It is the only one large enough to supply the water needs of a group this size. Sagebrush Spring is about one-half mile east of Gateway, and a little south, on land owned by Albert Quaale.

The early settlers of the area found it to be an excellent source from which to haul water for domestic use. Long before the white man came, it was an important spot to the Indian and his pony.

---

86 *Eugene Daily Guard*, August 16, 1919, narrative of D. G. Herren.

Chapter VII

BLUE BUCKET GOLD

LOST gold is captivating. While gold carries certain social and economic significances important to man, *lost* gold connotes much more—romance, mystery, adventure. It appeals to a basic human hunger to escape from the routine of everyday life to the world of imagination, of chance, of hope that the rainbow might be just around the corner.

Gold which mysteriously stays lost only adds to the attraction. The literature of the world amply illustrates this point; the legends of American folklore are crammed with lost treasures, lost mines, lost nuggets. The Blue Bucket is no exception.

However, into the fabric of the Blue Bucket legend there have been woven no stories of violence and mysterious death such as those associated with other lost mines of the West. The story, divorced from fabrication, is simple: a portion of the wandering Meek train discovered gold along the route. No member of the train was able to find the place again. Subsequent searches found gold in other locations, notably in Baker and Grant counties, but no definite proof that these strikes were the fabled Blue Bucket was ever shown. These parties of prospectors sometimes included members of Meek's train, were guided sometimes by diaries of the Meek emigrants or by conversations with survivors. After the excitement in California in 1848, through the 1860's and 1870's parties searched the interior of the state widely. Even Stephen Meek led an expedition, fruitlessly, from California in 1868. It was a time of gold discovery, and that, and the continued elusiveness of the Blue Bucket, together with the growth of a belief in the large volume of gold to be found, spurred men's interest.

Certainly, the idea of a bucket of gold is hypnotic and, even at this writing, individuals in the Pacific Northwest are still seriously searching.[87]

One article on State Archives microfilm entitled "Blue Bucket the First Gold Find" reads:

> Popular interest in the tale of the lost Blue Bucket mine serves as a reminder that Blue Bucket, wherever it was, in all probability was the first gold mine ever discovered west of the Rocky mountains in what is now the United States. It antedated by some three years the finding of gold in California which changed the current of our economic history and revolutionized social conditions in the west. If the pioneers who found Blue Bucket had been prospectors instead of home-seekers looking for farms in the Willamette valley, there would have been a different story to tell. Nobody recognized those nuggets as gold because gold was about the last thing the immigrants expected to find. The distinction of being the first El Dorado in the west went to California on a fluke.

Still the gold, apparently, has never been found. With modern advances in technology at the disposal of the prospector, it is distinctly puzzling that no discovery is made. It is equally puzzling that the large parties of miners, professional and amateur, who searched along the purported route

---

87 The authors encountered the general opinion that anyone searching for the Blue Bucket should be humored as mentally suspect. Questions about the trail or route were immediately considered to be leading ones about the gold's location. This reaction was followed by instant incredulous amusement, partially concealed behind a poker-faced exterior. We rather hated to ask, after a while.

failed to uncover any significant deposit. Perhaps the answer lies in the location of the search.

The writers feel that establishment of the Meek route, together with a grouping of the people involved at the time of discovery, might, in conjunction with some family material not available to us, reveal some aspects heretofore overlooked. With this thought in mind we offer this chapter.

Most printed sources acknowledge members of the Herren family to have been the original discoverers. There were many Herren children, most of whom told accounts differing in some details, but substantiating the Herrens as the finders. Some sources credit Solomon Tetherow with the find and, as the legend grew, other claimants arose.

In most of the accounts given, the gold was examined at camp, even "beaten upon a wagon tire" to test its malleability. These people are said to have been present (besides the Herrens), or participated in the examination: Solomon Tetherow, Isaac Simpson, John Durbin, Will Helm, W. G. T'Vault, Thomas R. Cornelius, James Terwilliger, Sanford Patch, H. D. Martin, and Theophilus Powell. Whether all these, and more, were actually present is open to conjecture.

At any rate, the geological speculation was not widely bruited at the time. One story had some of the skeptics proclaiming the nugget or nuggets as brass and throwing them away, for cares of the journey were more pressing than potential wealth. If this story is true, it makes sense in one way: it illustrates that the train was in difficulties *at this point*—which might more clearly indicate its location.

The gold discovery has been attributed to a number of places in Oregon from Jacksonville to Tygh Valley, but the reconstruction of route and wagon order which the writers have presented in the foregoing chapters eliminates most of these as possibilities. Two widely separated areas claim the majority of the sources.

The most intensive searching at the earliest date centered around an area of the North Fork of the Malheur River, because here is located the grave of Sarah Chambers. Later legend, widely believed, and quite possibly correct, associated the death of a woman emigrant with the gold find, and her grave as an important marker therefore. As stated in Chapter III, Mrs. Chambers' grave is the only one so marked along the whole route which now survives, to our knowledge. It is not surprising that it became the center of the prospecting target. However, no gold was found here in quantities sufficient to eliminate the mystery of the "Blue Bucket" location.

The other area lies between the South Fork of Crooked River and the Deschutes River. The writers believe this more likely and submit these statements as verification:

(1) Most accounts agree that the train was lost, separated, wandering, and confused at the time of the gold discovery—a condition which hardly fits the train's description at the comparatively early crossing of the North Malheur. It *does* fit the travel from Wagontire onward.

(2) If Tetherow was present, the location had to be after leaving Wagontire, for he had not caught the rest of the train before this time. Since the split involved Tetherow's train and, probably, some of the elements once led by T'Vault, this also makes for corroboration.

(3) The Herren accounts, more numerous and supposedly more authentic, fit this portion of the country more closely.

Lawrence McNary, in his presentation of Jesse Haritt's diary,[88] says that his father, Hugh M. McNary, then eighteen, witnessed the pounding of the gold upon the wagon tire, and that the find occurred September 17. If this date is accurate, and the writers have no reason to disbelieve it, then there are some deductions to be made from the combined sources. Lawrence McNary states that on the morning of the seventeenth, or the night of the same day, the discovery took place.

---

88 Lawrence A. McNary, "Route of Meek Cut-off, 1845," *OHQ*, XXXV (March, 1934), 8.

The McNary train, chronicled by Harritt, moves from Wagontire on the sixteenth, arrives at Buck Creek the morning of the seventeenth, and moves on to the South Fork of Crooked River that evening. Parker does substantially the same thing, so does Riggs.

These things would appear then: The discovery was made by some wandering group of wagons which joined the others on the seventeenth of September and who talked of the nuggets to few. This most closely fits the group in which Hancock and part of Tetherow's party were numbered, who left Wagontire, according to Field, on the afternoon of September 15, and who, in Hancock's words, traveled all the afternoon and night—all the next day, continued traveling all night and then into sunset of the third day.

The Herrens' later story that Meek was not with them is confusing and misleading; he was probably ahead of their party. Nevertheless the wandering of this group, together with the date, strongly indicates that the Herrens, separated from the main group of wagons, found the gold somewhere between Wagontire and the South Fork of Crooked River.[89]

A statement by D. G. Herren, appearing in the *Eugene Daily Guard* in 1919, in part, said:

> After turning to the north and traveling some days, they made a dry camp in a deep gulch or hollow, the oxen were driven to some pot holes 1½ miles from camp for water. The next morning two men went out to drive in the oxen and on their way they picked up some yellow metal. This they stored away in their shot pouches.

For substantiation the writers offer other Herren accounts, for what clues the reader may obtain. Though unrecorded in any material we have, there were, no doubt, deaths which

---

89   The area so described has seen gold finds. George Millican, one of the earliest settlers of the area, dug a nugget from a boulder above a spring at Hampton Butte.

occurred in this stretch of travel. There are reports of graves found by early ranchers, upon the line of travel—at Wagontire, on Hampton Butte, at Dry Lake, across Bear Creek—any one of which might be the grave of the woman connected with the Blue Bucket nuggets. W. H. Herren, son of W. J., gave these two versions:

I have always been under the impression that the location was some where near the head of Crooked River. The second day after finding the gold they were shown Pilot Butte by an Indian, and as they usually only traveled about 12 miles per day it could not be more than 20 or 25 miles from that point. They reached the Deschutes river, where the town of Bend is now located. If I were going to try to find the place again I would go to the summit of Pilot Butte, and look to the South East and see what point in the mountains in that direction it would be possible for them to have sighted Pilot Butte. My father's memorandum stated that the gold was found in the bed of a small creek, that was so near dry at that time that there was no running water, and that the creek as near as he could tell ran to the North, possibly a little to the North East.

They were hunting for water, and they found a place where there was moist gravel and dug with a shovel in the bed of the creek. The gold was found in the wet gravel at the place where it was found he stated that there had been a slide that had partially dammed up the creek. The only timber in the vicinity is described as a scattering growth of cedar trees, evidently Juniper.

From the point where they sighted Pilot Butte, there must be some pretty steep hills, as they stated that in order to get down into the valley they had to lower their wagons down with ropes. At the time the gold was found they were camped on a high ridge and were compelled to make a dry camp.

The Captain of the company ordered all the young men that had saddle horses to take pails and shovels and try and find water for the camp and their stock and in those days about the only pails they had was wooden buckets, and my father's bucket was painted blue, only three persons saw the place where the gold was found, as others found water much nearer the camp than that my father found. From Little Silver Lake on Silver Creek they traveled South west away out into the desert until they were in sight of the Cascade Mountains.

They reached some lakes that were so strong of alkali that it caused the death of a lot of their cattle.

They finally concluded that they had gone away south and were possibly passing around the head of the Deschutes river. They then traveled North and to the East and got back into the mountains, evidently the Maury Range, and it was while making their way up the East slope of those mountains that the gold was found, there fore it must have been on some of the tributaries of Crooked River, and near its source.

The company that my father crossed the Plains with used oxen mostly and with their heavy wagons and the slow oxen they only traveled some ten or twelve miles per day, and if I remember rightly the notes that my father gave me stated that it took them about ten days to reach the Deschutes after sighting Pilot Butte. They stated that they had a hard time getting down the Western slope of the mountains and that in places they were compelled to let their wagons down with ropes, on account of the steep places.[90]

The second Herren version, while inevitably repetitious, adds some details:

Several of the young men that had saddle horses scouted the country over and finally found a ridge that led to the summit of the mountain. They concluded that if they could once get their outfits up on to this ridge they could make it over the mountains. By hitching 10 and sometimes 12 yoke of oxen at a time to a wagon they finally succeeded in getting them up on to the divide.

There was no water on the divide so they had to make a dry camp. The captain of the company told all of the young people who had saddle horses to take buckets and go hunt for water. My father, who was then 23 years old, and his sister, who afterward became the wife of William Wallace,[91] took their old blue wooden buckets and started out to find water.

---

90 Letter to Mrs. J. E. Meyers, Prineville, no date. Original in possession of Mr. Bert Houston, Bend, Oregon. (Never before printed.)

91 Mr. Herren is in error. His father's sister, Susannah, was married May 25, 1841, in Platte County, Missouri, to William T. Wallace.

They finally found a dry creek bed which they followed until they found a place where a little water was seeping through the gravel, and while my father was digging for water his sister saw something bright and picked it up.

The account given me states that they found two good sized lumps or nuggets, and that there were many fine particles in the gravel. He was quite sure that it was gold at the time, and when he arrived at camp he showed it to some of the older men, who told him that if it was gold it would be malleable. So one of them took a hammer and hammered both pieces out flat into a saucer-like disk.

He had a tool chest with a secret drawer in it. He hid the gold in the chest, therefore no one but the members of the family ever knew what became of it.[92]

The account of Levi Herren's daughter (Mrs. Flora E. Bailey) contains additional information not generally given in other Herren accounts. Some of the story is contradictory, of course, as are all Blue Bucket stories:

No member of our grandfather Herren's company, which crossed the plains in 1845, has ever been able to describe the route traversed after crossing the Oregon Boundary, for the reason that they were lost and were travelling by the compass, making their road as they went.

The incompetent guide who had been employed to pilot them through to the Willamette Valley by what was known as "Meek's Cut-off" had lost his way, and after wandering aimlessly for many days had deserted them in the night, probably fearing he should be harshly dealt with.

The only thing to be done was to keep moving westward. They knew they should reach the Deschuttes river, and by that, the Columbia. So they were pressing on as rapidly as possible for provisions were nearly exhausted and winter approaching.

With their small daughter, Maria, they accompanied the Herrens on the Cutoff in 1845.
92 *Oregonian*, March 7, 1922. Reprinted in *Bend Bulletin*, August 16, 1950.

Some where on the eastern slope of the Blue Mountains,[93] on the head waters of the Malheur river or one of the small streams that form it, the weary company camped for the night. They turned the horses and cattle out to graze as was the custom.

The children of the party, always on the alert for something new, explored the region, and along the stream they found traces of Indians.

There was a group of small stone houses on a bench above the stream sheltered by a still higher bank, and by trees. *My father (then 10 years old) is the only one I have ever heard of who remembers these stone huts. He says they were round in shape and covered over the top and of different sizes,*[94] averaging six or seven feet in diameter. Of the many expeditions sent to locate this spot, no one has ever given any account of the remarkable little huts.

This makes it seem as if the right place had never been found, but there is a possibility, I suppose, that the upper bench might have slipped off in a land slide, and covered them.

It was along this stream, while rounding up the stock to move on, that my father's cousin Dan Herren saw a piece of yellow metal shining in a mound of fresh earth thrown up by a mole or gopher. It was oblong in shape, a little larger at one end than the other and about the size of a man's thumb.

He had never seen any virgin gold and picked it up as a curiosity, carried it to camp, beat it out on the wagontire with a hammer and found it malleable. Still not knowing what it was he dropped it into the tool box, and it was not until three years later when he went to the Feather River mines, that he knew that he had found the first gold in Oregon. But he, nor any one else has ever been able to re-discover it. He went back with a party (Uncle Noah was one of them) and would

---

93 In the pioneer concept the Blue Mountains embraced the elevations from the Snake to the Deschutes.

94 Mrs. Bailey's italics. Bert Houston, of Bend, relates that his cousin, Fred Houston, of Prineville, says he found a group of stone huts on upper Silver Creek. In one of them was a newspaper clipping containing the Dan Herren information!

probably have reached the spot but they were driven back by *the Indians.*

This is the true story, obtained from my father and from Dan Herren himself, who only died last July [1908].

Many romantic stories have gained circulation, and I have answered dozens, I might almost say *hundreds*, of letters for my father on the subject.

One Chicago physician asked if it were true that John Herren said he could have filled his wagon box with gold if he had known what it was. Water was carried from the stream to camp in a blue painted bucket and the old story that seemed to be most popular was that the children filled the blue bucket with nuggets and carried them to camp to play with. But Dan Herren says all these were fabrications, and all the golden stories started from *the one nugget picked up in a mole hill.*[95]

The "Blue Bucket" tag, as Ruby El Hult has pointed out in her fine chapter on the subject (in *Lost Mines and Treasures of the Pacific Northwest*), was added later. It was a fortunate choice, not only in alliteration, but in imagination. Volume is necessary to any good gold story, and "buckets of gold" is a concept readily grasped.

Perhaps there are buckets, under Dan Herren's molehill, but, if the reader will excuse us, this seems to be another application of the proverb.

Some of the later searches for the gold, notably the Griffin-Adams party who discovered paying quantities of the yellow stuff in Griffin Gulch in 1861, have been amply publicized. Many small expeditions from 1857 on received very little notice.

For example, Andrew McClure's diary of a mining expedition of 1858: The adventures he records are typical of the Oregon gold seeker of the fifties and sixties. Further, his

---

95 Account written in 1910 by the late Mrs. Flora Bailey, wife of George Bailey, Gladstone, Oregon; received from him September, 1960.

narrative serves to reinforce the theory presented by the writers about the location of the gold discovery.

Andrew McClure's party traveled from the Prineville Valley across Combs Flat to Crooked River, up Crooked River to Camp Creek, across the east side of the Maury Mountains to the Camp Creek Valley, where they prospected intensively. They traveled south from there to the South Fork of Crooked River and out into the desert for some miles before turning back west and north again. They numbered in their party a Jason Peters who had been with Meek in 1845. Apparently, Mr. Peters was not any more successful in recalling landmarks, for the 1858 expedition found little besides "color." Nevertheless it is significant enough for restatement that the party searched the area between the G. I. Ranch's present location and Crooked River, for here is where they expected to find the elusive nuggets. They made several attempts to trace the 1845 tracks, only to be thwarted by the factor of time eradication and confused by the presence of tracks which they identified as having been broken by Elliott's 1853 train. The track they found, and so identified, ran west-northwest from the South Fork, crossing *some deep ravines*, in one of which the prospectors camped because there was *a trickle of water*. Perhaps, ironically, the 1858 searchers were closer than they knew and the dim road marked the passage of those hardy souls who found the gold in 1845.

Now, over one hundred years after 1845, difficulties seem insurmountable. Tracks are meaningless. There has been a remarkable growth of juniper which hides landmarks. Man, with dams and erosion, has changed the face of the country. Therefore, the dry creek which ran "north or north east" may not be recognizable. The authors' best guess (and it is only that) is that the nuggets (or nugget) were found along a stream bed—wet or dry—between Hampton Buttes and Wagontire Mountain. The area of search should extend to Camp Creek

Valley but no farther east, and particular care should be taken to search along Clover Creek.[96]

A letter (courtesy Mrs. Donna Wojcik) from a son (Charles) of Isaac Butler, written April 4, 1934, to his daughters adds further information: "Your Grandpa told me that at that time when they saw the gold, one could look West and see a big slide on the East Slope of the Cascade Mts. from near the creek where they crossed and that could not be done from the Blue Bucket Creek that is marked on the new map. . . ."

With a reconstruction of the route available, and some idea about group involvement and organization the key may yet be found. In some attic trunk the yellowed pages of a diary may still exist which would lead to a successful conclusion. The Herren diary, and others highly significant, have, unfortunately, been lost or destroyed. On the one hand the writers hope that some record still survives which will come to light and end for all time the speculation on Oregon's famous Blue Bucket nuggets. On the other, such a romantic portion of the fabric of Oregon's pioneer history adds so much color that were the location positively identified something fine would be gone from Oregon legend and story. Perhaps, anyway, the legend is indestructible.

Note: Since first publication of *Terrible Trail,* Donna Clark found a fragment of one of the Herren diaries published in an Albany newspaper. We have included it (page 260) in this second edition for its flavor and general interest.

---

96 Searchers should determine ownership of land and avoid trespass.

Chapter VIII

THE LAST, LONG PULL

SAGEBRUSH Spring spills unobtrusively from a limestone formation and pours its sweet water north through an ever-deepening ravine to reach the Deschutes far below. Waste irrigation water has deepened and widened the original channel. A county road crosses the head of the spring and the casual traveler could easily miss it. The travel in the fall of 1845 was not casual. Still, the sweet water of Sagebrush Spring and the plentiful grass might have made a pleasant interlude under different circumstances. Of necessity the reunited train spent the twenty-seventh of September in rest here. Provisions were ever scantier, the livestock showing now the effects of the forced drives. The fast-weakening members of the train also felt the effects. Parker's entry says: "many codent [get] to water and water was taken to them 32 in number   heare we beried 6 persons[.]" The spring has since been the scene of much activity by man and animal. No sign of those six lonely graves remains today.

Almost due east of Sagebrush Spring (Sandstone Spring in the early accounts of Captain Wallen and Major Steen) is a natural gateway for travel to the north. This is Lyle Gap. Early Indian travelers passed this way; the fur brigades found it an advantageous entry on their way to the John Day and Snake River valleys. The present Highway 97 runs through it. It is the only practical avenue for travel north from the Agency Plain.

And north they must go—at least those elements who could. Travel on the twenty-eighth took the weary trains through Hay Creek Valley to Trout Creek where they camped a little south of the present Bolter place.

Ahead was the mass of Bull Mountain. Cow Canyon, the site of the present fine highway, was a rock-strewn impasse. A route to the east up Trout Creek was difficult and time-consuming. There was nowhere to go but up, and up they went the next day, swinging west up a side draw until they could reach the foot of a long, steep ridge which enabled them to attain the top of the Shaniko Flats. The ascent was horrendous; it looks unbelievable for wagons today.

> Sept. 29. This morning we ascended a huge mountain; ware compelled to double our teames   gained the top at 12 oclock   we continued our journey over the levle plain until 8 oclock when we encamped on the margin of a bluff down which we decended 200 feet and found a small stream of water shaded by a beautiful grove of pine trees   distance 10 ms   (Harritt)
>
> Sept. 29. all day giting up hill   laid with out water beried 3 heare   3 (Parker)

Harritt's entry shows that the McNary party climbed the hill early in the day. Parker, helping the train ascend, did not get his group to the top until late. Perhaps the condition of his people forbade any night travel.

On top, the travel was better, though stony. Scattered with the cussed rocks which the tired travelers had come to expect, a gently rolling expanse lay before them. The flats were almost barren but for scrub sagebrush and grass. Northward, keeping to the high ground which skirted the canyons and draws that run down into the Deschutes Gorge, past Bakeoven, the wagons came to a slope they could carefully follow down to the Deschutes River.

It is unfortunate that the James Field diary was not kept during this section of the journey for it could have contributed a great deal to our knowledge of the trail. Parker and Harritt disagree as to mileage here and their description of the way is almost totally lacking. Other sources offer little help. Parker gives fifty-six miles from the Trout Creek exit to the Deschutes River crossing while Harritt lists thirty miles for the same route. Perhaps the most accurate distance for this section is supplied by Louis Scholl who, in 1859, back-tracked the trail of these people from near the Deschutes River crossing to Trout Creek. Scholl made a map showing thirty-nine miles for this portion of the route and it is probably near the correct distance traveled by the Meek train.[97]

Skirting the upper reaches of Bakeoven Canyon, they came to the Deschutes River Canyon about two miles south of the mouth of Buck Hollow. The descent was down a long, smooth slope, one of the few rockless stretches along the river. Here the wagons were disassembled and taken across the river a wheel at a time. The train was several days in crossing the hurtling waters.

A 1905 account of the Deschutes Canyon and its tumultuous stream illustrates what faced the pioneers:

> The roaring Des Chutes, a greater obstacle to the early travel than the Cascades themselves, refused to allow passage of its precipitous banks or to allow any traveler to pass in safety over its waters, unless the tribute of great labor was performed to make a place of descent and a bridge to span it. No ferry could live in its wild flood. Like the water of Lodore it comes down in a maddening rush, roaring, booming, foaming, and fighting, like a wild tyrant, furious at any restraint, never quiet until its bewitched waters are held in the firm grasp of old Columbia, in whose mighty arms they find their way to the ocean's expanse. Beautiful and wild in a high degree, the waters of a heaven blue that beggars description, everything connected with the stream bespeaks a decisiveness in nature that finds expression with no tamed spirit or mellowed lines. The very rocks rise in sheer precipices that defy intrusion or hang in beetling cliffs where only the eagle's

---

97   Scholl information supplied by Priscilla Knuth, Oregon Historical Society.

aerie may be found. Through countless ages the busy waters have eroded these stalwarts until naked and bare they stretch hundreds of feet from the blue, galloping waters at their feet towards the clouds above. Only at remote intervals, even in this day of advanced civilization's skilled engineering, do the wise attempt to make a crossing of the untamed Des Chutes.[98]

Why the trains traveled into this chasm, abandoning a longer but easier route north to the Columbia, is a mystery in one sense. The crossing at the mouth of the Deschutes was easier. But that crossing was miles away and the urgency of their situation dictated a passage here.

Meek knew this path, for a little way upstream was "the crossing" of the trappers. It was also the most direct ford for travel on to The Dalles. Here he left the train. The wagons followed, compelled to get to The Dalles and help as quickly as possible. It was thirty miles and they would be five days making the journey.

Hancock writes:

> This is the De Shutes River, a tributary of the Columbia.... After making our way through this broken country for three or four days, along this river we arrived at a part of it where the banks were not too high to swim our cattle to the other shore, this being the direction of our travel; at this point Indians came to us and said we were within two days travel of the Columbia River, which we were rejoiced to hear though not positive of its authenticity. ...
>
> At this place, where we swam our cattle, the current of the river was very rapid, and we regarded it unsafe to launch our water tight wagon beds for ferrying ourselves and property across, so resolved upon another expedient, stretching a large rope from bank to bank and suspending a wagon bed beneath to work on rollers. With a rope attached to it from either side of the stream, we were enabled to cross without being exposed to the water; but before this was put in practi-

---

98 *History of Central Oregon* (Spokane, Washington: Western Historical Publishing Co., 1905), p. 256.

cable operation a man rode up in great haste and informed our guide that he would have to leave immediately, as two young men of the company had died, and their father had taken an oath that the guide should die before sundown; attributing the death of his sons to the unsatisfactory way we had been guided through the mountains since leaving Fort Boise.[99] The guide understanding the feeling existing towards him in the company, left with his wife and going to some Indians near by, told them to put them over the river at all hazards, several of us who were anxious to see his escape effected, following to witness his departure.[100]

Thus did Stephen Meek and his wife leave the train. The later accusations of desertion aimed at Meek stem, apparently, from those straggling elements who did not see him after Wagontire Mountain. Meek and Elizabeth rode to The Dalles from whence a relief party had already started. Palmer in his journal, continuing the story of the advance riders to The Dalles, says:

At this place they met an old mountaineer, usually called Black Harris, who volunteered his services as a pilot. He in company with several others, started in search of the lost company, whom they found reduced to great extremities; their provisions nearly exhausted, and the company weakened by

---

99 A biographical sketch of Henry J. Noble, in H. K. Hines, *An Illustrated History of the State of Oregon* (Chicago: Lewis Publishing Co., 1893), pp. 889-90, mentions the deaths of two sons, aged eighteen and eleven, on the Cutoff.

100 Hancock further states: "... they [Meek and his wife Elizabeth] had not been gone more than fifteen minutes when two men rode up with rifles and inquired the whereabouts of the guide. Being told that he had gone in the direction of our destination, the old man replied that it was perhaps well, as his sons were now buried." *The Narrative of Samuel Hancock*, edited by Arthur D. Howden Smith (New York: Robert M. McBride & Company, 1927), pp. 33-34.

exertion, and despairing of ever reaching the settlements.[101]

Neither Parker, nor Harritt, nor Hancock for that matter, mentions this party. What help it extended was to the latter, weaker groups.

Hancock, Parker, McNary, and Riggs all crossed the dangerous Deschutes at the mouth of Buck Hollow. It is likely that the Tetherow train did, too, although one source states that those wagons crossed the tablelands through Grass Valley to the mouth of the Deschutes.

Much detail of the crossing has survived. Samuel Parker, beset with private worry, described only a portion of the process which must have been laborious to the extreme:

> October 2. got to the deschutes river Missis Butts Dyed this day my wife and child and second daughter all sick 9
> October 3. Crossed the deschutes river in a wagon body and tuck the wagons Apart and tuck a wheale at a time by ropes this day my 2 small boys tuck sick gideon and george and susan my forth girl 6 of my family sick at one time

Harritt:

> October 3. spent the day in crossing the river had no timber to make boats ware compelled to make boats of our waggon beds to cross our families and goods.

G. W. Marquam, who was one year old when he traveled the Meek Cutoff in 1845, relates what his father and grandfather had told him:

> They followed down the Crooked river, to where Prineville now is, and from there down the Deschutes to the point now known as Sherar's bridge. Here they were obliged to cross the Deschutes, which was deep and swift. The wagon

---

101 Palmer, *Journal*, entry for September 30. In Thwaites' *Early Western Travels, 1748-1846* (Cleveland: The Arthur H. Clark Company, 1906), Vol. XXX.

boxes were converted into raftlike boats and one man swam across carrying a light line tied to a rope. Then he pulled the rope and attached it to a large rock, by which means the wagons were safely ferried across.[102]

Joel Palmer related what he had learned about the crossing in a typical, carefully descriptive passage:

They succeeded in finding a place where their cattle could be driven down to the river, and made to swim across; after crossing, the bluff had to be ascended. Great difficulty arose in the attempt to effect a passage with the wagons. The means finally resorted to for the transportation of the families and wagons were novel in the extreme. A large rope was swung across the stream and attached to the rocks on either side; a light wagon bed was suspended from this rope with pulleys, to which ropes were attached; this bed served to convey the families and loading in safety across; the wagons were then drawn over the bed of the river by ropes. The passage of this river occupied some two weeks. The distance was thirty-five miles to the Dalles, at which place they arrived about the 13th, or 14th of October. Some twenty of their number had perished by disease, previous to their arrival at

---

102 State Archives Microfilm, "Blue Bucket Mine"; C. M. Haskell, *Old Oregon*. There are numerous claimants to the honor of swimming the Deschutes. Goulder, in later years, still remembered the shock of the water: "In order to test the strength of the rope and the safety of this method of transit, the rope was passed around my body, just under the arms, and I was dragged through the raging torrent to the other side. I could but feel that I was in the hands of my friends, nor could I be insensible to the fact that the water was of icy coldness, just being lately arrived from the snowy brow of Mt. Hood. It has been my good fortune to enjoy some very cool and refreshing baths, but nothing in my experience ever equaled this one. I shall not stop here to inquire how the rest got across, further than to remark that several of the young men followed my example, while the main body of the company waited for more elaborate contrivances." Goulder, *Reminiscences of a Pioneer* (Boise, Idaho: Timothy Regan, 1909), p. 134.

the Dalles, and a like number were lost, after their arrival, from the same cause.[103]

To cross a river such as the Deschutes at Sherars, facing the mass of Tygh Ridge to the northwest, is to the writers the most amazing feat of all. Sick, tired almost beyond endurance, both men and animals were called upon for strength and stamina and determination which few present-day mortals could muster at any time. To have made this last, long, hard pull taxed them all severely, some to the limit. Parker wrote:

> October 5. day I got all over and went 3 miles to a small creek heare we beried missis Butts and 3 more

Harritt's entry for the day following the McNary party's crossing is less pathetic:

> October 4. rigd our waggons loaded up and travleed 3 m to a delight stream shaded by a fiew cotton wood trees where we encamped for the night

It took two days to ascend from the river. The first night was spent at a spring on the John Conroy ranch after threading a ridge directly across the Deschutes from the mouth of Buck Hollow.

The next day they climbed another ridge close to the route of the later freight road, built between Sherars Bridge and The Dalles. Mr. Conroy informed the writers that from his corral to The Dalles by the old freight road was thirty miles. This is the exact mileage given by Jesse Harritt for the same trip.

They emerged on top of Tygh Ridge near the point where a twin transmission tower stands today. Staying east of the rolling canyons, the train followed the bench parallel to the Deschutes, passing east of Dufur. Dropping down into Fifteen Mile Creek, then Eight Mile, they arrived at the mission at The Dalles.

---

103 Palmer, *loc. cit.*

In 1889, Hugh McNary, a member of the Meek party, pointed out to W. S. Campbell the old road and the final campground:

> It was along one of these aboriginal trails leading in from Tygh that a detail from the travel worn expedition of Meek rolled into The Dalles making their last encampment under the overhanging boughs of a lone pine tree which formerly stood on the farm owned, in 1889, by Mr. John Southwell, on Eight Mile Creek, ten miles south of The Dalles. Sixteen years ago traces of this now forgotten roadway were yet to be found.
>
> The first bunch-grass sod of the Inland Empire—at least in a large portion of it—was broken not one hundred yards from Meek's last camp on Eight Mile.[104]

Harritt arrived at The Dalles October 7, as did Parker, who sums up in his usual fashion:

> this morning nothing to eat   got to the mishion at dark 17   got in A house with my family   got something to eat   this was the first day we had done without something to eat   But some of the company had been with out bread fore 15 days and had to live on pore beef without anything else   I will just say pen and tong[ue]   will both fall short when they gow to tell the suffering the company went through[.]

104 *History of Central Oregon, op. cit.,* p. 90.

Chapter IX

THE DALLES OF THE COLUMBIA

IT TOOK days to gather and assist all the members of the trains into The Dalles. Parker and Harritt were among the forefront of the arrivals; Goulder, with the Ownbey party, arrived the fifteenth of October. Some sources indicate that a period as long as two weeks elapsed before the last stragglers passed the mission.

At The Dalles the exhausted survivors obtained aid and some provisions through the offices of the Reverend Alvin Waller, in charge of the Methodist Mission. Some of the pioneers in later accounts are bitterly critical of Reverend Waller:

> We found the missionary, Mr. Waller, ready to devour the poor starved emigrant by charging exorbitant prices for everything and very unaccommodating in every way, and nothing without specie or cattle at one third of their value. . . .[105]

In Morse's *Washington Territory* it is stated:

> In fact, it is the united testimony of all the old Pioneers, that for rank selfishness, heartlessness, avarice, and desire to take advantage of the necessities of the immigrants to the

---

105 H. D. Martin letter in the *St. Joseph* (Mo.) *Gazette*, August 21, 1846.

111

utmost, the Methodist Mission of the Dalles exceeded any other institution on the Northwest Coast. This is a terrible charge, but a conversation with 50 different pioneers who crossed the plains in an early day will satisfy any of the fact.[106]

No doubt these people were not in the happiest state of mind, and perhaps there is some justification for their complaint, but it must be stated in fairness that Waller's mission was completely unprepared for the arrival of such large numbers of sick and famished people. His responsibility to the mission must have warred with his Christian charity. To further complicate things for Reverend Waller, his wife was about to present him with a son, Edmund James, born at The Dalles October 19.

Certainly, from whatever sources—the mission, the Hudson's Bay Company, other more fortunate persons who had traveled the regular route—aid was forthcoming. Some starving survivors overate—one, Mr. Wilson, so excessively that death resulted.[107]

Lucy Hall Bennett remembered:

> At The Dalles we got our first dried peas and potatoes and one peck of wheat—all that was allowed to a family for bread so all could have a little.[108]

---

106 Bancroft, quoting Elisha Packwood from "Packwood biography" in Morse's *Washington Territory*, pp. i. 60-61.
107 Hancock says, "My most intimate companion on this journey died from the effects," *The Narrative of Samuel Hancock*, edited by Arthur D. Howden Smith (New York: Robert M. McBride & Company, 1927), p. 35. It is mentioned variously in H. K. Hines, *An Illustrated History of the State of Oregon* (Chicago: Lewis Publishing Co., 1893), p. 1031; Joseph Gaston, *Centennial History of Oregon, 1811-1911* (Chicago: S. J. Clarke Publishing Co., 1912), p. 602; and *Portrait & Biographical Record of Willamette Valley, Oregon* (Chicago: Chapman Publishing Co., 1903), p. 1183.
108 Lucy Bennett, "Captain Lawrence Hall," *Oregon Pioneer Association Transactions,* 1895, p. 102.

A biographical sketch of Jesse Harritt contains some information about food available (and prices):

> When they arrived at The Dalles they were happy in being able to replenish their rapidly decreasing food supply. This company found plenty of buffalo and were amply supplied with meat, but by the time the caravan had traversed Idaho and Eastern Oregon, where there was practically no game, their larder was pretty empty. It was not safe, because of Indians along here, to do much hunting. The price paid for flour at this time was $8 per hundred pounds. Dried beans were only 6 to 7 cents per pound, potatoes 62½ cents per bushel, wheat $1.50 per bushel, coffee 33⅓ cents per pound, while tea was $2 per pound. Sugar was 20 cents per pound.[109]

The emigrants who had arrived at The Dalles before the appearance of the survivors were not backward in sharing what little they had. They knew the trail's demands.

Sarah J. (Walden) Cummins, who, with her first husband, Benjamin Walden, and her father and family, had taken the regular route to The Dalles and was among the first emigrants to arrive in 1845, says:

> After the Walden party arrived at The Dalles and were camped there, resting up for the trip down the Columbia River, a man was seen coming slowly toward their camp. By his slow progress they could see he was in distress. Mr. Lemmon and others hastened out to meet him and found he was a Mr. Hull, one of those who had left the main train at Bear river. He was scarcely able to walk and had not tasted food for three days. After he had eaten and was able to tell his story, he said his wife and five other women had died. The children and remainder of the party were camped about one day's travel up the Columbia and were dying of starvation. Their teams had also been without food for some time and were unable to travel. Food was immediately packed on

109 Sarah (Hunt) Steeves, *Book of Remembrance of Marion County, Oregon, Pioneers, 1840-1860* (Portland, Oregon: Berncliff Press, 1927), pp. 36-38. Information from J. W. Harritt.

horses and Mr. Lemmon, accompanied by others, went to their rescue and found them as Mr. Hull had said. Several children had also died but in a few days the remnant of the train were again camped among friends, yet the reunion was one of sadness. One of their women had died while their train was going down a steep mountain, but for fear of Indians they did not dare stop until they reached the open country, where they buried her as best they could.

Mrs. Sam Parker, a mother of a large family, was one of those who died in this train.

Everyone set about, after the rescue, to do what they could to help these unfortunate ones and to keep families together. All had a chance to do their bit, a great test of human nature.[110]

Despite the generous efforts some members of Meek's party were too ill for recovery. How many died and were buried at The Dalles it has been impossible to ascertain. Joel Palmer says "some twenty of their number had perished by disease, previous to their arrival at The Dalles, and a like number were lost after their arrival from the same cause.[111]

Evidence of at least twenty-three deaths on the Cutoff is presented in the following entries from Parker's diary:

September 8—"one child beried heare"

September 23—"Beried 4 persons heare"

September 26—"heare we beried 6 persons"

September 29—"beried 3 heare"

September 30—"5 beried heare"

October 5—"heare we beried missis Butts and 3 more"

---

110 *Ibid.,* pp. 47-65.

111 Palmer, *Journal of Travels Over the Rocky Mountains,* in Thwaites' *Early Western Travels, 1748-1846* (Cleveland: The Arthur H. Clark Company, 1906), Vol. XXX. Entry for September 30.

A total of twenty-four deaths is realized when Sarah King Chamber's death (September 3) is added—a death Parker did not record. It is very possible that some persons died on the western swing through the Bear Creek country to Pilot Butte at Bend, to Sagebrush Spring, and it has been said by Daniel Dodge Bayley descendants that a woman died at Wagontire Mountain. We can be certain, however, that twenty-four or more persons perished before the trains reached the mission at The Dalles.

The known dead include Elkanah Packwood, baby son of Elisha Packwood, who died at Harney Lake from whooping cough September 8; Sarah (Mrs. Rowland) Chambers, who died September 3 and is buried near Castle Rock in Malheur County, eastern Oregon; Emaline McNemee, baby daughter of Job McNemee; Eliza Harris, thirteen-year-old daughter of Phillip Harris; two sons, ages eighteen and eleven, of Henry J. Noble; Mrs. John Butts, who died October 2 and was buried on the fifth, after the crossing of the Deschutes River at Sherars Bridge; Mrs. Robert Hull, of Ohio; Mrs. Alexander Liggett, who died near Dufur, in the vicinity of The Dalles.

Other possible Cutoff deaths are a Mr. Moore;[112] Mrs. Stevens (or Stephens), of Iowa; H. Belden, of Missouri; a Mr. Catching; J. Mallery (perhaps James Mallory of the Tetherow Train), Missouri; J. Patterson; Mrs. Jones (perhaps Mrs. Michael Jones), of Iowa; a daughter of Mrs. Jones, aged seventeen; John Harris; Mary E. Harris;[113] the baby daughter of David Pugh. Three deaths which occurred within families who took the Cutoff but cannot for certain be attributed to the trials of the route are a sister to Dulaney C. Norton; Tabitha

112 See William A. Barlow, "Reminiscences of Seventy Years," *Oregon Historical Quarterly, XIII* (September, 1912), p. 260; also Ellen Garrison Carlin, Vertical File, Oregon Historical Society.
113 It is possible that Mary E. Harris is the Eliza Harris, daughter of Phillip Harris, who died of mountain fever.

Fuller, daughter of Arnold Fuller; David Atcheson Tetherow, son of Solomon Tetherow, aged two.

Bitterly, Hiram Smith wrote a letter which appeared in the *St. Joseph Gazette*, St. Joseph, Missouri, Friday, July 17, 1846:

> Our emigration of 1845 would have gotten down in good time as a part did, if they had not been led astray by a pilot by the name of Stephen Meeks who undertook to pilot what was called the St. Joseph Company consisting of 214 wagons, a nearer route from Big Snake river to the Dalls on the Columbia. They were out near 40 days longer than they should have been if they had kept on the old road. They run out of provisions and then had to eat their poor cattle, which gave them a camp fever and were out of water 12 to 24 hours and had not sufficient for the sick or children which gave them intense suffering, and the loss of near 50 souls, old and young. The greatest number that died were children. . . . Those that traveled the old road got in well and in good time.

H. D. Martin added in his letter:

> . . . However we got through safe, with a good deal of suffering on the part of some for want of provisions and a good many deaths when we got to the mission where we took water.

Among the members of the train were several physicians. One, Dr. Ralph Wilcox, became the first physician in Portland in 1847.[114] These men's offices may have deterred the deaths of a greater number.

There are several firsthand accounts which illustrate the condition of these unfortunates; J. M. Bacon in his *Mercantile Life* recalled,

> The cutoff people came into Deshouts about 35 or 40 miles from the Dalles. That is the first place they knew where

114 O. O. Larsell, *The Doctor in Oregon* (Portland, Oregon: Binfords & Mort, 1947), p. 135.

they were. They went 400 or 500 miles out of the way. They expected to find themselves on this side of the mountains. If they could have gotten through the mountains into the southern part of Oregon they probably would have saved distance. We were there close to them when they came up—the most desolate looking people I ever saw in my life. They had travelled through the sage brush and over timbered mountains.[115]

One family's records have survived in part—enough to use for illustration. The clan of Nahum King, traveling with the original group led by T'Vault, later moved with various units and was in the company of the Nortons, Chambers, and Fullers. Misfortune dogged their steps from beginning to end. A letter home by Maria King, dated April 1, 1846, Luckiamute Valley, reads:

> Dear Mother, brothers, and sisters,
>
> After traveling six months we arrived at Lynnton on the Willamette November the 1st. We had beautiful weather all the way, no rain of any account. We got along finely until we came to Fort Boisen, within 3 or 4 [hundred] miles [east] of Lynnton, when along came a man by the name of Meiks, who said he could take us a new route across the Cascade Mountains to the Willamette river in 20 days, so a large company of a hundred and fifty or two hundred wagons left the old road to follow the new road and traveled for two months over sand, rocks, hills and anything else but good roads. Two third of the immigrants ran out of provisions and had to live on poor beef, but as it happened we had plenty of flour and bacon to last us through. But worse than all this, sickness and death attended us the rest of the way. I wrote to you from Fort Larima that the whooping cough and the measles went through our camp, and after we took the new route a slow lingering fever prevailed. Out of Chambers, L. Norton's, John's and our

---

115 Bacon himself was with Barlow, but his future wife was on the Cutoff. Bancroft Microfilm Pacific Series, Reel No. 2. Mrs. Bacon was the former Rachael Newman, daughter of the Reverend Samuel Newman.

family, none escaped except Solomon and myself. But listen to the deaths. Sally Chambers, John King and his wife, their little daughter Electra and their babe, a son 9 months old, and Dulaney C. Norton's sister are gone. Mr. A. Fuller lost his wife and daughter Tabitha. Eight of our two families have gone to their long homes. Stephen was taken the fever at Fort Boisen; he had not been well since we left Ohio, but was now taken worse. He was sick for three months, we did not expect him to live for a long time, was afraid he had consumption. . . .

Those that went the old road got through six weeks before us, with no sickness at all. Upwards of fifty died on the new route.

The Indians did not disturb us any, except stealing our horses. We have made our claim on the Luckiamute. . . .[116]

At The Dalles, Samuel Parker's personal part in the ordeal was not yet over:

. . . my wife and chils died and I staid till the 3 of November when I left fore Oregon City in a large canoe with four indiens for which I give sixty dollars when I started the wet wether had set in. I did not expect to git to the city with my fore sick children and my oldes girl that was sick I was looking all the time for hir to die I tuck my seete in the canoe by hir and held hir up and the same at nite when I come to the cascade falls I had to make a portige of 3 miles I put my sick girl in A blanket and pack hir and onely rested once that day we maid the portige with the help of my fore indiens and my oldest boy and oldest girl boath had never been sick one minet on the road on the 8 I land at O city wet hungry and all most wore out with my family most all sick the 3 youngest sone [soon] got well but it was 19 days after I landed till my oldest stood alone harty and well now . . . frome missory River to Oregon city 2083 miles.

They were hard miles. It took hard people.

The tragedies continued to mount at the mission. Few families escaped sickness, death, or mishap. Death claimed

---

116 Original on file at the Oregon Historical Society. John King's death is also recorded in the King family Bible.

Mrs. James Terwilliger, Mr. William Wilson, Mrs. Samuel Parker, daughter, Virginia, aged two, and the newborn Parker son, Samuel, Jr. John King, son of Nahum King, was drowned with his wife, Susan, and two children, rafting down the Columbia, October 26. Only their five-year-old son, Luther, was saved.

The James E. Hall family Bible records, "Elisha Hall was born on the 4th day of January A.D. 1845—and Departed this life on the 29th day of October A.D. 1845. Aged 9 months & 24 days—Died at the Cascades on the Columbia River on way from Missouri 1845."[117]

Hiram Smith sent a list of deaths with his letter to the *St. Joseph Gazette* which was quoted in this chapter. Of the thirty-two names listed, however, seven are known not to have been on the Cutoff; there are several uncertainties. Smith did not claim to have compiled a complete list of those perished, but his roster, nevertheless, is valuable.[118]

After The Dalles, there were others who perished during the following months as a result of their hard journey, and countless others never fully recovered.

Between The Dalles and Oregon City lay roughly one hundred miles of water travel (somewhat shorter by land). Barlow's toll road south of Mount Hood was only just being explored and was not for oxen and people in the condition of

---

117 Roelofson family papers, Oregon State Library, Salem.
118 Hiram Smith's death list reads: Mrs. Straighthoof; Mrs. Courtney; Mrs. Butts; John Sanders; Mr. Moore, Ill.; Mrs. Stevens, Iowa; Mr. Hull, Ohio; Mrs. Roland Chambers; H. Belden, Mo.; G. Davis; Mr. Earl, of Iowa; Mrs. Legit; Julian Straithoof; Duke Wilks; Mrs. Wilson, Mo.; Mrs. Bryant; J. Mallery, Mo.; E. Noble; Mrs. Tewilaker; J. Patterson; Mrs. Jones and daughter seventeen; Rev. Wm. Moore; John Harris; Mr. Pew and wife, son and daughter, Ark.; Mary E. Harris; John King, wife and child.

the survivors.[119] The alternatives were stark—abandon the wagons and go overland along the river or build rafts to carry the wagons and possessions down by water. Most of the emigrants chose the latter course, sometimes two weeks being consumed in preparation. Then launching onto the broad bosom of the Columbia, the crude floats entered the final phase of the journey. Some people were transported by Indian canoe, like Parker, some by the aid of Hudson's Bay men who were at The Dalles.

Goulder's closing comment we think especially appropriate:

> The men of our company were not all heads of families, or members of any of the families with whom we had so long journeyed. Many of us were young men, without relatives that we knew of anywhere west of the Alleghanies. We had traveled with the families by virtue of an agreement to stay with the immigration, and to help in all the tasks that came to hand, and to share with the families with whom we traveled in all that fortune, good or bad, might have in store for all. This agreement, as far as I know, was faithfully lived up to by all the parties concerned. The man with whom I traveled was a typical old frontier Missourian named Nicholas Ownby. He had a large family of sons and daughters, large herds of horses and cattle, and traveled with four well-equipped and well-provisioned wagons. During the long and trying journey of seven months he had uniformly treated the young strangers traveling with him as if they had been his own sons. He was of rough demeanor, but a real gem, for all that, and a man always ready and full of resources for every emergency. On the morning that we broke camp in Tualatin Plains, he said to us: "Well,

---

119 Powells and Centers were exceptions. See Palmer, *Journal*, entry for October 26. Barlow and party, including Palmer, were in progress across the south slopes of Mount Hood, making (with great difficulty) a trail which was to become the Barlow Road. The wagons of the 1845 people did not travel all the way to the valley, the emigrants having to ride horses and walk a great portion of the route. In 1846 the road was cut from the valley side and the first passage with wagons was made.

boys, I'm going away up into Polk County, wherever that may be, to see what I can find. It was agreed between us in St. Joe that you would stay with me till I found a place to settle down and help me to build cabins and get things started. You have been good boys, and I'm sorry to part with you, but we are all where we can take care of ourselves now, and I think it would be better for you to be hunting up your own claims, and building your own cabins. I'm not trying to get rid of you. If you want to go with me up country, well and good; but I wanted to tell you that you are free from any further obligation." We were nothing loath to take the old man at his word, and were glad to have a change from wagons, flocks and herds, cows, calves and crying babies.[120]

---

120 William A. Goulder, *Reminiscences of a Pioneer* (Boise, Idaho: Timothy Regan, 1909), pp. 138-40.

Courtesy Lowell Tiler.

PLATE XVIII: The view west from Stein's Ridge shows the old trace in the Camp Creek Valley. The train's exit was across this valley and up a draw on the opposite side. From here the emigrants moved to Crooked River, called "the Sandy" by Jesse Harritt.

Courtesy Priscilla Knuth..

PLATE XIX: Entry to Crooked River near the Pine Creek Cemetery.
Tracks of the train can be seen to the left in the picture.

PLATE XX: A very discernible trace down Stein's Ridge. This road, used by the Meek train, was subsequently traveled by Captain H. D. Wallen and Major Enoch Steen. Because of the incline, a new road

PLATE XXI: A drag log at the bottom of Stein's Ridge. Now rotten, this old juniper log long withstood the effects of time.

Courtesy *Lowell Tiller.*

PLATE XXII: Stewart Canyon, just west of the mouth of Camp Creek. Here the train took to the water.

Courtesy Web Loy.

PLATE XXIII: This giant red juniper carried the 1845 Lost Meeks inscription carved into a huge limb pointing north. On the south side a smaller limb had been placed to point to the west. At the base of the tree a small stone fire-circle held over a foot of dried juniper debris above charcoal. The tree vanished years ago, cut for firewood.

Courtesy Oregon Historical Society.

PLATE XXIV: Near Alfalfa, ten miles east of Bend, a member of the western split of the lost wagon train, carved in a tree limb, "1845 Lost Meeks." A scratch and a chipped-away piece make the "l" appear as a "y" in the picture. The carved figure between the words may be a direction marker indicating the line of travel or the direction of the Deschutes River.

Courtesy Mrs. Prince Staats, Bend, Oregon.

PLATE XXV: An old picture of the now almost destroyed juniper with "Sacred to the memory of Je—ie," near Alfalfa, Oregon.

Courtesy Child's Photographers, Redmond, Oregon.

PLATE XXVI: Three Sisters, looking west across the sagebrush flat, junipers in the foreground.

PLATE XXVII: Following almost to Buck Hollow, the train found a difficult but possible way down to the east bank of the untamed Deschutes a short distance above Sherars Falls. The top photo shows part of the later Bake-oven grade.

PLATE XXVIII: Buck Hollow at its mouth.

Courtesy Lowell Tiller.

PLATE XXIX: The site of the crossing of the Deschutes River at the mouth of Buck Hollow. A rope was stretched across to the rocks on the right and a wagon bed used to ferry some of the emigrants over. Wagons were taken apart and roped across, a "wheale at a time."

Courtesy Priscilla Knuth.

PLATE XXX: Tygh Ridge, the last barrier between the Lost Wagon Train and the mission at The Dalles. The ascent was made at the far right. With some improvements, the first freight road followed the tracks of the 1845 train.

Courtesy Lowell Tiller.

PLATE XXXI: Coming down Tygh Ridge on the northwest side, the emigrant and freight road is still in use by farmers and rock hounds.

PLATE XXXII: Artist's sketch of The Dalles Mission, 1849. To this small outpost came the emigrants in 1845 seeking assistance

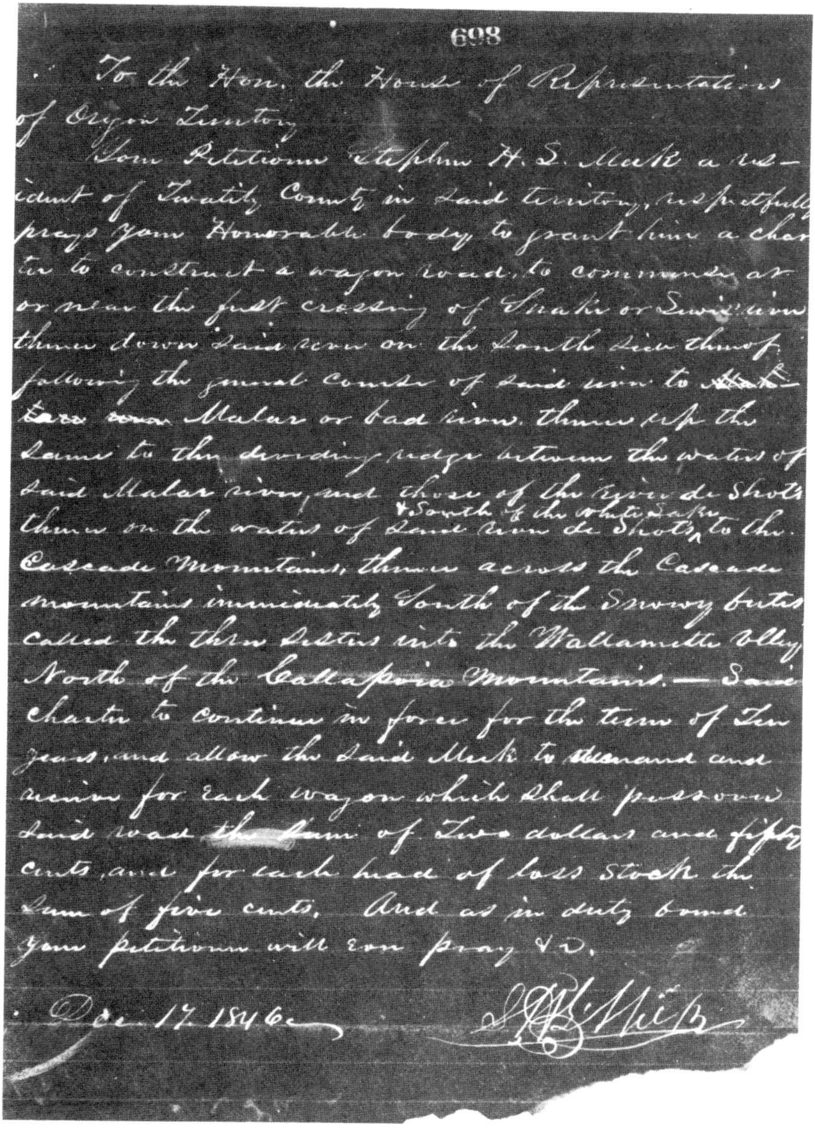
608

To the Hon. the House of Representatives
of Oregon Territory
Your Petitioner Stephen H. L. Meek a resident of Tualaty County in said territory, respectfully
prays your Honorable body to grant him a charter to construct a wagon road, to commence at
or near the first crossing of Snake or Lewis river
thence down said river on the South side thereof
following the general course of said river to
Malar or bad river. thence up the
same to the dividing ridge between the waters of
said Malar river, and those of the River de Shots
thence on the waters of said River de Shots & South of the White Lake to the
Cascade Mountains, thence across the Cascade
mountains immediately South of the Snowy buttes
called the three sisters into the Wallamette Valley
North of the Callapooia Mountains. — Said
charter to continue in force for the term of Ten
years, and allow the said Meek to demand and
receive for each wagon which shall pass over
said road ~~the sum~~ of Two dollars and fifty
cents, and for each head of loose Stock the
sum of five cents. And as in duty bound
your petitioner will ever pray &c.

Dec 17. 1846 S. H. L. Meek

Courtesy Oregon State Library.

PLATE XXXIII: Copy of Meek's road petition to the Territorial House of Representatives, 1846.

Chapter X

"A MAN'S A MAN"

IN ANY assessment of blame for tragedy all factors must be considered. Stephen Meek led an extraordinarily large group over an untried route, through unfamiliar country to near disaster. Depending on the point of view, his behavior might be termed inexcusable, negligent, or adventuresome.

That he had no right to gamble with the lives of those pioneers under his leadership is unquestionable; it is equally true that, faced with dissatisfaction, animosity, and threat, he stayed with the train until its arrival at The Dalles was assured.

Later accounts by some pioneers and their descendants show considerable aversion for Meek,[121] best illustrated by the repeated story that "Meek deserted them in the desert." Threats against his life are said to have culminated in a lynch attempt, dramatically terminated at the last minute by several different men. One description of this is in the A. J. McNemee account:

> While the immigrants were camped in "Stinky Hollow" many of the oxen lay down and refused to get up, for when

---

121 Jesse Applegate also received his share of opprobrium for the Applegate Trail. Lansford W. Hastings and Peter Lassen found enmity from many who used their routes to California, with some justification.

an ox is all in he quits. An ox will stay with it as long as he can, but when he finally gives up it is almost impossible to persuade him to get to his feet again. For three days, while the men were out hunting for the lost oxen, the party camped there, suffering from thirst. My father rode three horses till they were beat out looking for water. Upon his return to the camp he found three wagons had been placed facing each other in the form of a triangle, their tongues raised and tied together at the top. The sullen and angry men of the party had put a rope around Steve Meek's neck and were about to hang him. My father, pointing his gun at the men, said, "The first man that pulls on that rope will be a dead man. Steve Meek is the only man who has ever been in this part of the country before. If you hang him, we are all dead men. If you give him a little time he may be able to recognize some landmark here and find a way out." The men agreed to give Meek three days. Meek left during the night and made his way to The Dalles, where he appealed to the Missionaries for help."[122]

The repeated statement that Meek "deserted" the train deserves comment, in view of the evidence. The "desertion" and abortive "lynching" are located at various places along the route from Harney Valley to the Deschutes crossing—depending on the memories of those confused and wandering people during their time of trial. Lawrence McNary, in his "Route of the Meek Cut-off 1845," previously cited, says the "desertion" occurred about the night of September 15 and before reaching water at Crooked River. It will be remembered that, according to Field, Meek left Wagontire the afternoon of the fifteenth of September with "7 of Owensbys," and part of Tetherow's Train. In the subsequent disorganiza-

---

122 Fred Lockley, "The McNemees and Tetherows with the Migration of 1845," *Oregon Historical Quarterly,* XXV (December, 1924), 356. The decision to hang Meek, if it occurred at all, was far from unanimous. Besides McNemee, these pioneers are claimants to the honor of saving Meek's life: Samuel Hancock (*The Narrative of Samuel Hancock,* p. 30); J. I. Packwood (letter in writers' possession); Daniel D. Bayley (*The Munson Record,* p. 505).

tion and division it is likely many of the people in the train did not see Meek again. From other accounts as well, it would seem a probable deduction that Meek, while still with Hancock, did not make his presence obvious to the majority.

Hancock's *Narrative* is a most reliable source for Meek's action and it does not describe anything so dramatic as the McNemee account. W. A. Goulder's statement, while somewhat denunciatory, adds confirmation:

> It was somewhat amusing to think how diligently and persistently Meek had tried to play guide to the last, though a very few days from the start sufficed to prove that he was as badly lost as the rest. I heard it said in after years that, after the immigrants reached Des Chutes River, Meek's life was in danger from the indignation and anger of the people upon whom he had imposed. Had this been true, I must certainly have heard something about it, but I think I can affirm confidently that there never was a word of truth in the statement. Had it been worth while to dispose of Meek by an act of violence, that little piece of work could have been done in the depths of the wilderness, where only coyotes would have been witnesses.

Not all the emigrants condemned Meek. Bancroft recorded the following:

> Elisha Packwood also says that Meek was not so bad a man as he was pictured by the immigrants; and that at the very time they were so anxious to hang him, if they had submitted he would have brought them to the settlements.[123]

The writers found the following episode illuminating:

> I guess you have heard of Meek's cut off. Well, it came pretty nigh cuttin' off the ones who tried it. Our oxen died from drinking alkali water and we all wandered around in the desert till we knew we were lost and we struck out on the back

123 Bancroft, *History of Oregon* (San Francisco: The History Company, 1886), I, 514, footnote 16.

trail. In one place we went down a powerful steep place. When we got down there was no way of going forward so we had to double teams and pull up to where we had been. One of the men that happened to be just ahead of us said, "When I get to the top of this hill, if I ever do, I am going to hunt for Steven Meek and if I find him I'll kill him." Meek was sitting just above us back of a big sagebrush. He stepped out with his gun in his hand and said, awful slow and cool, "Well, you've found me. Go ahead with the killing." The man wilted down and didn't have spunk enough to kill a prairie dog. He was like a lot of other bad men—just a bad man with his mouth.[124]

Overall, Meek's projected route to the headwaters of the Willamette was more direct than the Old Oregon Trail. It is interesting to note that in 1846 Meek applied to the provisional legislature for permission to open a toll road.[125] Its route lay from Eugene City up the Willamette River and straight across the mountains, south of Diamond Peak, to the desert, then to Harney Lake and beyond. He felt the route was practical, and, except for sufficient water, it was.

Meek went out into the desert with his people, gambling that water would be found and his gamble failed. Failures were not popular on the frontier, but it was often a large amount of luck that separated the failure from the success. It was an age of gamblers. Had water in sufficient quantity been located twenty to twenty-five miles west of Wagontire Mountain, Meek would have established a new route down the Willamette to Eugene City, a route of almost incalculable value to the emigrants, bypassing the Blue Mountains-Columbia River passage.

Furthermore, Meek's information seems to have been based on fact, for water at Silver Lake and Paulina Marsh, about fifty miles southwest of Wagontire, was an actuality. It

124 Fred Lockley, "Impressions and Observations of a Journal Man," interview with Susannah Johnson Peterson, no date.
125 Oregon Provisional and Territorial Government Papers No. 698 (December 17, 1846).

seems probable that the pressures from the emigrants forced a halt to Meek's search before there was time to search far enough. There is a contemporary account by Joel Palmer which is interesting:

> Whilst I was at Fort Hall, I conversed with Captain [Richard] Grant respecting the practicability of this same route, and was advised of the fact, that the teams would be unable to get through. The individual in charge at Fort Bois [e] also advised me to the same purport. The censure rests, in the origin of the expedition, upon Meek; but I have not the least doubt but he supposed they could get through in safety. I have understood that a few of the members controlled Meek, and caused him to depart from his original plan. It was his design to have conducted the party to the Willamette Valley, instead of going to the Dalles; and the direction he first traveled induced this belief. Meek is yet of the opinion that had he gone round the marshy lake to the south, he would have struck the settlement on the Willamette, within the time required to travel to the Dalles. Had he discovered this route, it would have proved a great saving in the distance. I do not question but that there may be a route found to the south of this, opening into the valley of the Willamette.[126]

Finally it was over—that heartbreaking journey. The total 1845 migration doubled the population of Oregon. H. J. Warre and M. Vavasour, British agents then in Oregon who regarded the tide of American immigration with a somewhat jaundiced eye, were moved to comment:

> It is extremely difficult to discover the exact number of immigrants now arriving in the country, but from the best information we have estimated their numbers at about 2000 individuals. They have 570 wagons drawn by oxen, which are found to be preferable to horses for so long a journey, and, it

---

126 Palmer, *Journal of Travels Over the Rocky Mountains,* in Thwaites' *Early Western Travels, 1748-1846* (Cleveland: The Arthur H. Clark Company, 1906), Vol. XXX. Entry for September 30.

is stated that they started with 6000 cattle, including milch
cows, etc., etc., large numbers have died on the route. They
have a large number of horses and a few mules. Their wagons
are admirably adapted for the long rugged land journey.
That the gentlemen of the H. B. Company have not
exaggerated the lamentable condition of these emigrants on
former occasions is evident by the appearance on arrival of
this, said to be most wealthy and respectable of all the former.
Fever and sickness have made fearful havoc among them, and
many are now remaining in a helpless condition at the
"Dalles" and the "Cascades." They report 30 men, women
and children having died upon the journey.[127]

The compromise route of the Cutoff was established, in
spite of ill repute. Elijah Elliott's efforts in 1853[128] have been
mentioned. In 1859 Captain H. D. Wallen commanded an
army expedition from The Dalles to Salt Lake. Wallen's men
retraced almost exactly the 1845 route, and commented on
the tracks in places. Maps drawn by Louis Scholl, guide for
Wallen in 1859, and for the eastern branch of Major Steen's
1860 exploration, showed the wagon road. Other wheels
followed—the trader, the freighter, the miner, the settler. The
present highway from Vale to Bend marks, with improvements, the general line of march of some of those wagons.
When the Willamette Pass construction joined Highway 97,
the theoretical Cutoff became a reality. But Stephen Meek was
the first to lead a wagon company through the middle route.
He deserves that recognition.

---

127 Joseph Schafer, "Warre & Vavasour," *Oregon Historical
Quarterly*, X (March, 1909), 50.
128 For variations and improvements of the route, readers are referred
to "Cut-off Fever," Leah C. Menefee and Lowell Tiller, which
appears in six *Oregon Historical Quarterlies,* December 1976 -
Spring, 1978. The routes of the Elijah Elliott party and of the
William H. Macy train of 1854 are detailed. After the general
Indian uprisings in Oregon and Washington territories in 1855,
there was little use of the wagon roads by emigrants, although
army explorations in 1859 and 1860 retraced portions.

BIBLIOGRAPHY

DIARIES
AND
JOURNALS

FIELD, JAMES. Journal, 1845, "Crossing the Plains," *Willamette Farmer*, Portland, Oregon, beginning with the issue dated April 18, 1879, and ending with the issue dated August 1, 1879.

FINDLEY, WILLIAM. Diary of 1845, Coe Collection, Western Americana, Yale University, New Haven, Connecticut.

HARRITT, JESSE. Diary, 1845, *Oregon Pioneer Association Transactions, 1910-11*, Portland, Oregon, pp. 506-26; McNary, Lawrence A., "Route of Meek Cut-off, 1845," *Oregon Historical Quarterly*, XXXV (March, 1934), pp. 1-9. Original on file with the Oregon Historical Society, Portland, Oregon.

HERREN, JOHN. "A Diary of 1845," *Albany Daily Democrat*, January 1 & 2, 1891, Albany, Oregon.

HOWELL, JOHN EWING. "Diary of an Emigrant of 1845," *Washington Historical Quarterly, I (1906-7), 138-58.*

McCLURE, ANDREW S. Diary, 1853, reproduced by Lane County Pioneer-Historical Society, Eugene, Oregon, 1959.

_____. "Diary of a Mining Expedition, 1858," copy on file with Oregon Historical Society.

McCLURE, JAMES F. Diary, 1853, reproduced by Lane County Pioneer-Historical Society, Eugene, Oregon, 1959.

BIBLIOGRAPHY

PALMER, JOEL. *Journal of Travels Over the Rocky Mountains.* In Thwaites' *Early Western Travels, 1748-1846,* Vol. XXX. Cleveland, Ohio: The Arthur H. Clark Company, 1906.

PARKER, SAMUEL. Diary, 1845. Copy on file at Oregon Historical Society, Portland; original in possession of Parker descendants.

READING, PIERSON B. "Reading Diary," *Quarterly of the Society of California Pioneers*, Vol. VI (September, 1930), entries October 1-21.

SNYDER, JACOB R. "The Diary of Jacob R. Snyder" (1845), *Quarterly of the Society of California Pioneers.* San Francisco, California, 1931. VIII (1931), No. 4, 224-60.

TETHEROW: *Organizational Journal of an Emigrant Train of 1845 Captained by Solomon Tetherow,* reproduced by Lane County Pioneer-Historical Society, Eugene, Oregon; original in possession of Mrs. Vale Parker, descendant, Springfield, Oregon.

BOOKS

An Illustrated History of Baker, Grant, Malheur and Harney Counties. Spokane, Washington: Western Historical Publishing Company, 1902, pp. 138-39.

BANCROFT, H. H. *History of California (Works of Hubert Howe Bancroft,* Vols. XVIII to XXIV.) 7 vols.; San Francisco: History Company, 1884-90. Vol. III, appendix material of a biographical nature; Vol. IV, 577-78; V, 188-89, 526.

____. *History of Oregon,* "The Immigration of 1845." 2 vols.; San Francisco: History Company, 1886. I, chap. XIX, 508-41.

____. *History of the Pacific States.* San Francisco: History Company, 1884. XVI, chap. XXIV, 571-87.

BRIMLOW, GEORGE FRANCIS. *Harney County, Oregon, and Its Rangeland.* Portland, Oregon: Binfords & Mort, 1951, pp. 16-17.

CAREY, CHARLES H. *History of Oregon.* Portland, Oregon: Pioneer History Pub. Co., 1922, pp. 402, 442-43.

CLARK-McKITRICK, MARCIA & TIM. *Robert Newell: A Singular Life.* Champoeg, Oregon: De Press, July 1987.

CLARKE, S. A. *Pioneer Days in Oregon History*. Portland, Oregon: J. K. Gill, 1905.

COMBS, WELCOME MARTINDALE; ROSS, SHARON COMBS. *God Made a Valley*. Charleston, Oregon: The Empire Charleston Builder, 1962, p. 62.

CUMMINS, SARAH J. (WALDEN). *Autobiography and Reminiscences*. Milton-Freewater, Oregon, 1914; See also *Book of Remembrance of Marion County, Oregon, Pioneers, 1840-1860*, by Sarah Hunt Steeves, pp. 47-65.

DeMOSS CATHERINE CORNWALL. *Blue Bucket Nuggets*. Portland, Oregon: Binfords & Mort, 1939.

DeVOTO, BERNARD. *The Year of Decision*, 1846. Boston: Little, Brown, and Co., 1943, p. 362.

Dictionary of Oregon History, edited by Howard M. Corning. Portland, Oregon: Binfords & Mort, 1956, pp. 30, 164.

DOWNS, ROBERT HORACE. *History of the Silverton Country*. Portland, Oregon: Berncliff Press, 1926, pp. 29-30, 31, 33-35.

EL HULT, RUBY. *Lost Mines and Treasures of the Pacific Northwest*. Portland, Oregon: Binfords & Mort, 1957, pp. 47-60.

ELLISON, R. S. *Independence Rock, The Great Record of the Desert*. Casper, Wyoming: Natrona County Historical Society, 1930.

EVANS, ELWOOD. *History of the Pacific Northwest*, Vol. II. Portland, Oregon: North Pacific History Co., 1889.

FAGAN, DAVID D. *Illustrated History of Benton County, Oregon*. Portland, Oregon, 1885.

GASTON, JOSEPH. *Centennial History of Oregon 1811-1911*, Vol. III. Chicago: S. J. Clarke Publishing Co., 1912.

GOULDER, W. A. *Reminiscences of a Pioneer*. Boise, Idaho: Timothy Regan, 1909.

GREGG, J. R. *A History of the Oregon Trail, Santa Fe Trail and Other Trails*. Portland, Oregon: Binfords & Mort, 1955, Chapter 16. pp. 160-73.

____. *Pioneer Days in Malheur County*. Los Angeles: Morrison, 1950.

BIBLIOGRAPHY

HANCOCK, SAMUEL. *The Narrative of Samuel Hancock,* edited by Arthur D. Howden Smith. New York: Robert M. McBride & Company, 1927.

HINES, H. K. *An Illustrated History of the State of Oregon.* Chicago: Lewis Publishing Co., 1893.

History of Central Oregon. Spokane, Washington: Western Historical Publishing Co., 1905.

History of Linn Co., compiled by Workers of the Writers' Program in the State of Oregon, Sponsored by the Linn Co. Pioneer Mem. Association, pp. 4, 5, 42, 69.

History of Wasco County, Oregon, compiled by William H. McNeal. The Dalles, Oregon.

HULL, LINDLEY M. *A History of the Famous Wenatchee, Entiat, Chelan & Columbia Valley.* Spokane, Washington: Shaw & Borden Co., 1929, p.59.

Joint Abstract of Record, No. 16, Original, Supreme Court of the United States (October term, 1932), U.S.A. vs. State of Oregon, II, 1018-59.

KENNEDY, G. W. *The Pioneer Campfire.* Portland, Oregon: Clarke-Kundret Printing Co., 1914, pp. 116-18.

LANG, H. O. *History of the Willamette Valley.* Portland, Oregon: Himes and Lang, 1885.

LARSELL, O. O. *The Doctor in Oregon.* Portland, Oregon: Binfords & Mort, 1947, pp. 167-68, 135, 139-43.

LOCKLEY, FRED. *History of the Columbia River Valley,* Vol. I. Chicago, 1928, pp. 417-18.

_____. *Oregon Folks.* New York: Knickerbocker Press, 1928.

_____. *Oregon's Yesterdays.* New York: Knickerbocker Press, 1928.

McARTHUR, LEWIS A. *Oregon Geographic Names.* Portland, Oregon; Oregon Historical Society, 1952 edition, pp. 163, 389.

MEEK, STEPHEN HALL. *Autobiography of a Mountain Man, 1805-1889,* Glen Dawson: Pasadena, California, 1948, from *History of Siskiyou County,* Oakland, California: D. J. Stewart & Co., 1881, pp. 21-24.

147

MONTGOMERY, DONNA WOJCIK. *The Brazen Overlanders of 1845.* Bowie Maryland: Heritage Books, Inc., 1992 (Revised Edition). First publication was in 1976 by Donna Wojcik.

Polk County Pioneer Sketches, Vols. I, II. Dallas, Oregon, Polk County Itemizer-Observer, January 1, 1927 and October 1, 1929.

Portrait & Biographical Record of Willamette Valley, Oregon. Chicago: Chapman Publishing Co., 1903.

RHODES, GENEVA. *The Browns Family History II.* Newton, Kansas: Mennonite Press, 1992.

SCOTT, H. W. *History of the Oregon Country;* compiled by Leslie M. Scott. 6 vols., New York, 1924. Vol. II; Vol. III, p.338.

SHELLER, ROSCOE. *The Name Was Olney.* Yakima, Washington: Franklin Press, Inc., 1965.

STEEVES, SARAH HUNT. *Book of Remembrance of Marion County, Oregon, Pioneers 1840-1860.* Portland, Oregon: The Berncliff Press, 1927.

The Souvenir of Western Women, edited by Mary Osborn Douthit. Portland, Oregon: 1905, pp. 27, 44, 82.

WALLEN, CAPTAIN H. D., 4th Infantry, Commanding Wagon Road Expedition (1859). *Affairs in Oregon*, U.S. War Department Documents, April 12, 1860, pp. 211-219, 239-47.

WALLING, A. G. *History of Jackson, Josephine, Douglas, Curry and Coos Counties.* Portland, Oregon, 1884.

WHITE, ELIJAH. *Ten Years in Oregon—Travels and Adventures of Dr. E. White and Lady*, compiled by Miss A. J. Allen. Ithaca, New York: Mack, Andrus & Co., Printers, 1848, pp. 275-85.

PERIODICALS

Oregon Historical Quarterly:
BARLOW, WILLIAM A. "Reminiscences of Seventy Years," XIII (September, 1912), 240-86.

CLARK, ROBERT CARLTON. "Harney Basin Explorations, 1826-60," XXXIII (June, 1932), 108-11.

BIBLIOGRAPHY

DRURY, CLIFFORD M. "Some Aspects of Presbyterian History in Oregon," LV (June, 1954), 149-50.

JOHNSON, OVERTON, AND WINTER, WILLIAM H. "The Migration of 1843," VII (March, 1906), 93-94; VII (June, 1906), 165-66.

LOCKLEY, FRED. "Autobiography of William Henry Rector," XXX (March, 1929), 63-69.

_____ "The McNemees and Tetherows with the Migration of 1845," XXV (December, 1924), 353-77.

McARTHUR, LEWIS. "Early Scenes in Harney Valley," XXXII (June, 1931), 125-29.

McNARY, LAWRENCE A. "Route of Meek Cut-off, 1845," XXXV (March, 1934), 1-9.

NEDRY, H. S. "Notes on the Early History of Grant County," LIII (December, 1952), 236-37.

MINTO, JOHN. "Minto Pass: Its History, and an Indian Tradition," IV (September, 1903), 241-43.

SCHAFER, JOSEPH. "Warre & Vavasour 1845-6," X (March, 1909), 50.

SCOTT, LESLIE M. "Pioneer Stimulus of Gold," XVIII (September, 1917), 147-66.

_____. "Report of Lieut. Peel, 1845-6," XXIX (March, 1928), 75.

_____ "Where Was Blue Bucket?" XX (June, 1919), 219-20.

TEISER, SIDNEY. "Cyrus Olney, Associate Justice of Oregon Territory Supreme Court," LXIV (December, 1963), 311, footnote 14.

WOOLLEY, IVAN M., M. D. "Mt. Hood or Bust: The Old Road," LX (March, 1959), 5-88.

TERRIBLE TRAIL: THE MEEK CUTOFF, 1845

"Correspondence of Rev. Ezra Fisher," XVI (December, 1915), 406-11.

"Oregon Emigrants," (*Weston Journal*, March 15, 1845) IV (September, 1903), 278.

Vol. XXXI (June, 1930), p. 166, footnote 27.

Vol. XXXIX (June, 1938), p. 138, footnote 24.

Vol. XXXIX (September, 1938), p. 291, footnote 5.

Necrologies, birth dates, anniversaries, family reunions given in various issues.

Oregon Pioneer Association Transactions:
BENNETT, LUCY J. "Captain Lawrence Hall," 1895, 101-102.

HARRITT, JESSE. Diary, 1845, 1910-11, pp. 506-26.

STAATS, Address of HON. STEVEN, 1877, pp. 50-53.

Necrologies, 1876-1925.

"Register of Members of Oregon Pioneer Association," 1873-1886, pp. 75-98.

ROSTERS OF NAMES AND ADDRESSES
TAKEN AT THE REUNIONS OF THE OREGON PIONEERS ASSOCIATION, 1876-1925

Quarterly of the Society of California Pioneers:
READING, PIERSON B. "Reading Diary," Vol. VI (September, 1930), entries Oct. 1-21.

SNYDER, JACOB R. "The Diary of Jacob R. Snyder." San Francisco, Calif., 1931, VIII, No. 4, 224-60.

BIBLIOGRAPHY

Washington Historical Quarterly:
   HOWELL, JOHN EWING. "Diary of an Emigrant of 1845," I
      (1906-7), pp. 138-58.

   BEEBE, BEATRICE B. "Hunting for the Blue Bucket Diggings,"
      Overland Monthly, LXXXVII (August, 1929), 252-55.

   KEEN, PAUL. "Climatic Cycles in Eastern Oregon as Indicated by
      Tree Rings," *Monthly Weather Review*, Vol. 65, No. 5, May,
      1937.

   MEYERS, E. L. (ROY). "Wagon Trains Migration and Emigration,
      1832-1853," *Genealogical Forum of Portland, Oregon*, IX,
      No. 9 (May, 1960), 71.

NEWSPAPERS

The Oregonian:
   Lawrence Hall, obit., 2/2/1867.

   Charles Craft, obit., 7/24/1869.

   Stephen Meek, 4/30/1885, p. 2.

   "Found Blue Bucket Mine," Daniel Herren obit., 7/21/08, p. 10,
      col. 2.

   "Blue Bucket Mine is Believed Found," 3/26/16, sec 1, p. 1.

   Mrs. Rebecca Jane Thompson, obit., 2/24/18.

   Ruth Herren Leonard, letter, 4/28/19.

   "Discovery of Blue Bucket Mine Real," (Statement by George
      Millican) 4/27/19, sec. 2, p. 6, col. 1.

   W. H. Herren, letter, 3/7/22.

   "Tree Marks Old Grave," 4/25/26, p. 20.

TERRIBLE TRAIL: THE MEEK CUTOFF, 1845

Ted Boyer, letter, 3/10/33.

Mrs. Angelina Carter (100th birthday), 12/16/34, sec. 2, p. 2.

"Wagon Train Route Trailed, Identity of Pioneer Sought," 10/4/50.

"Pioneer Woman's Mystery Solved by Grandchildren," 10/5/50, sec. 2, p. 8.

John Phillips Family, 2/1/59.

Oregon Journal:
Fred Lockley, "Impressions and Observations of a Journal Man":

Susannah Johnson Peterson, date unknown.

Mrs. W. H. Rees (no date), James E. Hall descendant.

Mrs. Mary Stewart, no date.

Richard Watson Helm, 2/11/?.

John U. Smith, Bayley descendant, 8/27/?.

Sidney G. Dorris, Dorris-Bayley desc., 9/16/2?.

Mrs. Francis Large, Bayley desc., 2/27/22.

Sebastian Ritner, 2/28/22.

Mrs. J. F. Calbreath, Bayley desc., 10/3/24.

C. A. Sweek, 11/13/24; also appears in *Baker Morning Democrat*, 11/18/24.

Mrs. Lydia A. Steckel, Herren-Wallace desc., 12/11/24.

Thomas R. Cornelius, 6/2/25.

Mrs. T. C. Davidson, Gesner desc., 6/27/25.

Gabriel Preston Rush, miner of No. Calif., 10/16/25.

BIBLIOGRAPHY

Mary Elmira Hurley, Bayley desc., 8/16/25.

William H. Klum, Peterson desc., 3/26/26.

Mrs. Owen D. Hutton, Durbin desc., 10/23/26.

Stephen Hall Meek, 4/16/27; 4/17/27; 4/19/27.

Martha A. Belieu, 6/19/27.

H. C. Thompson, Lewis Thompson desc., 7/29/27.

N. A. King, 6/4/28.

Mrs. Strong, James Taylor desc., 6/18/28.

H. D. Randall and wife, King-Chambers desc., 4/13/29.

Carl G. Helm, 7/7/29.

Perry Read, 11/19/30.

Mrs. Martha E. Herren, 5/28/31.

Mrs. Nina Harris Stone, Philip Harris desc., 4/12/32; 4/13/32;
4/14/32.

Mrs. Elva Herren Estes, Herren desc., 5/17/32.

Herrens, Halls, and Rees, 5/18/32.

John H. McNary, Hugh McNary desc., 6/22/32.

Mrs. G. W. McLaughlin, James E. Hall desc., 7/7/32.

Frank Durbin, 7/14/32.

Cordelia Caroline Hubbard, Staats desc., 4/12/33.

Mrs. Fred Sherman, Helm desc., 3/28/34.

W. H. Newman, Newman-David Tetherow desc., 11/23/34.

Pierce Parker, Samuel Parker desc., 3/4/35.

Biography of Samuel Parker, 1845, 3/19/35.

Journal of Samuel Parker, 1845, 3/30/35.

Sol. Tetherow Wagon Train, 3/22/37, p. 10.

Mrs. Dale L. Torrence, Adam Smith Hamilton desc., 4/13/37.

Mrs. Ruth Elizabeth Martin Sayre, John Martin desc., 9/28/37.

Rev. C. O. Hosford, 3/21/38.

Fred Lockley, "In Earlier Days," Mrs. Ralph Wilcox, no date.

J. Ostergren, "Meacham Traces Death-marked Trail of 1845 Lost Wagon Train," 7/31/51, sec. 1, p. 3.

L. M. Scott, "Lost Migration," 9/24/45, sec. 2, p. 2.

"Watched Oregon Grow Up," Oliver Perry Henderson interview, Dec. 11, 1938, p. 9.

Other Newspapers:
"Notice of Death, Miss Julia Ann Stratuff," *Oregon Spectator*, 2/5/1846.

Letter to Editor, *Oregon Spectator*, signed "Oregonian," 2/18/1847.

Solomon Tetherow, letter, *Oregon Spectator*, 3/18/1847, p. 3, col. 2-3.

William Green T'Vault, obit., *Oregon Sentinel*, Jacksonville, Oregon, 2/6/1869.

"With the Emigrant Train, 1845," J. H. Walker, *Carleton-Yamhill Review*, 7/24/52.

Mrs. A. F. Rees, obit., *La Grande Observer*, 1/27/1899.

BIBLIOGRAPHY

"Oren E. Thompson," Rebecca Jane Hamilton desc., *Burns Times-Herald* 1/31/63.

"Group Believes Fabled Site Found in Lake County," *Lakeview Examiner*, 4/28/60, No. 23, pp. 1, 4.

"New Blue Bucket Story," *Lakeview Examiner*, 5/5/60, No. 24.

Elizabeth Orr, "James Foster Traveled with 'Blue Bucket' Wagon Train," *Lake County Examiner*, Lakeview, Oregon, 5/7/64, p. 8.

"Ontario Stirs When Tale of Mine is Told," *Caldwell Tribune*, Caldwell, Idaho, 4/14/22.

"Lost Emigrant Mines," *State Journal*, Eugene, Oregon, 11/23/1867.

D. G. Herren, statement, *Eugene Daily Guard*, 8/16/19.

"Finding of Blue Bucket Mine Told," *Redmond Spokesman*, 4/11/35.

Mary Glenn Butler, "Crook County Stage Station," *Central Oregonian*, Prineville, Oregon, 7/30/59.

J. M. Lawrence, "History of Bend's Development Has Many Interesting Features," *Bend Bulletin*, 7/3/12.

"Carved Inscription on Limb of Juniper Tree Puzzle to Central Oregon Historians," *Bend Bulletin*, 4/27/49, p. 9.

"Oregon Meeting," *St. Joseph Gazette*, St. Joseph, Mo., 5/2/1845, Vol. 1, No. 2, p. 2.

"The Oregon Emigrants," *Gazette*, St. Joseph, 5/2/1845, Vol. 1, No. 2, p. 2.

"Letters," *Gazette*, St. Joseph, 7/10/1846, Vol. 1, No. 52, p. 1.

Hiram Smith, letter, *Gazette*, St. Joseph, 7/17/1846.

TERRIBLE TRAIL: THE MEEK CUTOFF, 1845

H. D. Martin, letter, *Gazette*, St. Joseph, 8/21/1846.

Interview, Capt. T. M. Adams, *St. Louis Weekly Reveille*, 5/29/1845.

LETTERS

BAYLEY, BETSY, to her sister, Mrs. Lucy P. Griffith, of Charleston, Ohio, September 20, 1849. On file, Oregon Historical Society.

CARLIN, ELLEN GARRISON, Vertical File, Oregon Historical Society.

KING, MARIA, to mother, brothers and sisters, written from Luckiamute Valley, Oregon, April, 1846. First printed in an Illinois newspaper; see also *Gazette-Times*, Corvallis, Oregon, July 24, 1937, sec. 3, p. 1. On file, Oregon Historical Society.

BELIEU, LEANDER H., to wife and children, written en route to the gold fields in California, May 28, 1849. Original on file, Oregon Historical Society.

HERREN, W. H., to Mrs. J. E. Meyers, Prineville, Oregon, (no date) in possession of Bert Houston, Bend, Oregon.

MARTIN, H. D., to the *St. Joseph Gazette*, St. Joseph, Mo., Aug. 21, 1846.

SMITH, HIRAM, to *Gazette*, St. Joseph, July 17, 1846.

TETHEROW, SOLOMON, to *Oregon Spectator*, March 18, 1847, p. 3, col. 2-3.

MICROFILM

BACON, J. M., "Mercantile Life at Oregon City," 1878, Bancroft Pacific Series, Reel No. 2.

"Wm. W. Buck's Narrative," Oregon City, June 18, 1878, Bancroft Pacific Series, Reel No. 2.

HERREN, W. J., account of Meek's Cutoff and gold discovery, Bancroft Pacific Series, Reel No. 3.

"The Blue Bucket Mine," Oregon State Archives, Film 22-2.

BIBLIOGRAPHY

WPA FILES

Benton County, OSU & State libraries: Interviews:
Mrs. Rosetta Green, David Lewis desc.

Jesse W. Foster, son of John Foster & Mary Lloyd.

Mrs. Ollie Alcorn, Sebastian Ritner desc.

Pamela Fuller Brien & William E. Brien, Fuller-King desc.

Mrs. Angeline Belieu Carter.

Virgil Carter, Belieu desc., 7/25/38.

Elizabeth Currier, Foster information.

James Price, Norton desc.; King desc.

Mrs. Julia Price and sister Mrs. Alexander, daughters of Rowland Chambers-Lovisa King.

Thos. D. Reeves & Anna Charlotte Reeves Starr, desc. of Nancy Lloyd.

Mrs. Sarah Stewart, daughter of Prior Scott.

Mrs. Bertha Thompson, Norton-King desc.

Mrs. Lucy G. Yates, daughter of Martha Hughart.

News Item: "Haman Lewis," Feb. 15, 1925.

Deschutes County, University of Oregon, Interview:
Jess Tetherow, desc. of Sol. Tetherow.

News item: Inscription on tree, 1845-1846, GH XIV B.

Douglas County, University of Oregon:
  News Items:
    Umpqua Valley News, July 11, 1907, p. 3. Thomas Smith information concerning Thomas Cowan.

    Roseburg Review, Feb. 13, 1902, p. 3. Mrs. Martha Liggett Pearce obituary.

    Roseburg Review, Sept. 7, 1898, John Catching.

Jackson County, University of Oregon:
  News Items:
    Ashland Tidings, p. 3, col. 2, June 20, 1877, Solomon Tetherow; daughter, Mrs. Parker.

    Medford Mail, Dec. 11, 1908, William Bybee obit.; wife: Elizabeth Walker, daughter of Jesse Walker.

    Ashland Tidings, Oct. 20, 1911, p. 1, Elizabeth T'Vault Kenny obit.

Linn County, State Library, Salem: Interviews:
  Mrs. Lena Snyder Anderson, Peterson information.

  Mrs, Emma M. (Bates) Parrish, Henry Peterson family information.

  Mrs. Rachel Arminta Peterson, wife of David H. Peterson.

  Mrs. Emma Smeed, daughter of Hiram Smeed.

  Elias Walters-Naomi Williams information.

Marion County, University of Oregon:
  News Item:
    The Dalles Times Mountaineer, The Dalles, July 21, 1883, H. L. McNary obit.

Umatilla County, State Library, Salem:
  News Item:
    East Oregonian, Oct. 26, 1883, Vol. 9, No. 4, William Switzler obit.

BIBLIOGRAPHY

Washington County, State Library:
  News Items:
    The Hillsboro Argus, p. 1, June 3 and 10, 1926, "History of Wilkes
      Family—Among Earliest of County Pioneers."

  Obituaries taken from *Daily* and *Sunday Oregonian:*
  Margaret Ann Powell: Mrs. Rachael Walker.

  Argus, p. 3, June 2, 1904, "Pioneer Isaac Butler Died Here Yester-
      day."

  Argus, p. 3, June 29, 1899, "Col. T. R. Cornelius Has Passed Away."

  Argus, p. 3, September 22, 1898, "Grandma McKinney Has Passed
      Away."

  Argus, p. 1, August 14, 1919, "Pioneer Woman, Mrs. Mary H.
      Moore, Passes."

  Argus, p. 3, March 12, 1903, "Noted Pioneer Dies at County Farm,"
      obit. of Wheelock Simmons who married widow of the foun-
      der of Hillsboro, Lucinda Hill.

  Washington County News-Times, p. 1, "Across Plains in 1845,"
      sketch of Mrs. Zeruiah Large, Daniel Bayley's daughter.

  Information: Poll books' lists of voters for Eastern, Western and
      Middle precincts, Tuality County, 1845-46; Assessment
      Rolls, Washington County, July 27, 1846.

MAPS

State of Oregon Highway Department, County Series, 1960.

"Map of Reconnaissance for a Military Road from The Dalles of the
    Columbia to Great Salt Lake," Lt. Joseph Dixon, 1859, Oregon
    Historical Society.

"Map showing routes traveled by the Command of Maj. E. Steen, U.S.
    Drag.'s, 1860," Oregon Historical Society.

TERRIBLE TRAIL: THE MEEK CUTOFF, 1845

Maps drawn by Louis Scholl, in conjunction with Wallen and Steen
Expeditions; Miss Priscilla Knuth, Research Associate, Oregon
Historical Society.

Early Survey Records, Bureau of Land Management, Portland, Oregon.

Map compiled by Ralph M. Shane and Ruby D. Leno—Warm Springs
Indian Reservation, Warm Springs, Oregon; J. W. Elliott, Supt.,
April, 1949.

FAMILY RECORDS, CORRESPONDENCE

FAMILY	DESCENDANTS
Adams, Thomas	—Mildred Harms, Hillsboro, Oregon.
Allen, James Miller	—Mrs. Lois Allen Pierce, Shelton, Washington.
	—Pete Allen, Redmond, Oregon, "The Allens," 1957. (Mimeo.)
Bayley, Daniel D.	—A. Ray Dorris, Portland, Oregon, *The Munson Record*, New Haven, Conn. Privately printed.
Belieu, Leander	—Margaret Keyes, Bend, Oregon.
Burbage, Ezekiel	—See Marquam, Alfred.
Butler, Isaac	—Dale B. Sigler, Portland, Oregon.
	—Miss Zoa Bloyd and Mrs. Lucy Hutchinson, Cornelius, Oregon. (Letter written by Isaac's son to his grandchildren.)
Butts, John	—Mrs. F. R. Black, Vancouver, Washington, "Melva Butts McKenney." (Mimeo. from original, dated Oct. 1, 1925.)

BIBLIOGRAPHY

—Bob Templeman, Berrien Springs, Michigan.

Catching, William W.   —Betty Franklin, Medford, Oregon.

Center, Mary   —See Powell, Rev. Theophilus.

Chambers, Rowland   —Mrs. William Grant, Bellflower, California.

—C. E. Chambers, Sweet Home, Oregon.

—Paul K. Chambers, Jr., Corvallis, Oregon.

—Mrs. Mabelle Randall, Portland.

—Leah Chambers-Scott, Pasadena, California.

Cooley, Christopher   —Mrs. Paul E. Sharp, Seattle, Washington.

—Mrs. A. Bruce Steele, Santa Barbara, California.

Cornelius, Benjamin   —*Supplement to Cornelius Family in America*, Chapter XI, p. 72. (Privately printed.)

Cox, Anderson   —Mr. and Mrs. Lee Mantz, Waitsburg, Washington.

Cox, Isham   —Mrs. Stephen Dow Beckham, McMinnville, Oregon; information given by Stephen.

Craft, Charles   —Mrs. Virginia Scott-Morgan, Salem, Oregon.

—Mrs. Lawrence Scott, Salem.

161

Doak, Andrew	—Mrs. Meredith F. DeBuse, Portland, Oregon.
Durbin, John	—Barbara Leppe, Bend, Oregon.
	—Martha Agee, Dallas, Oregon.
Eaton, Jesse	—Miles Eaton, Portland, Oregon.
Foster, John and Nancy	—Mrs. H. O. Warren, Eugene, Oregon.
Fuller, Price	—Frances Maxine Bell (Mrs. Jesse E.), Eugene, Oregon.
Gillett(e), Joel	—Phyllis Denton, Clovis, California.
Glasgow, Thomas	—Mrs. Harold E. Mueller, Oklahoma City, Oklahoma; information from Harold.
Hall, James E.	—Bible, Roelofson Papers, Oregon State Library, Salem, Oregon.
Hamilton, Robert W.	—Oren E. Thompson, Burns, Oregon.
	—Mrs. Joseph B. Fine, Burns, Oregon.
	—Mrs. Leatrice Olfs, Wilbur, Washington. (Family Bible information.)
Hampton, John Jacob	—Mrs. Fay Robertson, Eugene, Oregon.
	—Mr. and Mrs. Lester Hampton, Lakeview, Oregon.
Hancock, Samuel	—Mrs. Carl P. Dean, Coupeville, Whidbey Island, Washington.
Harris, Leonard	—Mrs. William George, Eugene, Oregon.
Helm, William	—Herman Whitman Helm, Ashland Oregon.

BIBLIOGRAPHY

Henderson, Jesse   —Mrs. Dorothy Pea, Portland, Oregon.

          —Mrs. Margaret B. Parcel, Seattle, Washington.

Herren, John   —See Wallace, William T.

Holman, John   —Anna Clinkinbeard, Coos River, Oregon (through Mr. and Mrs. Dell Brunell of Coos River).

Johnson, Dr. Chas. M.   —Mrs. Neita Terry, Lafayette, Oregon.

Johnson, John   —Miss Lena Belle Tartar, Corvallis, Oregon.

King, Nahum   —Miss Bertha King, Corvallis, Oregon (Family Bible records, other information).

          —Mrs. Gardner A. King, Cottage Grove, Oregon.

          —Nathan King, Toppenish, Washington.

          —Dorothy King Young, Gualala, California.

          —Minerva Mueller, Portland, Oregon.

          —See also Chambers, Rowland.

Liggett, Alexander   —Viola Falk Menefee, Brownsville, Oregon.

Lloyd, John   —Helen Lloyd Shaffner (Mrs. Don K.), Dillon, Montana.

McKinney, William   —Mrs. Mabel Brooke Blum, White Salmon, Washington.

—Mr. and Mrs. Lee Mantz, Waitsburg, Washington.

McNary, James — Victor W. Jones, Redmond, Washington.

McNemee, Job — Mrs. John Upton, Hillsboro, Oregon.

Marquam, Alfred — W. M. Marquam, Del Paso Heights, Calif. (Family Bible information).

—Mrs. Dorothy L. Barber, Tillamook, Oregon, "Record of Marquam Family as Recalled by Mrs. Mary J. Marquam Albright Stockwell, March 28, 1917."

Meek, Stephen H. L. — Mrs. Grace Bottoms, Oakland, California.

—Joseph L. Meek, Washington, D.C., Joseph Meek descendant.

Norton, Lucius — Mrs. J. E. Norton, Kent, Oregon.

—Frances Maxine Bell (Mrs. Jesse E.), Eugene, Oregon.

—B. H. Plunkett, Wren, Oregon.

Officer, James — Mr. and Mrs. Joe Officer, Canyon City, Oregon.

—Wayne C. Stewart, John Day, Oregon.

—Mrs. John W. Murray, Dayville, Oregon.

—Mrs. Bertha Vaughan Johns, Fox, Oregon.

—W. O. Vaughan, Gladstone, Oregon.

Ownbey, Nicholas — Mrs. D. L. Ramsay, Stevenson, Washington.

BIBLIOGRAPHY

Packwood, Elisha —Mrs. Retta Hultgren, Shelton, Washington.

—Mrs. Ruth Ryser, Klamath Falls, Oregon.

—Mrs. Nellie Wiley Hartl, Tacoma, Washington (Wm. Packwood desc.)

Packwood, John I. —Clareta Olmstead Smith, Ellensburg, Washington.

—Mrs. Joseph Fejes, Vancouver, Washington.

Parker, Samuel —Florence Hedden, Eugene, Oregon.

Powell, Rev. Theophilus —Mrs. Arthur G. Elkins, Portland, Oregon, "The Trials and Tribulations of the Powells and Centers in 1845 while crossing the Plains from Illinois to Oregon." (Unpublished family account.)

Riggs, James Berry —The late Ralph R. Cronise, Albany, Oregon.

Ritner, Sebastian —Mrs. Rittie Kerber, Kings Valley, Oregon.

Simpson, Isaac —Paul B. Simpson, Eugene, Oregon.

Stewart, John —Mrs. N. C. Hiday, Salem, Oregon.

—Mrs. Alma Davis, Prineville, Oregon.

Switzler, John —Russell M. Turner, Roseburg, Oregon.

Tetherow, David —Margie Gard Gray, Wilbur, Washington.

—Mrs. Robert Braunwart, Wenatchee, Washington.

Tetherow, Solomon —Mrs. Vale Parker, Springfield, Oregon (original organizational journal of the Tetherow Train).

—Jess Tetherow, Redmond, Oregon.

—Claude L. Tetherow, Lincoln, Nebraska.

—Herbert H. Tutterow, Chattanooga, Tennessee.

Vaughan, William Greene —Jack R. Brandt, Sweet Home, Oregon.

Wallace, William T. —Mrs. Martha Susan Norland, Parma, Idaho.

—Wallace Stanciu, Richland, Oregon.

Walter, William —Mr. & Mrs. Lee Mantz, Waitsburg, Washington.

—Mrs. Mabel Brooke Blum, White Salmon, Washington.

Wheeler, Solomon —Mrs. H. O. Warren, Eugene, Oregon.

Wooley, Jacob —Geneva Rhodes, Gales Creek, Oregon.

—Carol Grover, Bend, Oregon.

Zumwalt, Christopher Peter —Mrs. Irene Foster, Dayton, Oregon. (Also provided material concerning many other 1845 emigrants.)

OTHER SOURCES

DONEGAN, JAMES J. "Historical Sketch of Harney County, Oregon," p. 1. (On file, office of *Burns Times-Herald*, Burns, Oregon.)

1850 U.S. Census Books for Oregon, Oregon Historical Society.

BIBLIOGRAPHY

Membership Files, Oregon Pioneers Association, Oregon Historical Society.

Scrapbooks, clippings, OHS.

Biographical index file, State Library, Salem.

Oregon Provisional & Territorial Government Papers, Nos. 581, 589, 613, 698, 699, 1043, pertaining to Stephen Meek, Oregon State Library, Salem.

Oregon Historical Quarterly Index, Vols. I to XL (1900-1939), Portland, Oregon, Oregon Historical Society, 1941.

Oregon Donation Land Claims, Vols. I, II, III, Genealogical Material, Abstracted by Genealogical Forum, Portland, Oregon, 1957-1962.

Oregon Spectator Index, 1846-1854, Vols. 1 & 2 (Sponsored by City of Portland), OHS, May, 1941.

Oregon State Archives, records of search, State Library, Salem.

Benton County Marriage Records, Sept. 1850-Feb. 1861.

Early Marriage Records—Clackamas Co., Wasco Co., Oregon, Vol, I, Tualatin Chapter, DAR, Oswego, Oregon, 1960.

1860 and 1870 census books prepared by Mrs. N. C. Hiday from microfilm at the Oregon State Library, Salem.

Membership records, Sons and Daughters of Oregon Pioneers, Portland, Oregon.

Marriages in Polk County, Oregon (Nov. 3, 1846-Dec. 24, 1865); Marion County, Oregon, Marriage Records (Feb. 13, 1849-Dec. 31, 1863); from *Beaver Briefs*, Willamette Valley Geneological Society, Salem, Oregon.

Marriage Record Book I (Jan. 1855-Aug. 1865), Multnomah County, Genealogical Forum of Portland, Oregon, Inc., Sept., 1970.

Polk County Cemeteries (Fir Crest, English, and small adjoining hillside cemetery at Monmouth, Oregon), Genealogical Records, Winema Chapter D.A.R., 1952.

ROSTER OF NAMES
—
Meek Train, 1845

THE FOLLOWERS OF MEEK

IN RETROSPECT, it would seem that the people involved in the adventure of the Cutoff, lost, exhausted, and discouraged as they were, could not possibly have retained enough strength to face the pioneer prospects of clearing land, building homes, making their way in the raw Oregon country. But here is another example of the paradox of human endurance. Most of them survived to become men of property. Not a few achieved distinction in various fields of endeavor besides that of the pioneer agriculturist.

W. G. T'Vault edited the first newspaper west of the Rocky Mountains, the *Oregon Spectator*; Ralph Wilcox was the first physician and first teacher in Portland; Lawrence Hall and Thomas Cornelius led troops in the Indian Wars of 1855; Samuel Parker served in both the Territorial and Oregon State legislatures, was appointed Prosecuting Attorney for the Territory in 1849, and United States Marshal in 1853. There are approximately 150 Territorial Documents at the Oregon State Library which bear Samuel's signature or name.

Some members of the Meek party, such as the Packwoods, Walters, McKinneys, Coxes, and Lloyds, found the Washington area to their liking. Notable, too, is Samuel Hancock, whose narrative of his adventures prior to his establishment on Whidbey Island makes amazing reading.

Associated with the 1845 party are some familiar place names: Ross Island and Terwilliger Boulevard in Portland; Cornelius Plains and the town of Cornelius in Washington County; Kings Valley in Benton County and King Heights in Portland; Hampton and Hampton Butte on the High Desert in central Oregon; Olney Creek at The Dalles; Tetherow Butte and Tetherow Bridge near Redmond. The list could go on.

But it was not just the men who made history; as Goulder suitably remarked of the women, "It was my privilege to see them all in the beautiful Willamette Valley, and to watch for successive years their quiet and devoted processes of home-building. If anybody asks you who 'saved Oregon,' tell them that it was the women who crossed the plains to Oregon during the fourth decade. Tell them that I said so, and add that my testimony is that of a perfectly impartial and disinterested witness. The task of 'saving Oregon' was not accomplished by diplomats nor politicians, nor by any school of missionaries of high or less degree, but it was the work of the women, who made it possible for the men to come and stay where the presence of both, women and men, was needed.[128]

Here, then, is our tribute to those remarkable people who suffered the trials of the Cutoff and then set about the business of strengthening and gaining the territory for the United States.

One can safely estimate that the Meek party numbered somewhere between 1,000 and 1,500 persons; our list numbers about 825. Now, over a century later, it is doubtful that a complete list can ever be compiled but the following roster is as accurate as our research can make it. Variance found in

---

128 William A. Goulder, *Reminiscences of a Pioneer* (Boise, Idaho: Timothy Regan, 1909), p.133.

the spelling of names and in the dates is the result of inconsistent records that were filed at the time.

The roster was compiled by Mrs. Keith Clark, of Redmond, but credit for much of the information contained herein must be shared with Mrs. Frank Wojcik (now Donna Montgomery[129]), of Portland. Their unswerving, laborious efforts in finding, analyzing, assessing, and piecing together the clues of genealogy deserve the unqualified thanks of the authors.

---

129 In 1976 Donna (Wojcik) Montgomery published *The Brazen Overlanders of 1845,* revised in 1992. Further information is available in her roster.

ROSTER
—
Meek Train 1845

*Person strongly believed to have been on the Cutoff; confirmation lacking.

Adams, Thomas—b. 18 March 1788, Hopkins Co., Kentucky; d. 16 February 1882, Monticello, California; took his family to California in 1848, lived in Yolo and Napa Co.

Adams, Sarah Frances (Cornelius)—b. abt. 1806, Christian Co., Kentucky; d. in California; sister to Benjamin Cornelius (see Roster); m. Thomas, 2 November 1826, Howard Co., Missouri; Thomas had m. 1st, Polly Davis 15 November 1809, Christian Co., Kentucky; Polly d. in 1826, Missouri.
Children:
See Cornelius, Elizabeth Adams (Mrs. Benjamin, Sr.); daughter of Thomas' first marriage.
*Thomas—b. abt. 1826, Missouri; settled in California; moved to Douglas Co., Oregon, abt. 1869; m. Martha ____, native of Ireland.
Wilson—b. 1828, Missouri.
Mary Jane—b. 1829, Howard Co., Missouri; m. Gabriel Chrisman, 19 January. 1847, Oregon Terr.; Donation Land Claim (DLC) No. 2114, Yamhill Co., Oregon.

Sarah B.—b. 1831/2, Howard Co., Missouri; m. Madison Mathiew Harbin, California, 1848/9.

John—b. 16 March 1834, Howard Co., Missouri; d. 10 September 1884, California; m. Polly Elizabeth Adams, 1 October 1854, California.

Missouri Ann—b. 1838; m. James Dallas, California.

*Allen, Benjamin—b. 1827, Kentucky; d. 29 October 1861, Eugene City, Oregon; m. Sarah Ann Howard, abt. 1848/9, Feather River, California; Sarah was b. 10 October 1835, Kentucky; listed as a private with the Tetherow Train.

Allen, James Miller—b. 2 October 1821, Cole Co., Missouri; d. 1 March 1887, Boyd, Oregon; DLC No. 4630, Polk Co., Oregon.

Allen, Hannah Jane (Riggs)—b. 10 January 1825, Morgan Co. Il.; d. 6 April 1860, Polk Co., Oregon; m. James, 19 November 1841, Platte Co., Missouri. He m. 2nd, Sarah Elizabeth Butler, 5 July 1860.
Children:
Cyrus Albert—b. 19 September 1843, Missouri; d. July, 1922; m. Margaret Caldwell, 9 March 1867.

Allred, Joseph—*see* Walter, William; Joseph was a grandson who had been orphaned.

Allred, Eliza (or Elizabeth)—*see* Walter, William; Eliza was a granddaughter who had been orphaned.

*Baggas, Henry—name appearing on the muster roll of the Tetherow Train.

*Barnes, Cyrus—listed as a private on the Tetherow Train roster.

Bayley, Daniel Dodge—b. 8 January 1802 (?), Concord, New H.; d. 29 March 1893, Tillamook Co., Oregon; DLC No.

4020, Yamhill Co.; later had land which is now the site of Garibaldi, Oregon.

Bayley, Elizabeth (Munson)—b. 29 February 1804 (?), Hartford, Connecticut; d. 1855, Yamhill Co.; m. Daniel, 14 February 1824, Madison Co., Oh.
Children:
> Timothy—b. abt. 1825, Springfield, Ohio; d. late 1850's, Yamhill Co., Oregon.
> Caroline Elizabeth—b. 2 March 1827, Springfield, Ohio; d. 12 May 1916, Lafayette, Oregon; m. Felix Dorris (*see* Roster), 25 December 1847, Yamhill Co., Oregon; m. 2nd, Dr. J. W. Watts, 1872.
> Mianda Nancy—b. 6 May 1829, Springfield, Ohio; d. 4 October 1918, West Chehalem, Oregon; m. Sidney Smith, 2 August 1846, Yamhill Co. Oregon.
> Bishop Asbury—b. abt. 1834, Springfield, Ohio, d. 1887, Tillamook, Oregon.
> Zeruiah—b. 11 June 1836, Springfield, Ohio; d. 24 June 1922, Forest Grove, Oregon; m. Francis Large, 27 July 1853, West Chehalem, Oregon; DLC No. 2956, Yamhill Co., Oregon.
> Iola—b. 14 February 1838, Ohio; m. 1st, Marcellus Wolff, 30 August 1851, Yamhill Co., Or; m. 2nd, Thos. B. Handley, 1867, Yamhill Co., Oregon.
> Delphine—b. abt 1841, Missouri; m. 1st, Robert Nixon; m. 2nd, Philip Buther; m. 3rd, T. J. Whalen, 1880.

*Bean, James Riley—b. 19 May, 1823, Todd Co., Kentucky, d. 12 April 1899, Seattle, Washington; DLC No. 2776, Yamhill Co., Or; m. Margaret J. Henderson (*see* Roster), 19 September 1850, McMinnville, Oregon.

Belieu, Rev. Leander—b. 1814, Tennessee; d. 15 August 1849, on board a sailing vessel en route from San Francisco, California, to Portland, Oregon; gave the first sermon in Benton Co.; DLC No. 4925, Polk Co., Oregon.

Belieu, Sarah (Liggett)—b. 7 April 1816, Missouri; d. 19 November 1894, Polk Co., Oregon; m. Leander, 15 December 1833, Clay Co., Missouri; m. 2nd, N. D. Jack, 25 September 1851; m. 3rd, H. J. C. Averill, 1 January 1861. *Children:*
Martha Angeline—b. 18 December 1834, Ray Co., Missouri; d. 24/25 February 1937, Wells, Oregon; m. Tolbert Carter, 22 August 1850, Polk Co., Oregon; DLC No. 4058, Benton Co., Oregon. Tolbert was b. 6 March 1825; d. 3 October 1899, Benton Co, Oregon.
Jesse Green—b. abt 1836, Missouri.
Rebecca E.—b. abt 1838, Missouri.
Elizabeth J.—b. 24 January 1839, Andrew Co., Missouri; d. 8 August 1905, Polk Co., Oregon; m. Calaway Hodges, 13 November 1851, Polk Co., Oregon.
Jonathan Wesley Asbury—b. 24 September 1841, Missouri; d. 29 December 1919, Post, Oregon; m. Lavinia Dennison, 24 December 1863, Polk Co, Oregon.

Bennett, William Harden—b. 18 April 1823, Middleton, Jefferson Co., Kentucky; d. 3 September 1889, Rockford, Spokane Co., Washington; DLC No. 398, Washington Co., Oregon; m. Lucy J. Hall (*see* Roster), 22 February 1849, Washington Co., Oregon.

*Bowman, Nathaniel—listed on the "armed men" list of the Tetherow Train; returned East, 4 March 1848.

Bullock, W.W.—said to have been with the Meek Train, organized a party to look in 1860 for gold (Blue Bucket Mine), but couldn't find it. (Information from Victor W. Jones, Redmond, Washington-—James McNary descendant, letter June 14, 1971.) No other Bullock information found.

Burbage, Ezekiel—b. 1778, Washington Co., Maryland; d. 22 November 1857; DLC No. 1682, Clackamas Co., Oregon.

Burbage, Elizabeth (Predwise)—b. 11 September 1789, Maryland; d. 22 November 1853, Marquam, Oregon; m. Ezekiel, 5 August 1820, Bourbon Co., Kentucky.
Children:
See Marquam, Olive Burbage (Mrs. Alfred).

Butler, Isaac—b. 13 June 1820, Al.; d. 1 June 1904, Washington Co., Oregon; DLC No. 393, Washington Co., Oregon.

Butler, Tabitha J. (Tucker)—17, b. Oh; d. 1869, Washington Co., Oregon; m. Isaac, 14 March 1845, Buchanan Co., Missouri; he m. 2nd Mrs. Polly C. Moore.

Butts, John—b. 1810, Pendleton Co., West Virginia; d. 1890, Forest Grove, Oregon; DLC No. 3330, Washington Co., Oregon.

Butts, Catherine (Bonnet)—d. on the Meek Cutoff 2 October 1845, at the crossing of the Deschutes River—what is now Sherars Bridge; m. John, abt. 1830, Virginia; he m. 2nd, Mrs. Jane Evans, 17 July 1850, Washington Co., Oregon.
Children:
Lewis—10, b. Iowa; d. abt 1880; Washington Co., Oregon; m. Elizabeth "Mary" Constable, 29 November 1862, Washington Co.
Mary Ann (Margaret)—b. 1836, Iowa; m. Sanford Wilcox, 4 October 1854, Washington Co., Oregon; DLC No. 4086, Washington Co.
Festus—b. 17 April 1838, Des Moines Co., Iowa; m. Susie Dunn, 30 March 1892, Baker Co., Oregon.
Jacob—5, b. Iowa; m. Sarah Dixon, 14 February 1867, Washington Co., Oregon.
Melva—b. 2 December 1840, Iowa; d. 10 June 1928; Benton Co., Oregon; m. Elijah McKinney, 12 June 1856, Washington Co., Oregon; he d. 13 April 1900 at 73 years.

Annice—3, b. Iowa; m. Isaac Newton McClanahan, 13 November 1859, Washington Co, Oregon.

Sarah—11 mos., b. Iowa; m. Benjamin E. Hall, 4 April 1860, Washington Co., Oregon.

Bybee, James F.—with wife Julia Ann (Miller) and youngsters, Robert and Elizabeth, were listed in earlier printings of *Terrible Trail* on the Meek Train Roster. Donation Land Claim No. 4319 gives arrival date in Oregon as 22 August 1847. Julia's parents Robert Emmett and Sarah Campbell Miller, and other relatives did arrive with the Meek Train in 1845. See the roster. (Obits do name Julie an 1845 pioneer.)

*Canby, Thomas (Dr.)—b. abt. 1788, Virginia; settled in Washington Territory. (In *The Brazen Overlanders of 1845*, author Donna M. Wojcik also lists on her roster a son, R. M. Canby, b. abt. 1826, Ohio.)

*Catching, Benjamin Holland—b. 1811, Kentucky; d. 19 July 1894, Washington Co., Oregon; DLC No. 3127, Washington Co., Oregon.

*Catching, Laura—b. 1814, Tennessee; d. 1860, Washington Co., Oregon; m. Benjamin, August 1833, Greene Co., Tennessee.
Children:
*William N.—8, b. Missouri.
*George—6, b. Missouri.
*Mary J.—5, b. Missouri; m. Watson E. Dixson, 10 June 1858, Washington Co., Oregon.
*Eliza—3, b. Missouri.

*Catching, John—died while crossing the plains, 1845. It is not known if death occurred on the Cutoff; b. abt. 1779, perhaps Tennessee.

*Catching, Jane (Warren); m. John, abt. 1810, prob. Kentucky; b. 1784, Tennessee; d. 2 May 1866, Douglas Co. Oregon.
Children:
See Catching, Benjamin Holland.
See Catching, William Warren.
*John—b. 18 September 1820, Kentucky; d. 27 August 1898, Riddle, Oregon; m. Margaret Wilson (*see* Roster), 10 May 1847, O.T.
*James Centers—b. 4 April 1827, Tennessee; m. Patsy Ellen Russell, 3 May 1854, O.T.; to Coos Co., 1871. DLC No. 189, Douglas Co. Oregon.

*Catching, William Warren—b. 12 March 1813 Knox Co., Kentucky; d. 10 October 1874, Riddle, Douglas Co., Oregon; DLC No. 3328, Washington Co., Oregon.

*Catching, Angeline F. (Yates)—b. 9 January 1825, Estill Co., Kentucky; d. 29 September, 1910, Portland, Oregon; m. William, 15 May 1839, Buchanan Co., Missouri.
Children:
*John—6, b. 30 May 1840, Missouri; m. Rhoda Leverage (Leverich?), 13 November 1863, Washington Co., Oregon.
*Joel P.—4, b. abt 1841, Missouri; m. Maria Evans, 17 December 1863, Washington Co, Oregon.
*William R.—b. abt 1844, Missouri; m. Susan Beckworth, 26 February 1873, Douglas Co., Oregon.

Center, Mary Fetter—b. January 1787, Pennsylvania; d. 6 August 1857, Marion Co., Oregon; widow of Ebenezer Center who had died 11 February 1835, Edgar Co., Illinois; DLC No. 79, Marion Co., Oregon.
Children:
See Powell, Rachael (Center) Tull (Mrs. Theophilus).
See Center, Samuel.

Jonathan E.—b. 1828, Edgar Co., Illinois; m. Amanda E. Johnson, 20 February 1862, Salem, Oregon; DLC No. 339, Marion County, Oregon.

Lucy—b. 1830, Illinois; d. young in Oregon.

Center, Samuel—b. 1824, Edgar Co., Illinois; d. 1888, Jacksonville, Oregon; DLC No. 271, Marion County, Oregon.

Center, Elizabeth (Evans) Dillon—m. Samuel, 20 June 1845, while crossing the plains.
Children:
Polly Amelia Dillon—b. 1841; daughter of Elizabeth. Polly's father had died at the beginning of the 1845 trip to Oregon.

Chambers, Rowland—b. 12 March 1813, Hamilton Co., Ohio; d. 6 January 1870; DLC No. 1610, Benton Co., Oregon; farmed and operated a gristmill in Kings Valley, Benton Co.

Chambers, Sarah (King)—b. 25 July 1823, Madison Co., Ohio; d. 3 September 1845, near Castle Rock in eastern Oregon, on the Meek Cutoff; m. Rowland, 17 August 1841. Rowland m. 2nd, Sarah's sister Lovisa King (*see* Roster), 22 February 1846, Washington Co., Oregon; she was b. 2 March 1828; d. 3 December 1889.
Children:
Margaret—b. 17 December 1842, Carrol Co., Missouri; m. Orthellow Bagley, 1859; he was b. 1830, N.Y.
James—b. September 1844, Missouri; d. 17 August 1883; m. Clarinda G. Kisor; professor at Philomath College, Philomath, Oregon.

Charlton, Joseph—b. 10 August 1825, Cole Co., Missouri; d. prior to wife's death; DLC No. 1913, Washington Co., Oregon.

Charlton, Margaret Catherine (Miller)—b. 13 January 1829, Hardin Co., Kentucky; d. 16 March 1913, Portland, Oregon; m. Joseph, 30 November 1842, Adair Co., Missouri.
Children:
Sarah Nancy—b. 2 October 1844, Adair Co., Missouri; m. Henry Ward Lamson.

Charlton, Silas—b. 1785, Virginia; father to Joseph (*see* Roster).

Cooley, Christopher Columbus—b. 6 August 1809, Christian Co., Kentucky; d. 14 November 1885; DLC No. 2083, Marion Co., Oregon.

Cooley, Nancy R. (Officer)—b. 20 March 1811, Tennessee; d. 21 August 1880, Marion Co., Oregon; m. Christopher, 30 September 1834, Clay Co., Missouri.
Children: (all b. Clay Co., Missouri.)
James Harvey—b. 15 November 1835; d. 31 December 1894, Marion Co., Oregon; m. Mary Ann Jones, 23 October 1859, Marion Co.; she was b. 28 December 1843, Iowa; d. 19 September 1909, Marion Co., Oregon.
Robert Franklin—b. 28 January 1837; d. 8 April 1916, Woodburn, Oregon; m. Rebecca Hubbard, 28 December 1860, Marion Co.; b. 23 May 1843, Pleasant Hill, Illinois.
Martha Loren—b. 22 February 1839; d. 17 November 1902; m. Foster Sylvester Mattison, 13 April 1856; DLC No. 1979, Marion Co., Oregon.
Helen Miriam—b. 1 February 1841; m. Judge Wm. C. Hubbard, 18 November 1859, Marion Co., Oregon. He d. 29 June 1929.
Mary Jane—b. 15 October 1844; m. Andrew Melvin.
*Eveline—b. 15 October 1844; twin to Mary Jane. d. en route to Oregon, or at The Dalles, October 1845.

Cooley, Eli C.—b. 1812, Howard Co., Missouri; d. 1886, Marion Co., Oregon; DLC No. 2082, Marion Co., Oregon; m. Lydia Bonney, 18 October 1849. Brother to Christopher, Jackson L. Cooley, and Eveline (Cooley) Officer.

Cooley, Jackson L.—b. 1816, Howard Co., Missouri; d. 16 August 1883, Hubbard, Oregon; DLC No. 2075, Marion Co., Oregon; m. Harriet L. Dimick, 13 November 1851, Marion Co.; b. 1834, Illinois; d. 1891, Hubbard, Oregon.

Cooley, Mathias—b. 26 August 1837, Ray Co., Missouri; an orphan in the care of William Wilson (*see* Roster) and a cousin to Christopher, Eli, and Jackson Cooley; cousin to Eveline (Cooley) Officer. m. Willamina Smith, 23 December 1868; settled near Silverton, Oregon; d. 8 December 1915 at Silverton. He was the son of Cornelius and Dolly (White) Cooley.

Cornelius, Benjamin—b. 9 February 1802, Christian Co., Kentucky; d. 13 December 1864, Washington Co., Oregon; DLC No. 31, Washington Co., Oregon.

Cornelius, Elizabeth (Adams)—b. 20 (27?) July 1811, Christian Co., Ky; d. 13 June 1880, Washington Co., Oregon; m. Benjamin, 14 November 1826, Howard Co., Missouri. *Children:*
Thomas Ramsey—b. 15 November 1827, Howard Co., Missouri; d. June, 1899; DLC No. 3327, Washington Co., Oregon; m. Florentine Wilks (Wilkes?), 14 February 1850; she d. 1864; m. 2nd, Missouri. Smith, 12 April 1866.
Jesse—b. 9 June 1829, Howard Co., Missouri; DLC No. 4921, Washington Co., Oregon; m. Julia Ann Mills, 26 January 1854, Washington Co., Oregon; m. 2nd, Caroline (Ingles) Freeman, 20 July 1869, Washington Co. (*see* Ingles, Roster).

Benjamin, Jr.—b. 13 January 1831, Howard Co., Missouri; d. 5 July 1881, Portland, Oregon; m. Rachael McKinney (see Roster), 15 July 1851; DLC No. 2139, Washington Co.

Mary Davis—b. 1 November 1832, Howard Co., Missouri; m. James Imbrie, 15/17 April 1851, Washington Co., Oregon; DLC No. 2987, Washington Co.

William Nelson—b. 31 March 1834, Howard Co., Missouri; m. Amanda S. Barrett, 10 September 1867, Washington Co., Oregon.

Hannah Ann—b. 31 December 1836, Howard Co., Missouri; m. Robert Freeman, 11 May 1854, Washington Co., Oregon; b. 1833, Tippecanoe Co. Indiana; DLC No. 3220, Washington Co.

Sidna C.—b. 8 January 1838, Howard Co., Missouri; m. William Kane, 5 September 1856, Washington Co., Oregon.

John Henry—b. 5 February 1843, Jasper Co., Missouri; m. Mary Ellen Freeman, 1866.

Frances Elizabeth—b. 19 February 1845, Jasper Co., Missouri; m. I. B. Darity (Dority?).

*Cowan, Thomas—b. 1805, Stewartry of Kirkcudbright Co., Scotland; d. early 1880's; DLC No. 312, Umpqua (Douglas) Co., at Yoncalla.

Cox, Anderson—b. 22 September 1812, Dayton, Ohio; d. 28 March 1872, Waitsburg, Washington; DLC No. 97, Linn Co., Oregon; moved to Washington, 1861; served in the legislatures of both Oregon and Washington; built roads from Walla Walla to Colfax and from Walla Walla to Fort Colville in Washington; appointed by Pres. Grant as receiver of the Walla Walla land office, 1871. His claim in Linn Co., Oregon, is now a part of Albany.

Cox, Julia Ann (Walter)—b. 29 March 1818, Indiana; d. 9 May 1891, Waitsburg, Washington; m. Anderson, 7 August 1836, Warren Co., Indiana.
Children:
Lewis—b. 9 May 1837, Attica, Indiana; d. 24 October 1905, Waitsburg, Washington; m. Caroline Bond, 29 August 1858; settled at Waitsburg, Washington.
Johanna—b. 7 December 1838, Warren Co., Indiana; d. 14 February 1915, Waitsburg, Washington; m. Sylvester Canon, June, 1856, Linn Co., Oregon; DLC No. 3519, Linn Co.; later moved to Waitsburg, Washington.
Philip W.—b. 1841, Warren Co., Indiana; settled in Whitman Co., Washington.
Sarah Jane—b. 1843, Indiana; d. August 1867, Jefferson, Marion Co., Oregon; m. John B. Looney.
Matilda—b. 19 August 1845, Kelly Hot Springs, Idaho, en route to Oregon. It is interesting to note that James Field said in his 1845 diary, entry for August 20, "Last night another member was added to our company by the birth of a child. Mother and child doing well." Matilda d. 1927, Waitsburg, Washington; m. William G. Preston.

*Cox, Isham—b. 2 February 1812, Knox Co., Ky; DLC No. 3594, Polk Co.; settled later in Curry Co., Oregon; d. 12 November 1877, Curry Co., Oregon.

*Cox, Mary Ann (Johnston)—b. 16 June 1816, Chilocothe, Ohio; d. 10 December 1890, Coquille, Oregon; m. Isham, 25 December 1834, Cook Co., Illinois.
Children:
*Martha Jane—b. 6 January 1836, Wabash Co., Illinois; m. William Hall, 5 October 1851, Polk Co., Oregon; DLC No. 3595, Polk Co.; settled in Coos Co., 1869.

*William—b. 13 May 1838, Illinois; d. 25 May 1917, Curry Co., Oregon; m. Mellissa Ann More; settled in Curry Co.

*Richard F.—b. abt 1840, Missouri; m. Lucy (Lynch) Gentry; settled in Curry Co.

*Margaline—b. 11 March 1844, Platte Co., Missouri; m. 1st, A.J. Elim.

Craft, Charles—b. 10 September 1803, Lycoming Co., Pennsylvania; d. 23 July 1869, Salem, Oregon; DLC No. 1164, Marion Co.; operated the Mission sawmill at Salem, cleared logs from the site of the city; operated a tannery on Mill Creek at Fifteenth Street between Chemeketa and Center Streets, Salem; built the first jail in Salem and dug the canal that connects the Santiam River with Mill Creek.

Craft, Rebecca (Jordan)—b. 14 March 1809, Pennsylvania; d. 4 November 1882, Salem, Oregon; m. Charles, March, 1829, Lycoming Co., Pennsylvania.
Children:
Sarah Elizabeth—b. 3 November 1829, White Sulphur Springs, Virginia (now West Virginia); d. 14 May 1907, Salem, Oregon; m. Joseph Watt (*see* Roster), 26 August 1846, Salem, Oregon; DLC No. 4774, Yamhill Co.; m. 2nd, Fabritus Smith, 1877, Salem, Oregon.
William Amos—b. 1832, Virginia; d. 1914, Seattle, Washington; m. Amanda Vanice.
Emaline Malinda—b. 1835, Virginia; d. at Prineville, Oregon; m. Octavius Pringle, 27 July 1854, Marion Co., Oregon; DLC No. 1106, Marion Co.
Virginia—b. 1843, Iron Co., Missouri; d. 1863, Salem, Oregon.

Craft, Sarah (Alward)—widow; husband, William Craft, d. 24 July 1818; Sarah was b. 1 June 1776; d. 1850, Salem, Oregon; walked across the plains at age sixty-nine.

Children:
See Craft, Charles.

*Cromwell, H.—with the McNary party; mentioned in Harritt's Diary, July 1, 1845; no other information known.

*Cunningham, Joseph—b. 1795, Worcester Co., Massachusetts; d. 14 March 1878, McMinnville, Oregon; DLC No. 1501, Washington Co.

*Cunningham, Caroline (Cramer)—b. abt 1812, Kentucky; m. Joseph, 12 May 1830, Cooper Co., Missouri.
Children:
*Philander—b. abt 1831, Missouri.
*Sarah—b. abt 1833, Missouri; m. Leonard W. Harris (*see* roster), 1851.
*Lucinda—b. abt 1836, Missouri.
*John—b. abt 1838, Missouri; d. 24 September 1855; killed by Indians, southern Oregon.
*Olivia Druscilla—b. abt 1840, Missouri; d. 28 July 1911, Portland, Oregon; m. Wm. W. Purdin, 13 November 1859, Washington Co., Oregon.
*Virginia Jane—b. abt 1843, Missouri; drowned, Sauvies Island, Oregon, 9 July 1859.

*Daviess, Abraham—appears as a private on the armed men list for the Tetherow Train.

*Dawson, William—b. 21 December 1816, Scotland; d. 1889, Monmouth, Oregon; DLC No. 1608, Yamhill Co.

*Dawson, Mary E. (Sercy)—b. abt 1823, Kentucky; d. 1862, Yamhill Co, Oregon; m. William, 28 December 1842, Platte Co., Missouri; William m. 2nd, Nancy (Baker) Rash, 17 January 1864.
Children:
*Phoebe—b. abt 1843, Missouri; m. John Hall; settled in Tacoma, Washington.

*Barbara Ann—b. 1845, Missouri; m. Archibald Sailing; settled at Waitsburg, Washington.

Dillon, Polly Amelia—*see* Center, Samuel; stepdaughter.

*Doak, ____ (Mr.)—name given by Packwood descendant.

*Doak, ____ (Mrs.)—name given by Packwood descendant; stated to have died "on the plains."
Children:
*Tom—age not known.
*Doak, Andrew J.—b. 1816, Campbell Co., Tennessee; DLC No. 4334.
*Doak, Rebecca—b. abt 1826, Missouri; d. 29 March 1854; m. Andrew, 8 December 1838, Pike Co., Missouri; he m. 2nd Elizabeth Hale, 16 April 1856, Polk Co., Oregon.
Children:
*Josiah—b. abt 1839, Missouri.
*Cynthia Jane—b. abt 1841, Missouri; m. John Angel, 18 May 1856, Polk Co.
*James Thomas—b. 1844, Bowling Green, Missouri.

Dorris, Felix G.—b. 1823, Franklin Co., Illinois; d. abt 1902; DLC No. 2481, Yamhill Co.; m. Caroline Bayley (*see* Roster), 25 December 1847. In 1879 Felix was cattle foreman for John Y. Todd, early central Oregon rancher. His cabin, built on the forks of Big and Little River of the upper Deschutes, later became known as the Dorris cabin. He ran packtrains from Umatilla Landing to the Boise Basin country and to the mining camps in Montana; raised horses and cattle.

Durbin, John—b. 13 September 1794, Washington. Co., Pennsylvania; d. 17 July 1897, Salem, Oregon; DLC No. 4281, Marion Co.

Durbin, Sarah (Fitting)—b. 8 October 1801, Pennsylvania; d. 31 March 1892, Salem, Oregon; m. John, Richland Co., Ohio.

Children:

Casper, J.—b. 26 April 1822, Richland Co., Ohio; d. 11 March 1905, Baker Co., Oregon; DLC No. 4556, Marion Co.; m. Julia Ann Draper, 1 March 1849, Council Bluffs, Nebraska.

Sarah Ann—b. 1828?, Ohio; m. George Sturges.

Solomon—b. 18 September 1829, Richland Co., Ohio; d. 24 May 1916; m. Martha Sophia Elgin, 9 March 1854, Marion Co., Oregon; settled at Salem, operated a livery stable at the corner of State and Commercial streets.

Isaac—b. 27 January 1832, Ohio; DLC No. 4280, Marion Co.; m. Olive Kays (Kaves?), abt 1855.

Daniel—b. 27 January 1832 (twin to Isaac), Richland Co., Ohio; d. 17 February 1893; DLC No. 4282, Marion Co.; m. Sally Ann Smith, 21 September 1854, Salem, Oregon.

Mary Jane—b. abt 1835, Ohio; m. Amos S. Starkey, merchant, 3 July 1856, Marion Co., Oregon.

Ruth Ann—b. abt 1839, Ohio; m. Richard A. Barker, teamster, 5 August 1856, Marion Co., Oregon.

(Another daughter, Fannie, came to Oregon in 1845 with her husband, John Martin, Jr., and baby daughter, but they did not travel by way of the Meek Cutoff. They chose to follow the regular Oregon Trail through the La Grande area to the Columbia River.)

Eaton, Jesse—b. 21 March 1826, Boone Co., Kentucky (possibly Indiana); d. 1902, Oregon; m. Mary E. Burden, 18 July 1850, Clackamas Co., Oregon; Mary also came in 1845, with her parents, but via the Oregon Trail. The Eatons first settled in Yamhill Co. (near Amity, Oregon), but in 1864 they built a stage station in Wasco Co. (now

Sherman Co.), at Spanish Hollow; Jesse was postmaster and a cobbler.

*Elkins, James E.—b. 1 June 1822, Culpepper Co., Virginia; DLC No. 4017, Polk Co.; m. Lucy J. Zumwalt, 22 May 1851, Polk Co.; d. 5 April, 1917, Independence, Oregon.

*Engle, William—b. 18 March 1789, Harper's Ferry, Virginia; d. 18 May 1868; DLC No. 1128, Marion Co., at Molalla; later settled at Silverton, died there.

*Engle, Martha Clark Chance—b. 20 April 1797/8; d. April, 1849; m. William, 12 February 1826, Madison Co., Illinois. William had m. 1st, Mary Butt, 1816, Virginia, who d. 1823; he m. 2nd, Mrs. Esther Hayes, 1824, who d. soon after; after death of Martha, he m. Susan _____, 4 April 1851, Mercer Co., Missouri.
Children:
  *Malvina—b. 21 March 1827, Illinois; d. 10 January 1906, Marion Co., Oregon; m. Mitchell Whitlock (*see* Roster), 2 July 1846, Clackamas Co.
  *Sarah—b. abt 1829, Illinois; d. 1854; m. George Rees, 3 February 1848, Clackamas Co., O.T.; DLC No. 293, Clackamas Co.
  *Samuel—b. 30 January 1831, St. Clair Co., Illinois; d. 1 March 1902, Molalla; m. Nancy Dunniway, 16 November 1854, Molalla; He settled on part of his father's donation claim on Molalla Prairie.
  *Christopher—b. 1834, Illinois; d. 1859; m. Nancy Jane Armpriest, 12 November 1857, Clackamas Co., O.T.; she d. 1859.
  *Augustus—b. 11 February 1837, Illinois; d. 1880, Clackamas Co..

*Fanning, Rebecca (Mrs.)—b. 1 January 1781; d. 6 February, 1881, Albany, Oregon.
Children:

*Levi—b. 8 February 1809, Wythe Co., Virginia; d. 5 June 1888, Albany, Or; DLC No. 1683, Linn Co.; m. Jane Gilliland, 30 August 1853, Linn Co., O.T.

Field, James—22, b. abt 1823, Port Chester, N.Y.; d. May, 1903, Port Chester, N.Y.; single in 1845, came with the James B. Riggs family.

*Fleming, John—b. 29 March 1795, Big Island, Lycoming Co., Pa.; d. 2 December 1872, Oregon City, Oregon; name appears on the muster roll for the Tetherow Train; he was a printer.

Flippin, James Allen—b. 17 March 1825, Weakley Co., Tennessee; nephew of Robert Hull (*see* Roster), served as cattle driver to A. Frier family (roster); DLC No. 4158, Washington Co.; m. Jane Amanda Patton, 26 February 1852, Tennessee. (Some sources say m. 19 December 1851.)

*Foster, Ambrose D.—b. 1816, Scott Co., Kentucky; d. 22 January 1860, Clackamas Co.; DLC No. 3261, Clackamas Co.

*Foster, Zerrelda Ememine—b. abt. 1817, Kentucky; m. Ambrose, 3 February 1836, Adams Co., Illinois; she m. 2nd, Cornelius A. Summers (Somers), 18 November 1860, Clackamas Co.
Children:
*Nancy Elizabeth—8, b. Texas.
*Martha Ann—4, b. Texas.
*Mary Jane—1, b. Missouri.

Foster, Andrew—b. 1789, Virginia; DLC No. 4779, Benton Co.

Foster, Elizabeth (Smith)—45, b. Pa.; m. Andrew, 29 December 1817, Coshocton Co., Ohio.
Children:

John—b. 3 March 1822, Ohio; d. at seventy-seven yrs., Benton Co., Oregon; m. Mary Lloyd (see Roster), 4 June, 1846, Oregon; m. 2nd, Eliza Buchanan; settled about twelve miles south of Corvallis.

James—b. 1827, Coshocton Co., Ohio; d. 19 December 1909, Lakeview, Oregon; DLC No. 4327, Benton Co.; m. Elizabeth Currier, December, 1849, Oregon Territory.

Isaac—b. May, 1829, Coshocton Co., Ohio; d. 12 December 1856; DLC No. 5184, Benton Co.

Maria—b. 1834, Ohio; d. 1859; m. Jacob M. Currier, 25 August 1850, Benton Co., O.T; DLC No. 1474, Benton Co. (Jacob m. 2nd, Helena Sarah Buchanan, 1863.)

*Foster, John (Sr.)—b. 1792, South Carolina; d. 22 March 1868, Clackamas Co., Oregon; DLC No. 4770, Clackamas Co.

*Foster, Nancy—b. abt. 1795; d. 7 June 1870, Clackamas Co.; m. John, 15 August 1814, Scott Co., Kentucky.
Children:
See Foster, Ambrose D.
*Isaac M.—b. 7 May 1819, Scott Co., Kentucky; d. 2 November 1893; DLC No. 1068, Clackamas Co.; m. Letha J. Beauchamp, 25 August 1849.
See Wheeler, Melissa Elizabeth Foster (Mrs. Solomon)
*John T.—b. 1822, Kentucky; DLC No. 4808, Marion Co.; m. Adaline Beauchamp, November, 1848, Clackamas Co., O.T.
*James—b. 1827.
*Thomas W.—b. abt 1833, Illinois.
*William J.—b. abt 1829, Illinois.
*Catharine—b. abt 1829, Illinois; perhaps m. Robert Arthur abt 1846; m. Laban Hicks, 2 July 1854, Multnomah Co., Oregon; he d. 14 October 1857. DLC No. 4041, Multnomah Co.; she m. 3rd Wm. Arthur (Sr.),

29 October 1862, Clackamas Co.; m. 4th _____ Severs.

Foster, Reason (Resin)—b. 20 January 1818, Howard Co., Missouri; d. 17 March 1908, Medford, Oregon; DLC No. 433, Douglas Co.; m. Eliza Jane Martin, 1846, divorced 1847; m. 2nd Margaret Noland, 16 August 1848, Washington Co., Oregon Territory.

Frier, Absalom—b. 1814, Madison Co., Kentucky; DLC No. 2315, Polk Co.; innkeeper.

Frier, Elizabeth—b. abt. 1820, Virginia; m. Absalom, April 1838/9, Cooper Co., Missouri.
Children:
Mary A.—5, b. Missouri.
John J.—4, b. Missouri.
Thomas J.—2, b. Missouri.
Martha J.—b. en route to Oregon, 1845.

Fuller, Arnold Wesley—b. 1802, Chenango Co., N.Y.; d. 27 June 1875, Benton Co.; DLC No. 169, Benton Co.; his wife (Sarah Greene) died 28 April 1845, in Missouri—the day the wagon train was to start for Oregon. He m. Mary Ann Elizabeth Lewis, 6 September 1848, Polk Co., O. T.
Children:
Price—b. 1826, Franklin Co., Ohio; DLC No. 168, Benton Co.; m. Abigail King, 23 August 1846, Benton Co., O.T. (*see* Roster).
Henry—b. 4 May 1829, Madison Co., Ohio; d. 8 May 1911, Nogales, Arizona; DLC No. 3773, Polk Co.; m. Malissa Ann Williams (*see* Roster), 16 August 1850, Polk Co., Oregon.
Samuel S.—b. 1832, Madison Co., Ohio; DLC No. 682, Douglas Co.; m. Ellen Jane Carlin, 3/5 October 1853, Douglas Co., Oregon.

Malinda—b. 25 May 1827, Ohio; d. 30 January 1887; m.
Amos N. King (*see* Roster), 8 March 1846, Washington Co.; DLC No. 3669, Washington Co.

Jasper—b. abt 1836, Ohio.

Tabitha—perhaps b. abt 1838, Ohio; d. 1845 en route to Oregon, date and place unknown.

Marion—b. abt 1840, Ohio.

Dyer—b. abt 1841, Missouri.

Geer, Joseph Carey, Jr.

Gesner, Reuben Alonzo—b. 17 May 1815, Schenectady Co., New York; d. 24 March 1888; DLC No. 61, Marion Co.

Gesner, Mary (Bailey)—b. 5 September 1821, Kentucky; d. 1903; m. Reuben, 6 April 1841, Charleston, Illinois.
Children:
Alonzo—b. 2 March 1842, Illinois; m. Rhoda Neal, 1875; surveyor; appointed Indian agent at Warm Springs Reservation by President Arthur, 1883.

Mary Elizabeth—b. abt 1843, Illinois; d. at sixteen years, unmarried.

*Gillett(e), Joel II—stated by Packwood descendant to have been on the Cutoff.

*Gillett(e), Judy (Packwood)—sister to John Packwood (*see* Roster) and Mrs. McKinley (*see* Roster); Mrs. Gillette m. 2nd, William Munz.

*Glasgow, Thomas W.—b. 1825, Huntingdon Co., Pa.; a private and cattle driver with the Tetherow Train; settled near Olympia, Washington; d. Whidbey Island, Washington. He m. Julia Patkanim, 1847/48 Washington Ty.; m. 2nd Helen Horan, 25 July 1858, Washington Territory.

*Glawser,____—young man mentioned by Jesse Harritt in his diary entry for August 11. A William Glaser appears on the 1845 immigration list prepared by Bancroft, the historian. Possibly this is the same man.

Goulder, William A.—b. 1821, Virginia; settled in Idaho; single in 1845, assigned to the Ownbey family (*see* Roster).

Hall, James Elliot—b. 8 January 1798, Madison Co., Kentucky; d. 2 June 1870, Butteville, Oregon; DLC No. 1856, Marion Co.

Hall, Cynthia Ann (Groom)—b. 2 October 1804, Clark Co., Kentucky; d. 20 June 1897; m. James, 24 July 1824, Clay Co., Missouri.
Children:
Benjamin Franklin—b. 15 November 1826, Liberty, Clay Co., Missouri; d. 2 November 1904, Woodburn, Oregon; DLC No. 612, Marion Co.; m. Mary Ann Johnson, 27 April 1854, Marion Co., Oregon Territory.
Amanda Malvina Fitzallen—b. 20 August 1828, Liberty, Missouri; m. Willard H. Rees, 21 January 1847, Marion Co., O.T.; DLC No. 1157, Marion Co.; d. 10 December 1916, Portland, Oregon.
Nancy Evaline—b. 22 September 1830, Missouri; d. 17 November 1905, Salem, Oregon; m. William J. Herren (*see* Roster), 14 October 1847, Marion Co., Oregon Territory; DLC No. 49, Marion Co.
Florinda Davidson—b. 21 April 1832, Missouri; m. George C. Lawton 1 June 1848; m. 2nd, William Porter Pugh (*see* Roster), 15 September 1857, Marion Co., Oregon; DLC No. 1110, Marion Co.; later lived at Cove, Oregon.
Adaline Eglentine—b. 11 September 1834, Missouri; d. 14 January 1913, Salem, Oregon; m. Andrew J. Vaughan, 22 November 1849, Marion Co., Oregon Territory; DLC No. 604, Marion Co.; m. 2nd (after death

of Andrew in 1852), Noah F. Herren (*see* Roster), 22 February 1855, Woodburn, Oregon.

Albert Galetain Wilson—b. 6 November 1836, Missouri; d. 22 August 1853. Butteville, Oregon.

James C. C.—b. 4 March 1838, Liberty, Missouri; d. 22 November 1915, Everett, Washington; m. Mary Elizabeth Garrison, 1866; m. 2nd, Mrs. Julia Davis, 1908, after death of Mary Elizabeth in 1904.

America Francis—b. 10 February 1841, Missouri; d. 20 January 1899, Cove, Oregon; m. McDonough B. Rees, November, 1856; resided in Marion Co. until 1864 when they moved to Cove.

William C.—b. 1842, Missouri; died in early manhood at Hall Farm, Marion Co., 22 September 1857.

Elisha—b. 4 January 1845, Missouri; d. 29 October 1845, at the Cascades on the Columbia River, en route from Missouri.

(A daughter, Angeline Moore who was b. 31 May 1825, Missouri, m. William McCulloch, 17 November 1842, Missouri. They did not come to Oregon until 1852/53; settled in Marion Co.; Angeline d. 31 May 1866, Harrisburg, Oregon.)

Hall, Lawrence—b. 10 March 1800, Louisville, Bourbon Co., Kentucky; d. 11 February 1867, Portland, Oregon; DLC No. 2191, Washington Co.; raised a company of volunteers in 1847/48 to fight in the Cayuse War; served in the legislature of the Provisional Government; chairman of the Committee on the Militia and a member of the Committee on Education.

Hall, Lucy Davidson (White)—b. 3 December 1803, Halifax Co., Virginia; d. 11 December 1865, Washington Co., Oregon; m. Lawrence, 19 September 1822, Kentucky. *Children:*

William F.—b. 1825, Cooper Co., Missouri; DLC No. 3748, Washington Co.; m. Susan R. Beauchamp, 29 July, 1849, Washington Co., Oregon.
John B.—b. 1827/8, Booneville, Cooper Co., Missouri; DLC No. 4819, Washington Co.; m. Mary L. Talbot, 15 July 1856, Multnomah Co., Oregon.
Allen W.—b. abt 1829, Missouri; m. Frances Imbler, abt 1863; settled in Union Co., Oregon.
David—b. abt. 1831.
Lucy Jane—b. 7 November 1832, Booneville, Missouri; d. 24 December 1925; m. William Hardin Bennett (*see* Roster), 22 February 1849, Washington Co., Oregon; DLC No. 398, Washington Co.
Berryman—b. abt. 1835.
Mary E.—b. abt 1837, Missouri; m. D. W. Ellis, 8 April 1873, Washington Co., Oregon.
George—b. abt. 1839, Missouri.
James—b. abt. 1841, Missouri.

Hamilton, Robert Wilson—b. 25 June 1805, Wilson Co., Tennessee; DLC No. 1082, Polk Co.

Hamilton, Rebecca Smith—b. 1 June 1811, Virginia; m. Robert, December, 1829, Sangamon Co., Illinois.
Children:
Adam Smith—b. 9 June 1832, Sangamon Co., Illinois; d. 8 August 1925, Diamond, Washington; DLC No. 1087, Polk Co.; moved to Whitman Co., Washington, 1885; m. 1st, Melissa Jane Ingram, 2 February 1854, Linn Co., O.T.; m. 2nd, Elizabeth Ann Hays Fountain, 19 March 1865, Polk Co., Oregon, after the death of Melissa, 2 January 1859, Linn Co., Oregon. Elizabeth d. 24 November 1878, Lane Co. Oregon. Adam was postmaster for sixteen years at Diamond; merchant.
William Porter—b. 8 May 1836, Illinois.
Rebecca Jane—b. 15 December 1839, Little Rock, Arkansas; d. 20 February 1918, Portland, Oregon; m.

David Thompson, 27 August 1857, Polk Co. Oregon; settled in Lane Co., Oregon where David d. 1913.

James Preston—b. 10 September 1840, Missouri.

Henry Bordean—b. 3 August 1844, Johnson Co., Iowa. (One of these daughters came with the family in 1845: Mary Jane, b. 7 November 1830; Harriett, b. 10 August 1834; or Martha Alean, b. 2 April 1838. It was probably Harriett, who married Adam Matheny, DLC No. 921, Yamhill Co., 6 May 1850, Polk Co., Oregon.)

Hampton, John Jacob—b. 15 October 1804, Garrard Co., Kentucky; d. 1884, Goshen, Oregon; DLC No. 1066, Yamhill Co.

Hampton, Elizabeth (Fickle)—b. 8 September 1809, Lee Co., Virginia; d. 2 April 1880, Goshen, Oregon; m. John, 9 November 1828, Lafayette Co., Missouri.
Children:
Liliburn—b. abt 1829, Missouri; d. at eighteen years near Sheridan, Oregon.

John Douglas—b. 8 September 1831, Lexington (Lafayette Co.), Missouri; d. 3 March 1899, Eugene, Oregon; DLC No. 1184, Lane Co.; m. Mary Eleanor Moore, 26 October 1854, Lane Co., Oregon.

James F.—b. 1833, Missouri; d. when a young man, unmarried, near Sheridan, Oregon.

Eliza—b. August, 1835, Missouri; d. 17 February, 1923, Harney Co., Oregon; m. Milton Scott Riggs (*see* Roster), 5 August 1851, Yamhill Co., Oregon; DLC No. 1807, Lane Co.

Mary A.—b. abt 1838, Missouri; d. 1859; m. Stanley Alexander Caldwell, 1855, Lane Co., Oregon. DLC No. 2054, Lane Co.

Jessie Green—b. 18 April 1840, Missouri; d. 8 September 1907, Eugene, Oregon; never married; lived on the

Joseph Lane Hampton stock ranch until 1901, near Paisley, Oregon, then moved to Goshen, Oregon.

Ralph—b. abt 1842, Missouri; d. in childhood. It is not known whether death occurred en route to Oregon (possibly on the Cutoff) or near Sheridan, on the family farm.

Andrew Jackson—b. 25 December 1844, Missouri; d. 20 June 1907; lived in Harney Co., then settled at Summer Lake to engage in stock raising; m. Mrs. Frances Elizabeth Smith.

Hancock, Samuel—b. 1819, Bedford Co., Virginia; d. 4 September 1883, Coupeville, Washington; settled on Whidbey Island, Washington, after many narrow escapes from the savages in the area; m. Susan Crockett, 1854. A tall granite marker, Whidbey Island Cemetery, says Samuel was born January 19, 1818; d. September 24, 1883. (Also: Susan Hunter Hancock, b. December 27, 1823, Montgomery Co., Virginia; d. January 9, 1902, Seattle, Washington, pioneer of 1851.)

*Harris, John—name appearing on an 1845 death list prepared by Hiram Smith, an 1845 pioneer. No other information is known.

*Harris, Leonard W.—b. 1814, Massachusetts; DLC No. 3153, Columbia Co.; m. Sarah R. Cunningham (*see* Roster), 12 October 1851, Oregon Territory.

*Harris, Mary E.—name appearing on an 1845 death list prepared by Hiram Smith, an 1845 pioneer. This may be the same person as Eliza Harris, daughter of Phillip Harris (*see* Roster). No other information is known.

Harris, Phillip—b. 21 January 1808, Cumberland Co., N.J.; d. 1892, Cheney, Washington; DLC No. 4073, Washington Co.

Harris, Sarah (Taylor)—b. 1810, Chillicothe (Madison Co.), Ohio; m. Phillip, 15 March 1827, Chillicothe, Ohio; d. 1904, Cheney, Washington.
Children:
See Johnson, Jane (Mrs. Hiram).
Eliza—b. 1832, Madison Co., Ohio; d. 1845, of mountain fever, on the Meek Cutoff.
William Melvin—b. 1835, Madison Co., Ohio; disappeared on a prospecting trip, 1860. Family never learned what became of him.
Stephen Morton—b. 17 September 1840 (or 1841?), Bowling Green, Missouri; d. August, 1923, Washington Co., Oregon; m. 1st, Virginia Shattuck; 2nd, Mary E. Stoughton; worked as a blacksmith.
Rhoda A.—b. 24 January 1843, Missouri; d. 8 February 1936, Goble, Oregon; m. 1st, _____ Richardson; 2nd, James Bothwell.
Ellen—b. 1845, Rocky Mountains, en route to Oregon; m. 1st, Zibbe Rowell; 2nd, _____ Ross.

Harritt, Jesse—b. 6 October 1818, Harrison Co., Indiana; d. 27 March 1888, on his farm near Salem, Oregon; DLC No. 1102, Polk Co.; m. Julia Franklin Lewis (*see* Roster), 1 October 1846; United Brethren minister.

*Hawkins, Henry, Sr.—b. Nelson Co., Kentucky; d. 7 July 1878, near Silverton, Oregon. DLC No. 1211, Polk Co.

*Hawkins, Martha (Crofton)—b. abt. 1794, Kentucky; m. Henry, 14 October 1810, Hardin Co., Kentucky.
Children:
See Hawkins, Zachariah.
*Henry, Jr.
*Nancy—b. abt. 1828, Kentucky; m. Lewis Hubbell Judson, 22 February 1846, Marion Co., Oregon; DLC No. 3704, Clatsop Co.
*America—b. abt. 1832, Illinois.

197

*Elizabeth—b. abt. 1835, Illinois; m. Jessie C. Wilkes, 1 February 1853, Clackamas Co., Oregon.

*Hawkins, Zachariah—apparently did not reach the Cutoff; available information states he died on the plains near the Snake River, abt. 12 August 1845. He was b. 6 January 1812, Hardin Co., Kentucky.

*Hawkins, Nancy (White)—b. 22 January 1815, Ohio; d. 25 May 1895, Benton Co., Oregon; m. Zachariah, 17 October 1832, Illinois; sister to Samuel Simpson White (*see* Roster) and Edward Newton White (*see* Roster); after Zachariah's death m. 2nd, Thomas Read, 10 November 1846. Read came to Oregon in 1845, but he took the regular Oregon Trail.

Children:
*Samuel Simpson—b. 3 October 1833, Illinois; d. 23 April 1907, Yakima, Washington; m. Cynthia Cahoon, 29 April 1858, Benton Co., Oregon.
*Mary J.—b. 29 August 1835, Lee Co., Iowa; d. 7 July 1870, Benton Co., Oregon; m. James Wheeler (*see* Roster), 27 June 1850, Benton Co.; settled near Soap Creek in Polk Co., Oregon.
*Martha—b. 11 October 1837, Lee Co., Iowa; d. 22 June 1893; m. Frank Pyburn, Polk Co., 17 June 1851, Polk Co., Oregon.
*Laura—b. 15 February 1840, Lee Co., Iowa; d. on the plains en route to Oregon, date and location unknown.
*Edward H.—b. 17 February 1842, Lee Co., Iowa; m. Susan C. Norton, 24 September 1866, Benton Co., Oregon; m. 2nd, Mary Taylor, 1882.
*Nancy—b. 18 February 1844, Lee Co., Iowa; d. 31 August 1885, Walla Walla, Washington; m. Jim Ford, Polk County, who d. 30 January 1875, Walla Walla, Washington; m. 2nd, Peter Wiggle, 18 March 1875.

Helm, William—b. 26 November 1800, Frederick Co., Virginia; d. 22 January 1890, Portland, Oregon; DLC No. 1698, Marion Co.; Methodist minister.

Helm, Martha Ann (Scoggin)—b. 1805, Virginia; d. 2 January 1890, Portland, Oregon; m. William, 26 October 1824, Shelby Co., Kentucky.
Children:
George Waulor—b. 6 August 1825, Kentucky; d. 15 November 1902, Calif.; DLC No. 775, Marion Co.; m. Julia Ann Henderson (*see* Roster), 18 August 1846, Yamhill Co., Oregon.
John Wesley—b. 19 May 1829, Kentucky; d. 23 July 1849, Linn Co., Oregon; m. Sarah S. Peterson (*see* Roster), 22 June 1847, Linn Co., Oregon.
William F.—b. 1 July 1834, Shelby Co., Kentucky; d. 10 December 1914, Portland, Oregon; m. Elizabeth Sager, 10 August 1855, Marion Co., Oregon; settled in Linn Co.
Joseph Benson—b. December 1836, Kentucky; d. abt 1853; m. Harriet Snyder, 1852; she m. 2nd, James Balch, Linn Co., Oregon.
Richard Watson—b. 29 May 1839, Kentucky; d. 13 April 1927, Josephine Co., Oregon; m. Eliza Barger, 4 December 1864, Salem, Oregon.
Mary J.—b. 18 September 1842, Platte Co., Missouri; d. 12 October 1923, Berkeley, California; m. John C. Cartwright, 25 December 1860, Marion Co., Oregon.
Asbury C.—b. 1845, Missouri; d. 23 October 1901, California; m. Josephine Payton, 3 March 1868, Marion Co., Oregon.

Henderson, Jesse Cloyd—b. 1802, Jefferson Co., Tennessee; d. 23 August 1867, Yamhill Co., Oregon; DLC 968, Yamhill Co.; m. Nancy Hughart, 5 April 1827, Callaway Co., Missouri; divorced 22 October 1842, Clinton Co., Missouri; m. 2nd, Elizabeth Moore (1 September 1846,

Yamhill Co.), widow of Alfred Moore who drowned
while attempting to pull a raft ashore on the Columbia
River below The Dalles, 1845; m. 3rd, Mrs. Nancy Ran-
som, 8 June 1857, Yamhill Co., Oregon.
Children:
James Oden—b. 1829, Callaway Co., Missouri; d. De-
cember 1865, Alamo, California; DLC No. 2037,
Yamhill Co.; m. Martha E. Moore, 18 May 1851,
McMinnville, Oregon.
Julia Ann—b. 1830, Callaway Co., Missouri; d. March
1891, Portland, Oregon; m. George Waulor Helm (*see*
Roster), 18 August 1846, Yamhill Co., Oregon; DLC
No. 775, Marion Co.; m 2nd Truman L. Hack, 10
October 1864, Seattle, Washington.
Mary Ellen—b. 17 July 1831, Callaway Co., Missouri; d.
25 February 1869, McMinnville, Oregon; m. James
William Rogers, 21 December 1848, Yamhill Co.,
Oregon; DLC No. 2534, Yamhill Co.
Margaret—b. 1833, Callaway Co., Missouri; d. 10 Sep-
tember 1917, Hope, B.C.; m. James Riley Bean (*see*
Roster), 19 September 1850, McMinnville, Oregon;
DLC No. 2776, Yamhill Co.
Alvin Mussette—b. 17 December 1836, Callaway Co.,
Missouri; d. 12 September 1909, Salem, Oregon;
never married.
Nancy Elizabeth—b. 10 February 1838, Callaway Co.,
Missouri; d. 11 October 1873, Idaho; m. James Barber
Foster, 1 April 1856, McMinnville, Oregon.
Martha Frances—b. 8 February 1840, Callaway Co.,
Missouri; d. 29 August 1915, McMinnville, Oregon;
m. John Joseph Collard, 21 May 1857, Yamhill Co.,
Oregon.

Henderson, Joseph—b. 1815, Greene Co., Tennessee; DLC
No. 4151, Polk Co.; later moved to Roseburg, Oregon,
area.

Henderson, Nancy (Holman)—b. 16 January 1817, Kentucky; d. 24 February 1907, Newberg, Oregon; m. Joseph, 28 September 1841, Clinton Co., Missouri.
Children:
Oliver Perry—b. 11 December 1843, Missouri; d. 28 January 1939, Portland, Oregon; m. Mary Smith, June 1872, California; she d. 1926.

*Henderson, William—Private on the list of armed men for the Tetherow Train; a William Henderson also appears on a list compiled by William Findley of the Hackleman Train. The list, dated June 11, 1845, notes that the train was then forty miles beyond the crossing of Little Blue. If this is the same William Henderson, it was not possible for him to have been on the Meek Cutoff for he was too far behind. It is possible, of course, that there were two William Hendersons.

Hening, _____ (Mr.)—name appears in the mining diary of A. S. McClure (August 29, 1858) as a prospector in the Crooked River area near Prineville, Oregon, and it is commented that he had been through in 1845 on his way to the Willamette Valley.

Herren, Daniel—b. 7 December 1824, Decatur Co., Indiana; d. 10 July 1908, on his farm; DLC No. 4136, Washington Co., m. Rebecca C. Westfall, 16 March 1854, Oregon; nephew to John Herren (*see* Roster). Rebecca was b. 1836; d. 1906.

Herren, John—b. 30 September 1799, Shelby Co., Kentucky; d. 2 March 1864, Marion Co., Oregon; DLC No. 1152, Marion Co.

Herren, Docia (Robbins)—b. 20 May 1804, Henry Co., Kentucky; d. 15 September 1881, Marion Co., Oregon; m. John, 13 June 1822, Henry Co., Kentucky.
Children:

William J.—b. 17 January 1824, Henry Co., Kentucky; d. 13 April 1891, Marion Co.; DLC No. 49, Marion Co.; m. Nancy Evaline Hall (*see* Roster), 14 October 1847, Marion Co., Oregon; commissioned sheriff, Marion Co., in 1850; built and managed Salem Flouring Mill at Salem.

Susannah—*see* Wallace, Susannah (Mrs. Wm.).

Berthia B.—b. 1827, Indiana; d. 1862, Marion Co., Oregon; m. Daniel Clark, 24 September 1846, Marion Co., Oregon; DLC No. 498, Marion Co.; he was b. Ireland, came to America at 4 years of age; came to Oregon, 1844; d. 1885.

John C.—b. 1828, Decatur Co., Indiana; DLC No. 2231, Marion Co.; m. Elizabeth Sharp, 26 July 1853, Marion Co.

Daniel S.—b. 1829, Decatur Co., Indiana; DLC No. 2065, Marion Co.; m. Susan S. Caton, 1 December 1852, Marion Co.

Mary Jane—b. 1832 (1831?), Indiana; m. John B. Keizer, 27 March 1851, Marion Co.; DLC No. 1100, Marion Co.

Noah Fowler—b. 7 September 1833, Indiana; m. Adaline Eglentine (Hall) Vaughan (*see* Roster, James E. Hall family), 22 February 1855, Woodburn, Oregon; settled at Woodburn, then Salem, Oregon.

Levi M.—b. 7 September 1835, Ind; m. Martha Mathews, 15 November 1860, Marion Co., Oregon; settled near Turner, Oregon; she was b. 15 January 1846.

Martha A.—b. 1837, Indiana; m. Nathan T. Caton, 14 April 1853, Marion Co.; DLC No. 5008, Marion Co.

Perry L.—b. 1840, Missouri; m. Selvina Havird (Howard?), 29 October 1858, Marion Co.

James R.—b. 1842, Missouri; m. Amanda McCulloch.

Elizabeth C.—b. 1845, Missouri; m. John Hastay, 2 February 1865, Marion Co.

Hiltibrand, Paul—b. 7 June 1823, Adams Co., Ohio; d. 29 September 1895, Polk Co., Oregon; DLC No. 3229, Polk Co.; m. Evaline Tetherow (*see* Roster), 3 July 1846, Polk Co.; farm was located near Airlie, Oregon.

Hinshaw, Isaac—b. 15 December 1813, Highland Co., Ohio; d. 4 July 1873, Sheridan, Oregon; DLC No. 3304, Polk Co.; came to Oregon as a widower—first wife, Mary Cox, had died in 1843; m. 2nd, Melissa Buell, 1 January 1850; brother to Luke (*see* Roster).
Children:
Sanford—b. 1841, Warren Co., Indiana; d. 15 October 1931, Mt. Vernon, Oregon; m. Elma C. Childers, 1878, Dallas, Oregon; farmed at Mill Creek in Polk County.

Hinshaw, Luke—b. 9 September 1819, Zanesville, Ohio; DLC No. 3770, Linn Co.; retail merchant in 1870: brother to Isaac (*see* Roster). A brother, George, d. abt. 12 August 1845, Glenns Ferry, Idaho; Luke m. Isabelle McKinney (*see* Roster), 23 December 1851, Washington Co., Oregon.

Hinshaw, William Lucas—b. 1823 Ross Co., Ohio; brother to Isaac and Luke (*see* Roster).

*Hipes, ____ (Mr.)—name appearing on the Bancroft 1845 immigration list. Perhaps husband to Emily (*see* Roster).

*Hipes, Emily (Olney)—b. 10 September 1824, Portage Co., Ohio; d. 8 March, 1911, The Dalles, Oregon; m. 2nd, Henry Marlin (*see* Roster), 10 May 1846, Washington Co., Oregon; DLC No. 3470, Clatsop Co.; settled at The Dalles later; after Henry's death, spent some time in California; returned to The Dalles in 1904.

Holman, John—came to Oregon with a son, Daniel Saunders, Daniel's wife, and child (William D.) with the immigration of 1843. John settled at McMinnville, and sent for his children, whose mother had died in 1841, Clay Co., Missouri (John and Elizabeth Betsy Duval married 1810, Woodford Co., Kentucky; Betsy was a daughter of Thomas Duval, born in North Carolina.) John Holman was b. 11 September 1787, Woodford Co., Kentucky; d. 15 May 1864, McMinnville. Son Daniel was b. 15 November 1822, Tennessee. Daniel's DLC No. was 1819, Yamhill Co.; apparently Daniel's wife died after reaching Oregon for he married Martha E. _____, 31 August 1847. His son William D. was b. abt. 1842, Missouri.

Children: Those who came, 1845.

See Henderson, Nancy Holman (Mrs. Joseph).

Susan Frances—b. 9 April 1821, Tennessee.

Woodford Carpenter—b. 18 March 1824, Tennessee; listed as the head of the family on the Tetherow Train roster, 1845.

Henrietta—b. 21 February 1826, Tennessee; m. H.H. Hyde, 1 September 1846, Washington Co., Oregon.

Isaac N.—b. abt 1830, Missouri.

Francis Dillard—b. 23 May 1831, Missouri; d. 2 December 1899, Portland, Oregon; minister of the Christian Church; m. Mary McBride, 25 September 1856; settled in Yamhill Co.

Mary Ann—b. 13 January 1833, Missouri; d. 5 February 1879; m. James Lyburn Clinkinbeard, 19 August 1849, Yamhill Co., Oregon; DLC No. 259, Douglas Co. James was b. 10 Nov. 1819, Kentucky; d. 5 February 1897.

(A son, James Duval Holman—b. 18 August 1814, Woodford Co., Kentucky; d. 1882—arrived in Oregon in 1846 with his wife, Rachael Hixson Summers—1823-1900—and children; a daughter, Rhoda Carpenter—b. 17 December 1815, Shelby Co., Kentucky—arrived in Oregon in 1846 with her husband, Robert Henderson, and children; they came via the Applegate Trail.)

*Hosford, Chauncey Osborn—b. 27 December 1822, Greene Co., New York; d. 1913, Portland, Oregon; DLC No. 1092, Polk Co.; m. Acenith Glover, March, 1849, San Francisco, Calif.; Methodist minister; brother to Erwin F. (*see* Roster).

*Hosford, Erwin F.—b. 6 August 1820, Greene Co., New York; d. 2 December 1892, Polk Co., Oregon; m. Mary Emmett, 1857, Oregon; resided on a farm in Polk Co.— near Salem, Oregon; brother to Chauncey Hosford (*see* Roster).

Hughart, Joseph T.—b. 13 February 1804, Clark Co., Kentucky; d. 17 May 1886, Benton Co., Oregon; DLC No. 4519, Benton Co.; settled at Philomath, Oregon.

Hughart, Martha Ann (Henderson)—b. 22 February 1808, Tennessee; d. 19 May 1846, Benton Co., Oregon; m. Joseph, 30 August 1827, Callaway Co., Missouri; he m. 2nd, Elizabeth Hicklin, 22 November, 1851, Marion Co. *Children:*
Eliza J.—b. 13 September 1828, Callaway, Co., Missouri; d. 20 April 1849, Benton Co., Oregon; m. Green Berry Smith (*see* Roster) 2 March 1848, Benton Co.
David E.—b. 1 September 1830, Callaway Co., Missouri; d. 22 April 1855, Benton Co., Oregon.
Martha Ann—b. 13 May 1833, Callaway Co, Missouri; d. 11 November 1895, Benton Co., Oregon; m. John Wiles, 8 June 1851, Benton Co.; he was b. 18 August 1822, Surry Co., North Carolina.
William T.—b. 1 May 1836, Buchanan Co., Missouri; d. 15 November 1857, Benton Co.
Mary F.—b. 1 March 1839, Buchanan Co., Missouri; d. 10 January 1856, Benton Co.
(Also with the Hughart family was Christopher Peter Zumwalt—*see* Roster—for whom Joseph Hughart was guardian.)

*Hull, Joseph—native of Ohio.

Hull, Robert (Colonel)—b. 1807, New York, New York; d. January 1890, near Olympia, Washington; DLC No. 1120, Clackamas Co.; uncle to James Allen Flippin (*see* Roster).

Hull, ____ (Mrs.)—d. 1845, on the Meek Cutoff; from Ohio. Names of children not known.

*Impiry, ____—appears on the Tetherow Train roster, 1845, as a cattle driver for Ownbey and Holman families; the name remains a mystery to the compiler. Perhaps this is James Imbrie, DLC No. 2987, Washington Co., who married Mary Davis Cornelius (*see* Roster); he was b. 1818, Trumbull Co., Ohio.

Ingles, DeWitt Clinton—b. 16 July 1813, Pittsburgh, Pa.; DLC No. 1151, Douglas Co.; owned property at 3rd and Main, Portland, Oregon, in 1855; killed by Indians, 16 March 1859, Chelan Co., Washington.

Ingles, Margaret Elizabeth (Wooley)—b. 1822, Louisville, Kentucky; d. 19 April 1851, Umpqua Valley, Oregon; m. DeWitt, 1835, Philadelphia, Pa. (DLC states m. 22 April 1836, Louisville, Kentucky.)
Children:
Catherine Jane—b. 10 January 1839, Kentucky; m. Jackson De Letts, 1853, Washington Co., Oregon, settled there.
William Stiles—b. 23 December 1840, Knox Co., Illinois; d. 5 December 1900, Forest Grove, Oregon; m. Mary Elizabeth Marsh, 4 September 1870, Centerville, Washington; she d. 1903.
Benjamin Reno—b. 23 February 1843, Knox Co., Illinois; d. 5 December 1885, Greenville, Oregon; m. Mary E. Mills, 1865.

Caroline—b. 17 March 1845, Boonville, Missouri; m. 1st, Clark Freeman, 24 December 1859; m. 2nd, Jesse Cornelius (*see* Roster), 20 July 1869, Washington Co.

*Jackson, James—listed on the Tetherow census as a private; also listed as a cattle driver for the James E. Hall family (*see* Roster).

*Jackson, Thomas—listed as a private with Tetherow Train; perhaps this is Thomas J. Jackson who settled in Washington Co., DLC No. 3587, b. abt 1820, d. 4 May 1853, Washington Co.; if so, it is possible he did not come via the Meek Cutoff but rather went to California in 1845, then arriving in Oregon in July, 1846. Bancroft, the historian, lists a Jackson (no first name) who came overland to California in 1845.

*Jennings, Berryman—nephew to Samuel White, Edward Newton White, and Mrs. Nancy (White) Hawkins (*see* Roster).

Johnson, Charles M. (Dr.)—b. 1797, Campbell Co., Virginia; DLC No. 2457, Yamhill Co.

Johnson, Elizabeth (Rude)—b. abt 1800, Pa; m. Charles, 10 June 1824, Indiana.
Children:
Sarah Ann—b. 1825, Indiana; d. abt. 1861; m.1st, Coswell (or Caswell) Davis, 10 December 1848, Yamhill Co., Oregon; DLC No. 4104, Polk Co.; he was b. 1816, Knox Co., Tennessee; d. 1852; m.2nd, Joe Hill.
James W.—b. abt. 1827, Ohio; never married; d. young on the family DLC.
John Freeman—b. abt. 1829, Ohio; d. 3 August 1868, Hood River, Oregon; DLC No. 2039, Yamhill Co.; m. Nancy E. ____, 3 October 1851, Yamhill Co.

Christopher Newton—b. abt 1836, Ohio; it is believed he married Louisa M. _____, and settled in eastern Oregon; the family received indefinite news that he had died there.

Charles Wesley—b. abt 1839, Missouri; went to eastern Oregon for awhile as an adult with his brother Christopher Newton; he m. Melissa Jane Hawn, 3 November 1861, Yamhill Co., Oregon; divorced, June 1870, Wasco Co.; m. Lucinda Walker, 11 March 1878, Washington Co.; Melissa m. 2nd, Charles Edwin Stillwell at The Dalles, 13 March 1871. (There is a C.W. Johnson buried in Sumpter Cemetery, Baker Co., who d. 10 July 1898, according to DAR records.)

Mary Elizabeth—b. abt 1842, Missouri; d. 28 May 1919, Yamhill Co.; m. Benjamin Franklin Lewis, 22 September 1859, Yamhill Co, Oregon; farmed two miles south of Dayton, Yamhill Co., until 1890; moved to Dayton.

Johnson, Hiram—b. 21 January 1820, Knox Co., Kentucky; d. 21 September 1891, Washington Co., Oregon; DLC No. 4700, Washington Co.

Johnson, Jane (Harris)—b. 30 March 1830, Madison Co., Ohio; d. 18 November 1857, Washington Co., Oregon; m. Hiram, 3 November 1843, Bethany, Missouri. She was the daughter of Phillip Harris (*see* Roster). First Johnson child was Thomas Franklin, b. 3 April 1846, Washington Co.

Johnson, John—b. 1816, Otsego Co. New York; d.1877, Pedee Oregon; DLC No. 4753, Polk Co.; m. Phoebe Taylor, 19 March 1854 Polk Co., O.T.; came as a single man with the Chambers-King-Norton families (*see* Roster).

*Johnston, Diana—15-year-old sister of John Johnston and Mary Ann Cox (Mrs. Isham Cox); see Roster. She came with the family, 1845, was killed that winter at Tualatin Plains while loading a gun.

*Johnston, John G.—listed on the muster roll of the Tetherow Train.

*Jones, Michael—b. 1804, Virginia; d. 21 March 1894, Speeleyah Prairie, Washington; DLC No. 477, Multnomah Co., Oregon.

*Jones, _____ (Mrs.)—probably the Mrs. Jones who died en route to Oregon in 1845; m. Michael prior to 1828.
Children:
  *Seventeen-year-old daughter who died en route to Oregon, name unknown.
  *Martha E.—b. 4 August 1837, Illinois; m. Abner E. Armstrong, 6 August 1853, Oregon, who d. 1887, Washington Territory.
  *Amanda—b. abt. 1841, Iowa.
  *Morris—b. abt. 1843, Iowa.

*Kent, Rodolphus—registered as a private with the Tetherow armed men; cattle driver for the John Ridgeway family (*see* Roster).

*Ketchum, Frederic—registered with the muster roll for the Tetherow Train; b. abt. 1828, New Brunswick; m. Josephine Smith, Clatsop Plains, Oregon, 19 February 1850; settled at Clatsop Plains.

*Ketchum, John—registered with the muster roll for the Tetherow Train.

King, John—b. 23 March 1813; d. by drowning in the Columbia River, 26 October 1845.

King, Susan (Cooper)—d. by drowning, same incident, 26 October 1845.
Children:

Luther—b. 10 October 1840, Missouri; DLC No. 3140, Benton Co.; m. Caroline Ladd, 20 August 1866, Benton Co.; only survivor of his family in the drowning accident on the Columbia; uncle, Amos N. King (*see* Roster) was appointed guardian 13 March 1857.

Electa (or Electra)—"little daughter"; d. 26 October 1845, in the drowning accident on the Columbia River with her parents and baby brother.

Nine-months-old son, name unknown—d. 26 October 1845, by drowning with parents and sister, Electa, on the Columbia River.

King, Nahum—b. 25 July 1783, New Salem, Massachusetts; d. 28 May 1856, Benton Co., Oregon; DLC No. 2713, Benton Co.; the beautiful land settled by Nahum and most of his children and in-laws became known as Kings Valley.

King, Sarepta (Norton)—b. 12 November 1791, Albany, New York; d. 14 July 1869; m. Nahum, 9 May 1807, Columbus Co., New York.
Children:
See King, John.
See Norton, Hopestill King (Mrs. Lucius Carolus).
See King, Stephen.

Isaac—b. 23 November 1819, Ohio; d. 22/23 November 1866, Benton Co., Oregon; DLC No. 2181, Benton Co.; m. Almeda Van Bibber, 22 March 1847, Benton Co.

Amos N.—b. 29 April 1822, Madison Co., Ohio; d. 12 November 1901; DLC No. 3669, Washington/Multnomah Co.; settled on King Heights, Portland; m. Malinda Fuller (*see* Roster), 8 March 1846, Washington Co.

See Chambers, Sarah King (Mrs. Rowland).

Lovisa—b. 2 March 1828, Madison Co., Ohio; d. 3 December 1889, Benton Co., Oregon; m. Rowland

Chambers, 1846, after the death of her sister, Sarah, who was Rowland's first wife. (*See* Chambers, Rowland.)

Abigail—b. 22 June 1829, Madison Co., Ohio; d. 28 May 1857; m. Price Fuller (*see* Roster), 23 August 1846, Benton Co., Oregon; DLC No. 168, Benton Co.

Lydia—b. 19 February 1831, Madison Co, Ohio; m. Jonathan L. Williams (*see* Roster), 23 December 1847, Benton Co., Oregon; DLC No. 4968, Polk Co.

Solomon—b. 26 February 1833, Madison Co., Ohio; d. 13 March 1913, Benton Co., Oregon; m. Anna Maria (Allen) King, widow of Stephen King, 20 November 1853, Benton Co., Oregon (*see* Roster.)

Rhoda Ann—b. 17 June 1835, Madison Co., Ohio; m. 1st, John Phillips, Benton Co., abt 1849; m. 2nd, Eli Summers, DLC No. 3885, Benton Co.

(Nahum's daughter, Lucretia, who was b. 5 July 1809, N.Y., came to Oregon with her husband, Heman Halleck, and several children in 1853. Lucretia and Heman were married 15/16 October 1827, Madison Co., Ohio. They took up a donation land claim, No. 2376, in Benton Co.; Lucretia d. May 1860.)

King, Stephen—b. 13 July 1818, Madison Co., Ohio; d. 28 November 1852; DLC No. 5196, Benton Co.

King, Anna Maria (Allen)—b. 26 March 1822, Massachusetts; d. 1905; m. Stephen, 25 December 1843, Madison Co., Ohio; m. 2nd, Stephen's brother, Solomon, 20 November 1853. (*see* Roster.)
Children: none in 1845.

*Kitchen, William—appears on the Tetherow Train roster as head of a family and a private with the armed men; no other information known about him.

*Kitchen, ____ (Mrs.)
Children:

*Three boys under sixteen years of age, names not known.
*One girl over fourteen years of age, name not known.
*One girl under fourteen years of age, name not known.

*Lewis, Haman C.—b. 31 January 1809, New York, New York; d. 17 April 1889, Benton Co., Oregon; DLC No. 177, Benton Co.

*Lewis, Mary (Moore)—b. 1 October 1821, Missouri; d. 22 February 1889, Benton Co.; m. Haman, September 1838/39, Cole Co., Missouri.
Children:
*Elizabeth—b. abt 1843, Missouri; m. James Buffington, 14 August 1859, Benton Co.
*Baby girl, name unknown—d. winter 1845/46 in the Willamette Valley from the effects of mountain fever which had attacked the family at The Dalles, Oregon.

Lewis, Julia Franklin—See McNary, James; Julia was a stepdaughter.

Liggett, Alexander—b. 1789, Wythe Co., Virginia; d. 25 April 1864, Benton Co., Oregon; DLC No. 183, Benton Co.

Liggett, Rachael (Mrs.)—d. at Fifteen Mile Creek near The Dalles, Oregon, October, 1845, en route to the Willamette Valley; Alexander remarried, m. Mrs. Barbara Happenstall, 5 July 1855, Benton Co., Oregon.
Children:
A girl, name unknown, b. abt. 1817; m. _____ Taylor. Perhaps this is Mary who m. Benjamin Taylor, 5 February 1849, Oregon. Benjamin's DLC No. 1786, Lane Co, shows a boundary conflict. The affidavit is signed for Benjamin by Elijah "Leggett."
Jonathan W.A.—b. abt. 1823, Arkansas.
Elijah—b. 1827, Arkansas; DLC No. 856, Benton Co.; m. Mary E. Mulkey, 26 July 1852, Benton Co., Oregon.
Hannah—b. abt 1830, Missouri.

Phoebe—b. abt 1832, Daviess Co., Missouri; m. Joseph Kelsey, 15 June 1851, Benton Co., Oregon; DLC No. 1416, Benton Co.

Martha—b. 20 October 1833, Daviess Co., Missouri; d. 3 January 1902, Deer Creek, Oregon; m. John Pearce, 31 May 1855; settled at Deer Creek, near Roseburg, where John d. 10 January 1892.

Another girl, name unknown.

Liggett, Jonathan—b. 7 March 1790, Wythe Co., Virginia; d. 26 November 1868, Dallas, Oregon; DLC No. 4495, Polk Co.

Liggett, Elizabeth (Fanning)—b. abt 1789, North Carolina; sister to Tabitha Ridgeway (*see* Roster); m. Jonathan, 19 October 1814, Blount Co., Tennessee.
Children:
See Belieu, Sarah Liggett (Mrs. Leander).
See Liggett, William P.
Thomas S.—b. 1823, Ray Co., Missouri; d. January 1850, Polk Co., Oregon; m. Nancy Zumwalt, 29 June 1848, Polk Co.; Nancy m. 2nd, Ed. N. Tandy, 3 January 1858.
Joseph—b. 1831, Ray Co., Missouri; m. Elizabeth Sleeth, 4 March 1853, Polk Co., Oregon.
(Two sons, Henry and Russell, may not have come to Oregon.)

Liggett, William P.—b. 1820/1, Ray Co., Missouri; d. 28 January 1851, Polk Co; DLC No. 4526, Polk Co.

Liggett, Julia Ann (Sampson)—b. abt 1821, Jefferson Co., Indiana; m. William, February 1840, Missouri; m. 2nd, Marvel Jones, 25 December 1851, Polk Co., Oregon.
Children:
Mary J.—b. abt 1841, Missouri.
John W.—b. abt 1843, Missouri.
William K.—b. 1844, Missouri.

*Lingenfelter, Josiah W. (later changed his name to Linn)—b. 1816, Fayette Co., Kentucky; DLC No. 3475, Washington Co.; m. Mary Pomeroy, widow of Franklin Pomeroy (*see* Roster), 8 July 1850, Washington Co., Oregon; Josiah appears on the muster roll of the Tetherow Train of 1845.

Lloyd, John—b. 22 August 1796, Caswell Co., North Carolina; d. 6 January 1877, Colfax, Washington; DLC No. 187, Benton Co. (near Monroe, Oregon).

Lloyd, Nancy (Walker)—b. 4 December 1798, South Carolina; d. 26 February 1853, Benton Co., Oregon; m. John, 10/13 March 1823, Caswell Co., N. C.
Children:
Mary Ann—b. 21 August 1825, N. C.; d. 22 August 1854, Benton Co., Oregon; m. John Foster (*see* Roster), 4 June 1846; settled in Benton Co.
Abner Thomas—b. 19 September 1827, Clay Co., Missouri; d. 1 May 1886, Colfax, Washington; DLC No. 4154, Benton Co.; m. Jane Rexford, 3 July 1853, Benton Co., Oregon.
Nancy Jane—b. 13 March 1829, Missouri; d. 5 July 1860; m. Thomas Reeves, 4 June 1846; DLC No. 190.
Eliza—b. 12 March 1831, Missouri; d. 4 March 1858, Benton Co., Oregon; m. William Miller, 4 June 1846; settled in Benton Co., Oregon; he d. 1853.
Malinda—b. 1834, Clay Co., Missouri; d. 4 July 1850, Benton Co., Oregon.
Julia—b. abt. 1834, Clay Co., Missouri; m. _____ Starr.
Albert Gallatin—b. 25 July 1836, Missouri; d. 5 January 1915, Waitsburg, Washington; m. Lois Jasper, 20 May 1858, Benton Co., Oregon.
John Calvin—b. 2 October 1838, Clay Co., Missouri; d. 6 January 1880; m. Mary Cantrell, 4 January 1863.
William Walker—b. 21 February 1841, Missouri; d. 1 January 1874, Benton Co., Oregon; m. Lucinda Davis, 14 February 1866, Benton Co., who d. 4 June

1869, Benton Co.; he m. 2nd Mary F. Goodman, 7 December 1869.

Logsdon, Mary Elizabeth—*see* Wilson, G. Anthony; a step-daughter.

McCarver, Mary Ann (Jennings)—came to Oregon in the care of Samuel Simpson White (*see* Roster); Mrs. White was a sister to Mary Ann whose husband, Morton M. McCarver, had arrived with the 1843 immigration; DLC No. 1010, Clackamas Co.; the McCarvers were married, 6 May 1830, Monmouth, Illinois; Mary Ann (b. 1809, Kentucky) d. 19 November 1846, leaving two children; Morton m. 2nd, Julia Ann Buckalew, 20 January 1848, Clackamas Co.; instrumental in settling Tacoma, Washington. The McCarver home still stands at Oregon City, restored by Mrs. Albert H. Powers, of Portland.
Children:
Thomas Jennings—b. 26 April 1833, Knox Co., Illinois; d. 4 December 1881; m. Mary Goodlief, 18 April 1852, McConnelsville, Ohio.
Mary Ann—b. 15 December 1842, Springfield, Illinois; d. 5 August 1919, Santa Barbara, Calif.; m. Richard Hurley, 17 November 1858, Clackamas Co., Oregon.

*McKinley, ____ (Mr.).

*McKinley, ____ (Packwood)—Mrs.; sister to John Packwood (*see* Roster) and Mrs. Gillette (*see* Roster); stated, by a Packwood descendant, to have been on the Cutoff in 1845.

McKinney, Daniel—b. abt 1805, Indiana; d. 1864, Multnomah Co., Oregon; never married; a private on the armed men list for the Tetherow Train; cattle driver for the Ownbey family; settled on Ross Island with nephew, Sherry Ross (*see* Roster); brother to James II and William McKinney (*see* Roster).

McKinney, James II—b. 1796, Montgomery Co., Kentucky; d. 16 July 1867, Douglas Co., Oregon; DLC No. 988, Douglas Co.; brother to Daniel and William McKinney (*see* Roster); came alone, sent for his wife Mary "Polly" (Little) and children at a later date. He m. Polly 14 March 1819, Wayne Co., Indiana.

McKinney, William—b. 30 April 1802, Ross Co., Ohio; d. 8 January 1889, Hillsboro, Oregon; DLC No. 643, Douglas Co.; brother to Daniel and James II McKinney (*see* Roster).

McKinney, Henry Ann (Walter)—b. 20 September 1806, Middleton (Washington Co.), Pa.; d. 21 September 1898, Portland, Oregon; m. William, 5 November 1828, Wayne Co., Indiana. (*See* Roster: Wm. Walter family.)
Children:
Charles C.—b. 1 February 1830, Wayne Co., Indiana; d. 11 June 1902; DLC No. 644, Douglas Co.; m. Mary E. Barton; lived in Washington Co., 1870.
Isabelle—b. 31 March 1831, Indiana; m. Luke Hinshaw (*see* Roster), 23 December 1851, Washington Co., Oregon.
Rachael—b. 10 June 1833, Indiana; d. 22 February 1918, Washington Co., Oregon; m. Benjamin Cornelius, Jr. (*see* Roster), 24 July 1851; DLC No. 2139, Washington Co.
James Montgomery—b. 7 August 1834, Indiana; settled in Washington Territory; m. Mrs. McNal, 1887, Okanogan Co., Washington.
William II—b. 5 May 1836, Indiana; d. 1 December 1924, Washington Co., Oregon; m. Sarah Jane Paulson, December, 1865, Oregon; settled in Washington.
Jasper Newton—b. 26 December 1839, Iowa; d. 8 May 1919; m. 1st, Jane Cornelius, who was the daughter of Benjamin Cornelius, Sr. (*see* Roster) 2 February 1865, Washington Co., Oregon, and was b. 1846 in

Oregon; Jane d. 1871, and Jasper m. 2nd, Sarah Brown abt 1873; settled at Waitsburg, Washington. She d. 1892.

McNary, Alexander—b. 26 December 1798, Lexington, Fayette Co., Kentucky; DLC No. 3, Polk Co.

McNary, Ladocia (Stockton)—b. 1802, Tennessee; d. 26 February 1875, Eola, Polk Co.; m. Alexander, September 1824/5, Morgan Co,, Illinois.
Children:
Sarah Eleanor—b. abt 1825, Illinois; d. 1901, Fresno Co., Calif.; m. Alva C. R. Shaw, 22 January 1846, Polk Co., Oregon; DLC No. 4735, Polk Co.; he was b. 1817, New Jersey.
Hugh M.—b. 15 May 1827, Morgan Co., Illinois; d. 17 August 1891, Salem, Oregon; DLC No. 4803, Polk Co.; m. Catherine Frizell, April, 1854, Polk Co., Oregon; she d. 1911.
Alexander W.—b. 3 March 1833 (some sources say 1832), Morgan Co., Illinois; d. 1898, Polk Co., Oregon; DLC No. 4267, Polk Co.; m. Celta Grubb, 1857, who d. 1862. He m. 2nd, Mrs. Elmer J. Miller, October 1874.
Nancy Catherine—b. abt 1834, Illinois; d. 1861, Polk Co., Oregon; m. John C. Allen, 30 April 1851, Polk Co., who was b. 7 July 1825, Cooper Co., Missouri.
Davis—b. abt 1838, Illinois; d. abt 1862, Polk Co., Oregon.

McNary, James—b. 28 February 1790 near Lexington, Fayette Co., Kentucky; d. 11 October 1871, Marion Co., Oregon; brother to Alexander and to Catherine L. "Kitty" Whitley (*see* Roster); DLC No. 93, Clackamas Co. He m. 1st. Elizabeth Sharp, b. 1795, d. 1840, Illinois. She was mother of the James McNary children. After her death he married Nancy M. Lewis Brookes.

McNary, Nancy M. Lewis Brookes—b. abt 1800, Kentucky; m. 3rd, James, 21 February 1841, Illinois.
Children:
Harriett Vanneva—b. 19 August 1819, prob. Harrison Co., Indiana; d. 7 October 1879, Clackamas Co., Oregon; m. Alanson Perry Smith (*see* Roster), May 1847, Clackamas Co.
Rachel Emaline—b. 9 February 1821, prob. Harrison Co., Indiana; d. 1889, Walla Walla, Washington; m. Isaac Lasswell, 6 January 1848, Clackamas Co., Oregon, an 1843 immigrant (b. 1820, Vigo Co., Indiana), DLC No. 4559, Clackamas Co.
Rosanna—b. 4 January 1827, prob. Shelby Co., Illinois; m. William D. Cole, 25 March 1847, Clackamas Co., Oregon; DLC No. 1084, Polk Co.
Hugh Linza—b. 30 August 1829, prob. Shelby Co., Illinois; d. 18 July 1883, Salem, Oregon; m. Mary Margaret Claggett, 21 December 1854, Marion Co., Oregon; she d. 1878; DLC No. 4918, Linn Co. He m. 2nd, Julia Johnson, 2 January 1890, Clackamas Co., Oregon.
Eliza—b. 14 November 1831, Shelby Co., Illinois; m. Francis Marion Phillips (brother to John Phillips; *see* Roster), 7 June 1858, Clackamas Co., Oregon.
Elizabeth—b. 29 August 1836, either Morgan or Pike Co., Illinois; d. 11 January 1861, Polk Co., Oregon, never married.
Julia Franklin Lewis—b. 9 November 1827, Ky; d. 15 March 1888; m. Jesse Harritt (*see* Roster), 1 October 1846; DLC No. 1102, Polk Co.; stepdaughter to James McNary.
_____ Lewis—stepdaughter to James McNary.

McNary, John W.—b. abt. 1828; d. 1850, Polk Co., Oregon (estate notice in *Oregon Spectator,* November 14, 1850; prob. a nephew of James and Alexander, and Catherine L. Whitley; *see* Roster).

McNemee, Job—b. 14 October 1812, Ohio; d. 1 October 1872, Portland, Oregon.

McNemee, Hannah (Cochrane)—b. 29 January 1815, Ross Co., Ohio; d. 15 September 1872, Pacific Co., Washington; m. Job 1832, Ohio; sister to Mrs. Frederick Waymire (*see* Roster).

Children:

Frances—b. 4 November 1837, Ray Co., Ohio; d. 1893, Portland, Oregon; m. Edward J. Northrup, 11 May 1856, Portland.

Moses Dimit—b. 11 October 1839, Fairfield Co., Ohio; d. 1905; m. Elizabeth Corbin.

Adam—b. 17 September 1841, Missouri; d. 29 March 1919; never married.

William G.—b. 8 April 1843.

Emaline—b. 25 December 1844, St. Joseph, Missouri; d. 1845 on the Meek Cutoff.

McWilliams, Mary Helen—*see* Wilson, William; Mary Helen was a stepdaughter to William.

*Mallory, James—a private on the Tetherow Train armed men list; a J. Mallery, Missouri, is listed on a death list compiled by Hiram Smith in 1845, showing immigrants who succumbed en route to Oregon or soon after; no other information known.

Marlin, Henry—b. 22 June 1822, Perry Co., Pa.; DLC No. 3470, Clatsop Co.; m. Emily J. (Olney) Hipes (*see* Roster), 10 May 1846, Washington Co., Oregon; settled at The Dalles in 1866—an incorporator with The Dalles Woolen Mills.

Marquam, Alfred—b. 14 March 1817, Hagerstown, Frederick Co., Maryland; d. 23 February 1887, Clackamas Co., Oregon; DLC No. 1693, Clackamas Co.; furniture maker.

Marquam, Olive Wise (Burbage)—b. 17 March 1824, Bourbon Co., Kentucky; d. 26 February 1893, Clackamas Co., Oregon; m. Alfred, 6 November 1842, Clay Co., Missouri. (*See* Roster—Ezekiel Burbage family.)
Children:
Mary Jane—b. 13 September 1843, Liberty, Missouri; m. 1st, Daniel Albright; settled in Clackamas Co.; m. 2nd, Rev. Charles W. Stockwell.
George W.—b. 7 November 1844, Liberty, Missouri; m. Mina Covey.

Martin, Hardin D.—b. 1810, Knox Co., Ky; DLC No. 377, Yamhill Co.

Martin, Eveline—b. abt 1811, Virginia; m. Hardin, October 1838, Clay Co., Missouri.

Martin, John (Sr.)—b. 1800, Spotsylvania Co., Virginia; d. at eighty-four years of age at Salem, Oregon; DLC No. 1085, Polk Co.

Martin, Malinda (Smith)—b. abt 1820, Virginia; d. at Salem, Oregon; m. John, September, 1834, Warren Co., Illinois.
Children:
Eliza Jane—b. abt. 1833, Illinois; m. Resin D. Foster (see Roster), 1846; divorced, 1847; m. 2nd John N. Chambers, 17 April 1848, Clackamas Co., Oregon; DLC No. 2410, Polk Co.
Mary—b. abt 1840, Iowa; m. 1st Joseph Allred (*see* Roster), 4 September 1853, Polk Co., Oregon; m. 2nd, John Pearson, who farmed and d. in Klamath County, Oregon; m. 3rd William Miller, 22 August 1900; settled at Salem, Oregon.
Emily—b. abt 1841, Iowa; m. ____ Howell; settled at Crescent City, Calif.
John (Jr.)—b. abt 1844, Iowa; d. at Jacksonville, Oregon, of smallpox in the 1860's, probably 1864/5.

Martin, William—Perhaps the William Martin who was b. 1813, Kentucky; m. Harriet ____; settled at Cow Creek, Douglas Co., Oregon; shown on the Tetherow Train roster as a member of the muster roll and a cattle driver for the John Martin family (*see* Roster).

Meek, Stephen Hall L.—b. 4 July 1805, Washington Co., Virginia; d. 11 January 1889, Etna, Calif.; mountain man, trapper; guide for the 1842 immigration and guide for a portion of the 1845 immigration; guide on the Meek Cutoff.

Meek, Elizabeth (Schoonover)—b. 16 May 1827, Canada; d. 31 October 1865, Jackson, California; m. Stephen, 18 May 1845, Territory of Kansas, en route to Oregon; they settled in Calif.

Melvin, William—appears on the muster roll for the Tetherow Train; apparently alone, without family.

*Miller, James.

*Miller, ____ (Mrs. James).
   Children:
   *Isabel—abt. 16 years old.
   *Eliza Ann—b. 1834, Illinois; m. P. Orchard, 18 September 1851.
   *Perhaps other children.

Miller, Robert Emmett—b. 1783-5, Ireland; d. 18 March 1856, Jackson Co., Oregon; came to the United States (Kentucky) when two years of age; DLC No. 1577, Jackson Co.

Miller, Sarah Campbell (Fitzgerald)—b. 29 June 1792, Hardin Co., Kentucky; d. 15 June 1867, Salem, Oregon; m. Robert, 1 April 1818, Elizabethtown, Kentucky (Some records state 1810.)
   Children:

See Walker, Nancy M. (Mrs. Jesse).

John F.—b. 30 April 1825, Hardin Co., Kentucky; d. 1901; DLC No. 1863, Jackson Co.; m. Zerilda (or Zerella) Hockson, 25 March 1849, Randolph Co., Missouri. (DLC states John arrived 1847.)

See Bybee, Julia Ann (Mrs. James F.).

James Napper Tandy—b. 10 October 1826, Hardin Co., Kentucky; d. 18 September 1900, Jacksonville, Oregon; DLC No. 113, Jackson Co.; m. Elizabeth Ann Awbrey, 22/23 August 1853, Lane Co., Oregon. She was b. 1832, Missouri; d. 24 February 1918.

See Charlton, Margaret (Mrs. Joseph).

Parthena Elizabeth—b. 1830; m. James Menzies, 5 February 1849, Washington Co., Oregon; DLC No. 2153, Washington Co. He was b. 1820, Perthshire, Scotland, arrived in Oregon, 1 September 1848.

Robert E.—b. 1832, Henry Co., Missouri.; DLC No. 959, Jackson Co.

William P.—b. 12 March 1836, Missouri; m. Sarah E. Raffety, 21 September 1864; lived in the Yakima, Washington, area from 1869 to 1877; appointed warden for Oregon State Prison in 1878.

(Another daughter, Narcissa M., b. 1822, came to Oregon at a later date. She and her husband, Horace J. McIntyre, were in the territory in 1850; he probably either returned to Missouri for his family or sent for them after that date. The McIntyres were married, 6 July 1842, in Missouri. All of the Miller family, including five sons-in-law, first settled on Sauvies Island near Portland, Oregon In 1854 they moved to Jackson Co.)

*Monroe, William—listed as a private with the Tetherow Train.

*Moore, John—appears on the Tetherow Train roster as a cattle driver for the H. M. Knighton family and as a member of the muster roll. If he stayed with the Knighton family, he traveled the regular Oregon Trail—not the Cutoff.

*Moore, Reverend William—d. in Oregon Territory, 1845, en route to the Willamette Valley. No further information is currently known, but there was a Moore family who experienced the trials of the Meek Cutoff. William Barlow in his *Reminiscences* states that his family went the regular trail while the Geers, Moores and Sweets said goodbye and took the Cutoff. He further mentions the loss of two or three members of these families, no names given.

*Moreland, Zachariah—registered as the head of a family with the Tetherow Train, listed on the muster roll. He is listed on Tuality County census, 1849; a claim of 640 acres in Tuality County, situated on Gales Creek about 4 miles from Gales Mill, was recorded 30 October 1847 (Provisional Govt. Land Claim Book, No. 6, p. 104). He served as grand juror, September, 1847, session of Circuit Court, Tuality Plains. All trace of this family is lost after 1849. Perhaps, the members were attracted to California and the gold rush.

*Moreland, ____ (Mrs.).
Children:
*Francis M.—cattle driver of 111 loose cattle for the family; under sixteen years of age.
*Three other boys under the age of sixteen.
*Three girls under the age of fourteen.
*One girl over fourteen years of age. Prob. Margaret Jane who m. Jehu Davis, 16 August 1846, Washington Co.

Newman, Rev. Samuel—b. New York, ?; d. 1848/9; killed by Indians in the gold fields of California; John and Rebecca Newman appointed as administrators of the estate, September, 1850.

Newman, Mary—b. 15 March 1807; d. 22 February 1868, Oregon City; m. Samuel, 1825, prob. Ohio. A Mary Newman m. Isaac Blanton, 25 July 1850, Clackamas Co., Oregon.

Children:

John W.—b.1829, Indiana; DLC No. 2849, Clackamas Co.; m. Edith Elizabeth Tetherow (*see* Roster), 20 May 1851, Linn Co., Oregon.

Rebecca—b. 20 May 1832, Indiana; d. 19 May, 1867, Lewiston, Idaho; m. Robert Newell, 28 June 1846, Marion Co., Oregon. DLC No. 2051, Marion Co.

Rachel W.—b. 19 November 1833 Indiana; d. 26 June 1902, Oregon City; m. John M. Bacon, 16 March 1851, Clackamas Co., Oregon; DLC No. 1538, Clackamas Co.; John was postmaster and merchant at Oregon City.

George—b. abt. 1841, Lee Co., Iowa; d. 16 August 1869, Portland, Oregon; resided at Oregon City, Oregon; m. Addie Foster, 9 March 1875.

Noble, Henry J.—b. 1805, Allegheny Co., Pa.; d. 1885, Portland, Oregon; DLC No. 3002, Yamhill Co.

Noble, Mary Ann (Layton)—b. 1 February 1803, South Carolina; d. 20 February 1870, Washington Co., Oregon; m. Henry, May, 1826, Jefferson Co., Indiana.

Children:

John—b. 1827, Indiana; d. of mountain fever, 1845, on the Meek Cutoff.

Rebecca Jane—b. 1830, Indiana; d. 12 April 1852, Yamhill Co., Oregon; m. Israel Stoley, November 1847, Yamhill Co.

Henry J.—b. 1832, Kentucky; d. 21 July 1907, Newberg area; m. Martha Boyles, 24 May 1857, Oregon; settled on a farm near Newberg, Oregon; she was b. 1842, Missouri.

Mary—b. 1833, Indiana; d. 1860-70, Yamhill Co., Oregon; m. John Richason, 20 February 1851, Yamhill Co.

A boy (E. Noble), eleven years old—d. of mountain fever, 1845, on the Meek Cutoff.

Nancy—b. abt 1838, Missouri; m. Thomas Benton Nelson, 30 July 1857, Yamhill Co.

Norton, Lucius Carolus—b. 26 December 1818, Madison Co., Ohio; d. 6 May 1859, Kings Valley, Oregon; DLC No. 2765, Benton Co.

Norton, Hopestill (King)—b. 7 February 1815, Ohio; d. 16 November 1893, Norton's Station, Lincoln Co., Oregon; m. Lucius, 9 October 1839, Franklin Co., Ohio; after Lucius' death, Hopestill ran a stagecoach way station in the Coast Range, west of Corvallis.
Children:
Isaac—b. 22 February 1842, Carrol Co., Missouri; m. Olive Harris (1842-1887), 20 February 1867, Benton Co., Oregon.
Wiley—b. 27 March 1844, Big Bend, Carroll Co., Missouri; d. 1933, Kings Valley, Benton Co., Oregon; m. Nancy A. Zumwalt, 18 May 1865, Benton Co.; farmed at Blodgett's Valley until 1900, then farmed near Lewisville in Polk County. Nancy was b. 25 May 1847, Tualatin Plains, Oregon.

Officer, James—b. 12 June 1801, Overton Co., Tennessee; d. 16 March 1893, Clackamas Co.; DLC No. 469, Clackamas Co.

Officer, Eveline (Cooley)—b. 7 December 1807, Kentucky; d. 14 June 1878, Clackamas Co., Oregon; (*see* Roster— Mathias Cooley); m. James, 19 February 1828, Clay Co., Missouri.
Children:

Martha Ann—b. 5 February 1828, Clay Co., Missouri; d. 22 June 1884, Clackamas Co., Oregon; m. John K. Dickey, August, 1847, Molalla, Oregon; DLC No. 1119, Clackamas Co.

Eli Casey—b. 24 January 1831, Clay Co., Missouri; d. 29 November 1896, Dayville, Oregon; DLC No. 5094, Linn Co.; later settled in Baker Co., Oregon (was there in 1870); m. 1st, Sarah Howard, 28 November 1852, Clackamas Co., Oregon; m. 2nd, Martha Jane (Woods) Thorpe, 9 January 1862; m. 3rd, Mary Ann Steele, 1879; m. 4th, Mrs. Mary Rounds, 10 November 1892.

Susan Mary—b. 3 March 1833, Missouri; d. 11 April 1911, Clackamas Co.; m. William Hatchett Vaughan, 27 August 1847; took the first donation land claim (No. 731) in the Molalla area—16 miles southeast of Oregon City, along the Molalla River. A portion of the claim was still in the hands of a descendant, Mrs. Bertha Vaughan Johns in 1966, and has been honored by the State of Oregon as a Century Farm.

John E.—b. abt 1835, Missouri; m. Sarah Trullinger, 16 December 1857, Clackamas Co., Oregon; divorced, 1867.

Robert V.—b. abt 1837, Missouri; d. 1916, Izee, Oregon; m. Viana Bunton, 9 December 1859, Wasco Co., Oregon; settled near Molalla, Oregon, in Clackamas Co.; located in Grant Co., 1884; mayor of John Day, Oregon, 1911. Viana was b. 15 May 1845; d. 1 January 1889.

Francis Marion (Frank)—b. abt 1839, Missouri; m. Louise Mary Tarter.

Joseph Thomas—perhaps b. abt 1841, Missouri; his name does not appear in the 1850 census, may have been deceased.

Nancy E.—b. 18 March 1843, Missouri; d. 2 November 1931, Beagle, Oregon; m. Aaron Wyland, 12 December 1860, Clackamas Co., Oregon; settled in the Molalla area.

Missouri—b. 13 August 1845, Ash Hollow, Wyoming, en route to Oregon; d. 2 September 1916; m. Allen P. Snyder, 6 December 1876, Dayville, Oregon; farmed at Dayville, in Grant Co.

Olney, Nathan—b. 1824; d. 28 (or 15?) September 1866, Attanum (Ft. Simcoe area), Washington Ty, result of an Indian arrow wound received ten years earlier; first came to Oregon in the 1843 immigration. His second trip, in 1845, was made with the McDonald party. Somewhere between Fort Laramie and Fort Boise he joined Stephen Meek, drew a map for the immigrants, and took the Cutoff. Nathan settled at The Dalles in 1847, the first permanent resident. He built a store on the bank of Mill Creek—later (1850) built another on Olney, or Chenowith Creek; established a ferry at the mouth of Deschutes River, 1852, to aid the immigrants; served as Indian agent, guide, and interpreter during the Yakima Indian War of 1856; m. Annette Hallicola (sometimes referred to as Jeanette by descendants), daughter of Chief Chalalee of the Wasco Indian tribe; they were first married by tribal custom, then by a justice of peace-the latter ceremony taking place, 23 January 1859; Nathan had married, 1 April 1857, the widow of James Sinclair who had been killed by Indians at the Cascades in 1856, but the marriage lasted only a month. He obtained a divorce, took back his Indian wife, Annette.

Ownbey, Nicholas—b. 1794, Rutherford Co., North Carolina; DLC No. 181, Benton Co.

Ownbey, Lucy—b. abt 1806, Kentucky; m. Nicholas, 23 May 1821, Cooper Co., Missouri.
Children:

Jesse—b. 1824, Missouri; DLC No. 852, Benton Co.; m. Elizabeth Jasper, 7 December 1848, Missouri. She was b. 21 July 1829.

John—b. abt 1827, Missouri.

William—b. 1831, Missouri; DLC No. 854, Benton Co.; m. Martha Jane Langston, 2 December 1852, Clackamas Co., Oregon Territory.

Powell—b. 22 February 1834, Missouri; DLC No. 3216, Benton Co.

Mary—b. abt 1839, Missouri; m. William C. Jasper, 8 January 1854, Benton Co.

Nicholas—b. abt 1842, Missouri; m. Louisa J. Zevely abt 1864; a resident at Cove (Union Co.), Oregon, in 1870. (*See* DLC 3635, Benton Co.)

Lucy—b. abt 1844, Missouri.

*Packwood, Charles—brother to Elisha, John, Larkin, and Robert Tait Packwood (*see* Roster); historian H. H. Bancroft states that Charles came in 1845, but some Packwood descendants say he did not. Charles was b. 14 November 1816, Patrick Co., Virginia; d. 4 December 1866, California.

Packwood, Elisha—b. 2 July 1805, Patrick Co., Virginia; d. 27 May 1876, Everett, Washington; took his family to Calif. in 1848, returned to the Northwest about 1862; settled on the Snohomish flats, 1868—an area now known as Packwood Landing in Washington.

Packwood, Paulina (Prothero)—b. 28 April 1816, Kentucky; m. Elisha, 12 February 1832, Jackson Co., Indiana.

Children:

Samuel Tait—b. 29 December 1832, Jackson Co., Indiana; d. 1910, Tacoma, Washington; m. Matilda Wardle, 6 January 1861, Santa Clara, California, settled on the Snohomish flats in Washington, 1868.

Chiletha Emma—b. 9 May 1841, Platte Co., Missouri; m. Marcelus Barnett; settled at Ellensburg, Washington.

Elkanah—b. 24 December 1843, Platte Co., Missouri; d. 8 September 1845, from whooping cough, near Harney Lake, on the Meek Cutoff.

*Packwood, James—cousin to Charles, Elisha, John, Larkin, and Robert Tait Packwood; killed by Indians near The Dalles, 1848; name appears on the Bancroft 1845 Oregon immigration list.

Packwood, John I.—b. 22 February 1804, Patrick Co., Virginia; d. 1879, Barry Co., Missouri; moved his family to California, 1848. In later years John and some of his family returned to the East. He was a brother to Charles, Elisha, Larkin, and Robert Tait Packwood.

Packwood, Abigail (Tinder)—b. 1810, Kentucky; d. 1852, Salmon Falls, California; m. John, 1831, Jackson Co., Indiana; he m. 2nd, Jane Stamps abt. 1854, Missouri, who d. 1880.

Children:

See Shaser, Margaret Packwood (Roster—Mrs. George).

Orpha—b. October 1833, Indiana or Missouri; d. in Kansas during Civil War.

Lucinda—b. 1835, Indiana/Missouri; she m. Frank Proctor, Texas farmer.

Malenda (Malinda)—b. 20 January 1837, Platte Co., Missouri; d. 20 August 1913, Olympia, Washington; m. Geo. W. or John Smith; 2nd Thomas Nixon; 3rd Charles Gaillac.

Mary—b. abt. 1838, Missouri; m. abt. 1865, William H. Packwood, Los Angeles, California.

Isaac—b. abt. 1839/40, Missouri; d. young.

Samuel Tate—b. 4 July 1842, Platte Co., Missouri; d. Ellensberg, Washington; m. Margaret F. Holmes, 24 December 1860, Rocky Comfort, Missouri.

Ann—b. ca. 1844, Platte Co., Missouri; d. abt. 1903, Newton Co., Missouri.

*Packwood, Larkin—brother to Charles, Elisha, John, and Robert Tait Packwood; name appears on the Bancroft 1845 immigration list.

*Packwood, Robert Tait—brother to Charles, Elisha, John, and Larkin Packwood.

(William and Samuel Packwood, brothers to the 1845 Packwood brothers, arrived in Oregon with the 1844 immigrants. William and family settled at Tumwater—near Olympia, Washington. The town of Packwood and a neighboring lake in the Cascade Range bear his name.)

Parker, Samuel—b. 27 January 1806, Franklin Co., Virginia; d. 12 September 1886, Aumsville, Oregon; DLC No. 2989, Marion Co.; his claim was the site of the Oregon State Penitentiary; Speaker of the House during the first territorial legislature of Oregon.

Parker, Elizabeth (Sutton)—d. at The Dalles after arriving in October, 1845. She m. Samuel abt. 1828, in Virginia. Samuel m. 2nd, Rosetta Spears English, widow of William English who d. 1845, after arriving near The Dalles by way of the Oregon Trail. They were married November, 1846, Marion Co., Oregon.
Children:
Sarah Sutton—b. 16 August 1829, Parkersville, Virginia; d. fall of 1917, Washington Co., Oregon; m. John B. Jackson, 4 July 1846, Clackamas Co., Oregon; DLC

No. 1354, Washington Co. He was b. 14 March 1820, Virginia; d. 22 December 1869, Centerville, Oregon.

Priscilla—b. abt 1833, Parkersville, Virginia; d. Portland, Oregon; m. Perrin Whitman, nephew of Dr. Marcus Whitman, 5 February 1854, Marion Co.; settled in Marion Co., Oregon.

Newton O.—b. 19 March 1835, Virginia; m. Sophie S. Cornelius, 13 November 1865, Marion Co., Oregon.

Amanda L.—b. 3 November 1836, Parkersville, Virginia; d. 25 October 1920; m. Green B. Cornelius, 6 March 1860, Marion Co., Oregon; settled near Turner, Oregon; farmed.

Susan Kale—b. abt. 1838, Van Buren Co., Iowa; m. George W. Ferrel, 16 June 1853, Oregon Territory; DLC No. 527, Washington Co.; he was b. 1822, Kentucky.

Gideon Jasper—b. 1839, Van Buren Co., Iowa; m. Genella Jones; settled in Idaho.

George L.—b. abt. 1841, Van Buren Co., Iowa; m. Mary Usher; he lived in Grant Co. in 1870, later in Portland.

Virginia—b. abt 1843, Van Buren Co., Iowa; d. at The Dalles, 1845, from the effects of the Meek Cutoff.

Samuel, Jr.—b. and d. at The Dalles, 1845, after his parents arrived via the Cutoff.

Patch, Sanford—a member of the Herren group, said to have been present at the gold find and to have kept a diary; he returned to the East and died there. (Statement made by Willard Herren, son of William J.)

*Patterson, Abraham—b. December 1817, Greene Co., Tennessee; d. September 1872, Douglas Co., Oregon; DLC No. 484, Douglas Co.; settled in the Camas Valley area.

*Patterson, Lovey—m. Abraham, 6 March 1845, Andrew Co., Missouri.
Children:

231

*Martha—b. 1845, Missouri; m. John H. Lee, 29 October 1865, Douglas Co.

*Patterson, J.—name appearing on the Hiram Smith death list for 1845.

Patterson, John—b. 5 June 1804, Pa.; d. 1869; DLC No. 5133, Marion Co.; m. 2nd Sarah Stout Pickering (widow), 2 June 1853, Marion Co.

Patterson, ____ (Mrs.)—It is not known whether this Mrs. Patterson was John's wife, but she was accompanied by her husband and children.
Children:
Three girls, names unknown.
One son, old enough to help his father manage the raft on the Columbia.

Peters, Jason—b. 8 October 1820, Andrew Co., Tennessee; d. 3 January 1894, Portland, Oregon; DLC No. 920, Yamhill Co.; m. Eleanor C. McCullough, 31 August 1852, Yamhill Co., Oregon; returned to central Oregon with the McClure mining party, 1858; helped in identifying the 1845 tracks.

Peterson, Asa H.—b. 12 April 1822, Lewis Co., West Virginia; d. 13 September 1898 at Lebanon, Oregon; DLC No. 2246, Linn Co.; physician and dentist at Albany, Oregon.

Peterson, Susannah (Johnson)—b. 16 November 1826, Kentucky; d. 20 April 1917, Lebanon, Oregon; m. Asa, 2 July 1843, Clark Co., Missouri.
Children:
David H.—b. 23 May 1844, Iowa; d. 9 January 1929, Linn Co.; m. Rachel Arminta Powell; settled in Linn Co., Oregon.

Peterson, Henry J.—b. 1800, Pendleton Co., West Virginia; d. 25 April 1864, Linn Co., Oregon; DLC No. 1594, Linn

Co.; Peterson Butte in Linn Co. named after him and his family.

Peterson, Eliza (Allen)—b. 1802, Virginia; d. 1861, Linn Co.; m. Henry, 15 February 1821, Lewis Co., West Virginia. *Children:*
See Peterson, Asa H.

Lydia M.—b. abt 1824, West Virginia; d., Linn Co., Oregon; m. Gamaliel Parrish, 25 February 1847, Linn Co., Oregon; DLC No. 1726, Linn Co.

William A.—b. 1828, Lewis Co., West Virginia; d. June, 1894, Albany, Oregon; DLC No. 2374, Linn Co.; m. Eliza Ann Smelser, 10 March 1853, Linn Co., Oregon; carpenter, built one of the first two brick buildings in Albany, three stories high.

Sarah—b. 11 July 1830, Lewis Co., West Virginia; d. 14 May 1869, The Dalles, Oregon; m. John Wesley Helm (*see* Roster), 22 June 1847, Linn Co., Oregon; m. 2nd Caleb Brooks, 30 October 1851, Linn Co.; DLC No. 2019, Linn Co.

Marshall—b. abt 1832, West Virginia; d. 6 January 1895, Portland, Oregon; m. Maggie Marshall, November 1864, Portland; settled in eastern Oregon; veteran of the Rogue River Indian wars.

Laura—b. abt 1834, West Virginia; m. Walter Ketchum, 30 October 1851, Linn Co., Oregon; DLC No. 2422, Linn Co.; was living in Pomeroy, Washington, 1903.

Martha—b. 30 June 1836, Weston, West Virginia; d. 21 April 1907, Portland, Oregon; m. Charles O. Barnes, 24 December 1862; settled in Linn Co., Oregon.

Henry J.—b. abt 1838, Ohio/Indiana; was living at Plainview in Linn Co., Oregon, 1903.

Eliza—b. abt 1840, Kentucky/Indiana; m. ____ Walker; lived at Athena, Oregon, 1903.

(Granville—b. 1843, d. en route to Oregon, on the Green River cutoff; available information indicates he was buried beside the river.)

*Phillips, John—b. 25 November 1814, Wiltshire, England; d. 1 July 1892, Polk Co., Oregon; DLC No. 569, Polk Co.; cabinetmaker.

*Phillips, Elizabeth (Hibbard)—b. 17 July, 1820, Shaftesbury, Dorsetshire, England; d. 18 May 1901/2; m. John, 11 February 1839, New Orleans, Louisiana.
Children:
    *Sarah Ann—b. 14 August 1842, Missouri; d. 1871; m. Edwin Dane, 24 February 1859, Polk Co.
    *John E.—b. 15 August 1844, St. Louis, Missouri; settled at Zena, Oregon.

Pierce, M. N.—known in later years as "old man Pierce," an avid miner.

Pitman, Lee Monroe—b. abt 1814, Virginia; d. 1 December 1880, Silverton, Oregon; DLC 713, Marion Co.

Pitman, Mary—b. abt 1814, Virginia; m. Lee, July 1827, Lancaster Co., Virginia.
Children:
    George W.—b. 1828, Lancaster Co., Virginia; d. August 1857, Marion Co.; m. Emily _____, November 1851, Marion Co., Oregon; DLC 1086, Marion Co.
    Lucius—b. 1832, Virginia; m. Julia Woolen, 3 July 1864, Marion Co.
    William—b. 1834, Illinois.
    Lloyd—b. 1836, Missouri.
    Mary J.—b. 1839, Missouri; m. John F. Cox, 27 October 1853, Marion Co.
    Catherine—b. 1841, Missouri; m. James H. Sawyer, 16 November 1856, Marion Co.
    Virginia—b. 1843, Missouri; m. Thomas F. Burford, 26 August 1858, Marion Co.
    Albany—b. 1845, place unknown, on the Plains to Oregon.

*Pollard, William—a private with the Tetherow Train; no other information.

*Pollock, Thomas—b. 1816, Erie Co., Pa.; DLC No. 1067, Umpqua Co.; m. Jane ____; name appears on the muster roll for the Tetherow Train.

*Pomeroy, Franklin—d. early spring, 1850, Tuality Plains, Oregon; listed with the Tetherow Train as a private and the head of a family.

*Pomeroy, Mary (Catching)—b. abt 1827, Tennessee; d. 1859, Oregon; she probably m. Franklin abt 1842/3; m. 2nd, Josiah Lingenfelter (Linn)—*see* Roster—8 July 1850, Washington Co., Oregon; DLC No. 3475, Washington Co.
Children:
*Lydia Jane—b. 1844, Missouri; m. Kenyon Crandall, 3 February 1858, Washington Co., Oregon.

Powell, Theophilus—b. 12 August 1792, Montgomery Co., Virginia; d. April, 1861; DLC No. 18, Marion Co.; Methodist minister.

Powell, Rachael (Center) Tull—b. 14 April 1819, Ohio; d. 1890, Clackamas Co., Oregon; m. Theophilus, 1 November 1841, Van Buren Co., Missouri; m. 3rd, Jacob Roop, 23 July 1862.
Children:
William Tull—b. 8 January 1838, Illinois; d. 31 July 1866, Clackamas Co., Oregon; Rachael's son, first marriage.
Mary Ann—b. 30 August, 1841, Independence, Missouri; d. 22 March 1903, Clackamas Co., Oregon; m. 1st, William Roberts; m. 2nd, George R. H. Miller, 1873; resided at Oregon City, Oregon.
Isaac—b. 19 April 1843, Missouri; d. 5 September 1921; m. Adelia Culver, 18 January 1870.

*Prothero, Samuel—father of Paulina Prothero Packwood (*see* Roster).

*Pugh, William David—d. at Forest Grove, Oregon, 3 January 1846, Washington Co., Oregon.

*Pugh, Jeanette (Donaldson)—b. 1798, Wilson Co., Tennessee; m. David, 16 February 1815, Wilson Co., Tennessee; DLC No. 44, Marion Co.
Children:
  See Smith, Sarah N. Pugh (Mrs. Alvis).
  See Pugh, William Porter.
  *John M.—b. 1820, Sullivan Co., Indiana; DLC No. 25, Marion Co.; m. Sarah Ann (Sallie) Claggett, 31 August 1854, Marion Co.
  *Silas George—b. 27 February 1830, Warren Co., Indiana; d. 17 May 1909, Marion Co., Oregon; DLC No. 314, Marion Co.; m. Sara Rose, 1857, Marion Co.
  *David Hall—b. 22 February 1833, Indiana; d. 10 December 1912, Salem, Oregon; contractor and builder at Salem; m. Catherine Entz, 24 October 1860, Salem.
  *Amanda (Mandy) Anne—b. 22 February 1833, Indiana; twin to David; m. E. E. Wheeler about 1851/2; settled in Linn Co., Oregon. She d. 1911.
  *Andrew—b. abt. 1838, Indiana or Arkansas; d. after arriving at Forest Grove, winter of 1845/6.
  *A girl—b. 1836, Indiana or Arkansas; d. winter of 1845/46, Washington Co., Oregon.

*Pugh, William Porter—b. 9 March 1818, Sullivan Co., Indiana; d. 2 February 1878; DLC No. 1110, Marion Co.; William's wife d. en route to Oregon at Big Sandy River in Wyoming; he m. 2nd, Mrs. Florinda Davidson (Hall) Lawton, daughter of James E. Hall (*see* Roster), 15 September 1857, Marion Co., Oregon.
Children:
  *Andrew—b. abt 1843, Arkansas.

(Two sons d. en route to Oregon at Big Sandy River in Wyoming.)

*Ridgeway, John—b. 30 March 1808, Lincoln Co., Kentucky; d. abt 1871, Polk Co., Oregon; DLC No. 3593, Polk Co.; first settled near Dallas, then Buell, Oregon.

*Ridgeway, Tabitha—b. 20 May 1822, Kentucky; d. 4 November 1877, Sheridan, Yamhill Co., Oregon; m. John, 22 April 1836, Sangamon Co., Illinois; sister to Elizabeth Liggett (*see* Roster).
Children:
*John—b. abt 1841, Buchanan Co., Missouri; d. 1 May 1914, near Buell, Oregon.
*William—b. 3 September 1842, Buchanan Co., Missouri; d. 6 August 1911, Polk Co., Oregon; m. Matilda J. Blair, 30 July 1878; settled at Mill Creek, Polk County, Oregon, where he farmed.
*Lindsey—b. abt 1844, Buchanan Co., Missouri.

Riggs, James Berry—b. 21 March 1802, Adair Co., Kentucky; d. 15 August 1870, Dallas, Oregon; DLC No. 2301, Polk Co.

Riggs, Nancy C. (Anderson)—b. abt 1803, South Carolina; d. July 1869, Polk Co.; m. James, 28 April 1824, Lawrence Co., Illinois.
Children:
Milton Scott—b. 18 January 1825, Morgan Co., Illinois; d. 26 November 1893, Burns, Oregon; DLC No. 1807, Lane Co.; m. Eliza Hampton (*see* Roster) , 5 August 1851, Yamhill Co., Oregon.
See Allen, Hannah Riggs (Mrs. James). She was a twin to Milton.
Rufus Anderson—b. 27 November 1827, Morgan Co., Illinois; d. 3 April 1898; DLC No. 2351, Polk Co.; m. Evaline H. Nicklin, 21 November 1851, Polk Co., Oregon. She was b. 1830, Virginia.

Marion L.—b. 17 May 1830, Illinois; d. 1847, Polk Co., Oregon.

Washington L.—b. 14 August 1833, Illinois; DLC No. 1628, Lane Co.; m. Matilda S. Robinson, 29 January 1850, Polk Co., Oregon.

Silas T.—b. 17 April, 1836, Missouri; m. Sarah M. Butler, 4 November 1857.

Louisa M.—b. 28 February 1839, Missouri.

Silbey A.—b. 5 March 1842.

Ritner, Sebastian R.—b. 1815, Helvetic Confederacy, Switzerland; d. 10 September 1887, Pedee, Oregon; DLC No. 4582, Polk Co.; m. Sarah (Woodling) Ritner, widow of Sebastian's brother John, 20 October 1854, Benton Co., Oregon.

Ross, Sherry—b. 11 February 1824, Wayne Co., Indiana; d. 4 January 1867, Portland, Oregon; DLC No. 3122, Clackamas Co.; m. Rebecca F. Deardorff, 20 November 1851, Milwaukie, Oregon; Sherry owned the land now known as Ross Island at Portland, Oregon; shared the claim with his uncle, Daniel McKinney (*see* Roster).

St. Clair, Wayman—b. 1816, Kentucky; d. 11 January 1872, Corvallis, Oregon; DLC No. 3821, Benton Co.; m. Mahala Jane Johnson, 21 September 1851, Benton Co., Oregon.

*Sanders, John—name appears on the Hiram Smith death list of 1845; the Alfred Marquam family (*see* Roster) records report, "Alfred Marquam with his family, wife and two children, his father-in-law and mother-in-law, Ezekiel and Elizabeth Burbage, lived one year at Oregon City. They lost all their clothing and everything they had except the clothes they were wearing. All was upset in the Clackamas rapids at the mouth of the Clackamas River in sight of Oregon City, a haven of rest after the long and tedious journey of nine months of peril and hardships from being lost on Meek's Cutoff . . . a man by the name of Sanders was drowned when the raft upset in the Clackamas rapids." It has not been established that the drowned man was John Sanders, but it is certainly possible.

*Schoonover, Peter—b. abt 1805, N.Y.; d. sometime after 1884, California; owned land at Table Bluff, Humboldt Co., California, by 1866; believed to be the father of Elizabeth (Schoonover) Meek (*see* Roster) and stated by Meek descendants to have made the trip to Oregon in 1845.

*Schoonover, _____ (Mrs.).
Children:
It is not presently known if there were other children with the Schoonovers besides Mrs. Stephen H. L. Meek.

Scott, Prior—b. 18 January 1825, Switzerland Co., Indiana; d. 1891; DLC No. 841 Benton Co.; m. Mary Jones Scott, widow of Prior's brother, 15 February 1852, Benton Co., Oregon; operated blacksmith shop in Corvallis, Oregon. Mary d. 23 February 1886 at 57 years, 10 months, 11 days.

Shaser, George Washington—b. 15 July 1815, Erie Co., N.Y.; d. 1899, Thurston Co., Washington, where he had settled; a trapper, guide, scout, before his trip to Oregon.

Shaser, Margaret (Packwood)—b. 28 April 1832, Indiana; d. 17 March 1921, Thurston Co., Washington; m. George, on the plains, 7 May 1845 (now Brown Co., Kansas).

Simpson, Isaac M.—b. 4 July 1813, Oglethorpe Co., Georgia; d. 11 July 1887, Oregon; DLC No. 1252, Polk Co.

Simpson, Martha (Jackson)—b. 8 November 1815, Tennessee; d. 22 November 1912, Polk Co.; m. Isaac, 16 August 1835, Lawrence Co., Arkansas.
Children:
Amos Carol—b. 1836/7, Lawrence Co., Arkansas.

Marshall W.—b. 13 July 1838, Lawrence Co., Arkansas; d. 26 August 1930, Benton Co., Oregon; first settled in Polk Co., then located at Elk City, Oregon, where he was proprietor of the Simpson House, postmaster, and storekeeper; m. Joice A. Bevens, 14 June 1859, Polk Co., Oregon.

Eliza—b. 25 January 1841, Arkansas; d. 1 October 1922, The Dalles, Oregon; m. Lafayette W. Loughary, July, 1858. He was b. 2 September 1832; d. 20 July 1915.

Simpson, Rice W.—b. 1 September 1808, Oglethorpe Co., Georgia; d. 14 March 1883, Polk Co., Oregon; DLC No. 1251, Polk Co.

Simpson, Rebecca—b. 8 October 1812, Tennessee; d. 22 March 1865, Airlie, Oregon; m. Rice, 7 October 1828, Franklin Co., Tennessee.
Children:
Sophia—b. 1837, Arkansas; m. Burres Hastings, 5 March 1854, Polk Co., Oregon Territory; DLC No. 3377, Polk Co.

Henderson—b. 30 January 1841, Franklin Co., Arkansas; d. 1904; went to Montana at twenty years of age to engage in mining; settled near Airlie, Oregon, where he m. Martha Faulkenberry; began a logging business operation on Luckiamute River in 1883. In the 1850 census Henderson's name is not given; but the name "Alfred" is and the age given was Henderson's. The compiler feels the name refers to Henderson rather than another Simpson child.

Albert—b. abt 1843, Arkansas.

Smeed, Hiram N.—b. 26 November 1824, Cattaraugus Co., N.Y.; DLC No. 989, Linn Co.; m. Rachael Jane Wood, 17 February 1849, Linn Co.; second man to locate on the site of Albany, Oregon.

*Smith, Adam—appears on the Tetherow roster as cattle driver and a member of the muster roll; m. Elizabeth Comer, 9 June 1841, Missouri; she did not come with him. They were divorced May, 1847, Oregon. It appears he was traveling with Ezekiel Smith (*see* Roster) and other relatives. He was b. 1828, Bavaria.

Smith, Alanson Perry—b. 1815, Union Co., Indiana; DLC No. 1074, Clackamas Co., Oregon; m. Harriet Vanneva McNary, 15 May 1847, Clackamas Co. (*see* Roster). According to James McNary descendant, Victor W. Jones, Redmond, Washington, Alanson joined with the McNary famiy on the 1845 trip.

Smith, Alexander—d. 1851, Honolulu, Sandwich Islands; came with his brother, Green Berry (*see* Roster).

*Smith, Alvis—b. 1808, Orange Co., North Carolina; DLC No. 2702, Marion Co.

*Smith, Sarah N. (Pugh)—b. 18 May 1814, Tennessee; m. Alvis, 17/18 May 1832, Warren Co., Indiana; sister to John, William, and Silas Pugh (*see* Roster).
Children:
*Nancy—b. abt 1834, Indiana.
*Sarah Ann—b. 3 December 1837, Arkansas; m. John Quincy Wilson, 13 May 1858, Marion Co., Oregon.
*Polly—b. abt 1839, Arkansas.
*Eliza—b. abt 1841, Arkansas.
*Mariah—b. 1845, on way to Oregon.

*Smith, Ezekiel—appears as a cattle driver for the Adam Smith group, Tetherow roster.

*Smith, ____ (Mrs.)—believed to be along with the Tetherow Train.
Children:
See Martin, Malinda Smith (Mrs. John).

*Adam Smith (*see* Roster), believed to be a son.

Rebecca Hamilton (*see* Mrs. Robert Hamilton), believed to be a daughter.

*Smith, George—appears as the head of a family on the Tetherow roster, and a Private with the train.

*Smith, ____ (Mrs.)—believed to be along with the Tetherow Train.
Children:
*George W.—listed as a private with the Tetherow Train; believed to be a son to George.
*Two girls, under the age of 14, names unknown.
*Three boys, under the age of 16, names unknown.

*Smith, George D.—b. 1824, Ohio; settled in Marion Co.; shoemaker; listed with the Tetherow Train as a private.

Smith, Green Berry—b. 10 September 1820, Grayson Co., Virginia; d. 7 May 1886, Corvallis, Oregon; DLC No. 2322, Benton Co., on Soap Creek near Corvallis; engaged in stock business in 1862 in what is now Gilliam Co.; retired on his ranch at Corvallis fifteen years later; m. 1st, Eliza Hughart (*see* Roster), 2 March 1848; after Eliza's death m. 2nd, Mary Baker, 21 February 1850, Benton Co. Green Berry was a brother to Alexander Smith (*see* Roster).

*Smith, James Preston—b. 1819, Hopkins Co., Kentucky; DLC No. 828, Polk Co.

*Smith, Rebecca (English)—b. Kentucky; m. James, 14 March 1839, Des Moines Co., Iowa.
Children:
*Levin Nelson—b. 1840, Missouri.
*Ellen—b. 1842, Missouri.
*William—b. en route to the Willamette Valley, Oregon Territory.

Smith, Paschal (Pascal)—b. September 1823, Sangamon Co., Illinois; DLC No. 4814, Polk Co.; m. Eliza Ann ____, 22 September 1851, Polk Co., Oregon.

Smith, "Pack Horse"—reported by the Herrens to have been with them in the finding of water on the Cutoff. He is never further identified.

Stewart, John—b. 12 February 1799, Washington Co., Virginia; d. 28 February 1885, Corvallis, Oregon; DLC No. 175, Benton Co.

Stewart, Mary (Scott)—b. 1 June 1821, Switzerland Co., Indiana; sister to Prior Scott (*see* Roster); d. 31 December 1913, Corvallis, Oregon; m. John, a widower with several children, 7 January 1842, Holt Co., Missouri. She was the first white woman to live in the area now known as Corvallis—the original name of the city, Marysville, being applied in her honor.
Children:
Archimedes (Kim)—b. 1827, Tippecanoe Co., Indiana; DLC No. 176, Benton Co.; m. Matilda Grimsley, 19 October 1848, Benton Co., Oregon; m. 2nd, Margaret J. Walker, 21 March 1860, Linn Co.
Minerva A.—b. abt 1829, Indiana; m. Elizie (or Elgy) C. Dice, 28 September 1848, Benton Co., Oregon; DLC No. 1209, Polk Co.; he was b. 1816, Adair Co., Kentucky; they lived in Umatilla Co. in 1870.
Hugh—b. abt 1834, Indiana; killed by Indians in southern Oregon while driving cattle to the mines in California, September, 1854.
Elizabeth—b. abt 1838, Indiana; m. 1st, L.M. Rininger, Whitman Co., Washington; m. 2nd, ____ McDonald, Washington Territory.
John W.—b. 18 August 1841, Holt Co., Missouri; m. Mahala Stewart (cousin); settled near Tacoma, Washington.

Calvin N.—b. 5 February 1843, Holt Co., Missouri; d. 2 May 1915, Albany, Oregon; m. Barbara A. ____; settled in Benton Co., Oregon. She was b. 6 June 1836; d. 24 June 1890, Benton Co.

*Sullivan, Isaac—listed on the Tetherow roster as a private; apparently single or alone.

Sweet, Zara (Zana) T.—b. 2 November 1815, Pittsburgh, Pa.; d. September 1892, Mapleton, Oregon; DLC No. 1798, Lane Co.; at times lived in California.

Sweet, Sarah Maria (Stephens)—b. 12 September 1819, Montreal, Canada; m. Zara, July, 1840, Stark Co., Illinois; d. 25 March 1884 at Mapleton, Oregon.
Children:
Wallace G.—b. 14 October 1843, Knox Co., Illinois; lived in Lane Co., Oregon.

Switzler, John—b. 29 September 1789, Orange Co., Virginia; d. March 1860; m. 1st, Elizabeth Lee, 1811—she d. in 1826, leaving three children; DLC No. 137, Clackamas Co.

Switzler, Marie (Robinson)—b. abt 1808, Warrensburg, Missouri; d. May 1850, Clackamas Co.; m. John, 12 April 1827, Warrensburg, Missouri.
Children:
See Wilson, Sarah Switzler Logsdon (Mrs. G. Anthony Wilson).
Joseph Robinson—b. 26 September 1829, Saline Co., Missouri; d. 22 February 1865, Clackamas Co., Oregon; m. Mary Wolf, 9 March 1848, Clackamas Co.; m. 2nd, Elizabeth ____, 21 April 1861, Clackamas Co.; located south side of the Columbia River; DLC No. 1322, Clackamas Co.
Jehu Robinson—b. 3 September 1831, Boone Co., Missouri; d. 4 February 1908, Mesa, Arizona; m. 1st,

Margaret Eleanor Nye, 27 April 1861; m. 2nd, Eliza-
beth Kuykendall, 11 June 1877; lived in Clackamas,
Multnomah, and Umatilla counties; DLC No. 2305,
Multnomah Co.

William B. G.—b. 7 December 1834, Saline Co., Missouri; d. 23 October 1883, Umatilla, Oregon; per-
formed services as a scout and interpreter for the
government; was a merchant at Pendleton in 1869; m.
1st, Elizabeth Hale, 1870; m. 2nd, Ellen Catherine
O'Hearn.

Cynthia Charity—b. abt 1836, Saline Co., Missouri; d.
1881 at Vancouver, Washington; m. 1st, John Wirt
Nye, 31 August 1851, Vancouver, Washington; m.
2nd, Benjamin F. Shaw, 1871.

Martha Frances—b. abt 1838, Saline Co., Missouri; d.
abt. 1856, Multnomah Co., Oregon.

John B.—b. 16 May 1839, Saline Co., Missouri; d. 6
October 1924, Umatilla, Oregon; m. Mary Ann
Smoot, 3 January 1866, Montana; she d. 20 April
1914; lived in California, eastern Oregon (1875), and
Walla Walla, Washington; raised horses and engaged
in real-estate business.

Harriet Jane—b. 29 June 1844, Saline Co., Missouri; m.
Adam Wirt Nye, 18 November 1865, Portland, Oregon; her husband operated a furniture business in
Pendleton, Oregon; he also had orchards and farmland
at Pendleton, once served as sheriff of Umatilla Co.

Mary Ann Margaret—d. at eighteen years of age.

Terwilliger, James—b. 3 October 1809, Ulster Co., N.Y.; d.
1 September 1892, Portland, Oregon; DLC No. 1078,
Multnomah Co.; blacksmith; built his shop and cabin on
a lot at First and Morrison streets, the first buildings in
Portland.

Terwilliger, Sophronia Ann (Hurd)—d. October 1845, at The
Dalles, after arriving from the Meek Cutoff trip. She m.

James, 1833, Tompkins Co., New York; James m. 2nd, Mrs. Philenda Lee Green, April, 1848, who d. 1873.

Children:

Lorenzo—b. abt 1834; reputed one of a ring of horse thieves, killed with two others by Indian members of the gang on the headwaters of Deschutes River (not Rogue River), 1851. The posse which found the bodies apprehended the Indians with the horses at Columbia River.—*Oregon Spectator,* November 11 & December 16, 1851.

John—b. abt 1836; d. 1849 in the California gold diggings of quinsy (tonsillitis).

Hiram—b. 6 March 1840, Vernon, Ohio; d. 1918, Portland, Oregon; m. Mary E. Edwards, 13 July 1869, Tillamook, Oregon; operated a dairy business at Tillamook for six years, then returned to Portland to help his father with real-estate sales.

Charlotte Ann—b. 21 December 1842, Chicago, Illinois; d. 20 July 1915; m. 1st, Walter Moffett, 12 April 1860, Multnomah Co., Oregon; m. 2nd, Charles M. Cartwright, 8 March 1887; her first husband died at sea in 1878; she and her second husband lived in Eastern Oregon.

*Terwilliger, Ruth—1845 pioneer listed by Sarah Walden Cummins in her *Reminiscences*; no other information known.

Tetherow, David—b. abt. 1805, French Broad River, Tennessee; brother to Solomon (*see* Roster); settled at Hillsboro, Oregon; d. 1846.

Tetherow, Ruth (Southwood)—b. abt 1814, Kentucky; after husband David's death, she m. John G. Wilson, 15 August 1850, Benton Co., Oregon; settled in Linn Co.; DLC No. 2680.

Children:

Mary Ann—b. abt 1831, Illinois; m. Randal Yarbrough, 13 May 1849, Linn Co., Oregon; DLC No. 2095, Linn Co.

George W.—b. 2 April 1834, Burlington, Lee Co., Iowa; m. Elizabeth Miller, 11 November 1857, Linn Co., Oregon; moved to Josephine Co., 1861, where he farmed.

Edith E.—b. abt 1835, Burlington, Lee Co., Iowa; m. John W. Newman (*see* Roster), 20 May 1851, Clackamas Co., Oregon; DLC No. 2849, Clackamas Co.; freighted from The Dalles to Canyon City in 1862.

John—b. abt 1838, Missouri; m. Lily Foland; buried, Waterville, Washington.

Solomon S.—b. 26 March 1841, Clay Co., Missouri; d. 2 May 1926, Wenatchee, Washington; m. Nancy Jane Crossley, 20 April 1865; settled in Lane Co. She was b. 31 December 1849, Mercer Co., Missouri.

Ellen—b. abt 1844, Clay Co., Missouri; m. Joel T. Broiles, 9 July 1860, Clackamas Co., Oregon.

William Henry—b. 1845, Rocky Mountains, en route to Oregon; m. Polk Co., Oregon widow; he is buried at Tieton, Washington.

Tetherow, Solomon—b. 28 March 1800, French Broad River, Tennessee; d. 15 February 1879, Polk Co., Oregon; DLC No. 3567, Polk Co.; his land was on the Luckiamute River, his home destroyed when the U.S. Government purchased the land for Camp Adair during World War II days. Solomon had accompanied General Ashley on his expedition to the headwaters of the Missouri and Yellowstone rivers, operated a trading post for American Fur and was a pilot of the first steamboat on the upper Mississippi before coming West.

Tetherow, Ibba (Baker)—b. 15 September 1806, North Carolina; d. 25 March 1869, Polk Co., Oregon; m. Solomon, 2 April 1823, Clay Co., Missouri.

Children:

Amos—b. 21 January 1827, Missouri; d. young.

Evaline—b. 27 March 1828, Missouri; d. 26 February 1916, Airlie, Oregon; m. Paul Hiltibrand (*see* Roster), 2 July 1846, Polk Co., Oregon; DLC No. 3229, Polk Co.

Lucinda—b. 1 August 1830, Missouri; m. William Glenn Parker, 25 January 1847, Polk Co., Oregon; DLC No. 3445, Polk Co.

Matilda—b. 30 October 1832, Missouri.

Andrew Jackson—b. 20 June 1834, Daviess Co., Missouri; DLC No. 3540, Polk Co.; m. Sophronia Crow, 23 April 1854, Polk Co.; settled in central Oregon in 1879; operated a ferry on the Deschutes River at what is now known as Tetherow Bridge, near Redmond, Oregon.

Samuel Houston—b. 6 March 1836, Platte Co., Missouri; settled at Dallas, Oregon; d. 1925 Fall City, Oregon; m. 1st, Henrietta Griffith, 16 December 1858, Polk Co., Oregon; m. 2nd, Isoline Holman, 3 September 1891.

Thomas Benton—b. 12 February 1838, Platte Co., Missouri; d. 3 March 1918, Polk Co., Oregon; settled at Monmouth, Oregon; m. Martha McLoughlin, 18 November 1858, Buena Vista, Oregon. She was b. 24 May 1842; d. 6 December 1920.

Emily—b. 21 January 1840, Missouri; d. 5 January 1910; m. Harry (Henry?) Christian, 4 December 1856. He was b. 17 July 1832; d. 31 August 1910; DLC No. 551, Umpqua Co., Oregon.

David Acheson—b. 12 February 1843, Missouri; d. 31 May 1845, "on the plains," en route to Oregon (Nebraska Territory).

William Linn—b. 12 February 1843, Missouri; twin to David Acheson; m. Angeline Johnson, 5 December 1861, Polk Co., Oregon.

*Thompson, Lewis—b. 1809, Covington, Kentucky; d. 18 October 1897, Oakland, California; DLC No. 2975, Clatsop Co.; m. Sarah Ann Sheadle, 18 October 1848, Oregon; organized the second Presbyterian church in Oregon, Warrenton, on Clatsop Plains.

*Thompson, William—listed as second lieutenant with the Tetherow Train. There is a William Thompson, 51, b. Kentucky, listed in the Douglas Co., Oregon, 1870 Census, with wife Susan (Indian), 27, b. California, and 4 children (b. Oregon).

Tull, William—*see* Powell, Theophilus; William was a stepson.

T'Vault, William Green—b. 23 March 1806, Davidson Co., Tennessee; d. 4 February 1869, Jacksonville, Oregon, from smallpox; first editor of a newspaper on the Pacific Coast, *The Oregon. Spectator* at Oregon City; later edited *The Sentinel* at Jacksonville, and other papers.

T'Vault, Rhoda Boone (Burns)—b. 1811, Kentucky; d. 4 June 1886, Jacksonville, Oregon; m. William, 11 July 1829, Warrick Co., Indiana; niece to Daniel Boone.
Children:
Elizabeth—b. 14 December 1834, Warrick Co., Indiana; d. 20 October 1911, Jacksonville, Oregon; m. Daniel Kenney, 18 February 1855, Jackson Co., Oregon.
Marian—b. 1836, Indiana; d. 1870, Portland, Oregon.
George—b. 1838, Indiana; d. 1857, Jacksonville, Oregon.

Vaughan, William Tyler—b. 22 October 1808, Cabell Co., West Virginia; d. 18 November 1888, Lane Co., Oregon; m. Phoebe (Phebe) Hazlett, 26 December 1827, Cabell

Co., West Virginia; DLC No. 1500, Linn Co.; came alone in 1845; returned in 1846 to bring his family to Oregon, 1847, acting as captain of a wagon train.

*Walker, Clairbourn C.—b. 1 March 1819, Wythe Co., Virginia; d. 30 December 1902, at Spring Valley, in Polk Co., Oregon; DLC No. 821, Polk Co.; m. Louisa Purvine, 4 July 1850; brother to Wellington B. Walker (*see* Roster) and a cousin to Andrew J. Doak (*see* Roster).

Walker, Ellis—b. 1819, Missouri; brother to Jesse Walker (*see* Roster); DLC No. 2996, Washington Co.; m. Sarah Ann Bozarth, 23 September 1847, Oregon.

Walker, Jesse—b. 1815, Howard Co., Missouri; d. 18 August 1855; DLC No. 956, Jackson Co.; brother to Ellis (*see* Roster).

Walker, Nancy Magaha (Miller)—b. abt 1816, Kentucky; m. Jesse, 28 April 1834, Howard Co., Missouri.
Children:
James William—b. 8 February 1836, Howard Co., Missouri; m. Mary Harrell, 1866; settled in Clatsop Co., Oregon.
Elizabeth Ann—b. 1837, Howard Co., Missouri; d. 1899; m. William Bybee, 16 November 1854; settled in Jackson Co., Oregon, 1854.
Sarah Jane—b. 1842, Howard Co., Missouri; m. Eli Ledford; settled in Jackson Co., Oregon.

*Walker, Thomas—b. 1830, Missouri; probably a brother to Jesse and Ellis Walker (*see* Roster); was living with Jesse and family in 1850.

*Walker, Wellington B.—b. 1824, Wythe Co., Virginia; DLC No. 2127, Polk Co.; m. Catharine ____, 20 September 1849, Marion Co., Oregon; brother to Clairbourn Walker (*see* Roster) and cousin to Andrew J. Doak (*see* Roster).

Wallace, William T.—b. 1813, Shelby Co., Kentucky; d. 1899, Lincoln Co., Oregon; DLC. No. 3161, Yamhill Co.; later went to California and southern Oregon.

Wallace, Susannah R. (Herren)—b. 1826, Shelby Co., Kentucky; d. 1906, Lincoln Co., Oregon; m. William, 25 May 1841, Platte Co., Missouri.
Children:
Maria Jane—b. 6 March 1842, Weston, Missouri; d. 4 December 1863; m. Norval Thomas, 8 July 1858.

Walter, William—b. 25 October 1780, Baltimore, Maryland; d. abt 1868, Hillsboro, Oregon; DLC No. 62, Washington Co.

Walter, Rachel (Doddridge)—b. 10 May 1783, Pennsylvania; d. October 1849, California; m. William, 1804, Washington Co., Pennsylvania.
Children:
See McKinney, Henry Ann Walter (Mrs. William).
Sarah—b. 1812, Washington Co., Pennsylvania; never married.
Phillip D.—b. 25 January 1816, Wayne Co., Indiana; never married; d. 2 July 1900, Waitsburg, Washington.
See Cox, Julia Ann Walter (Mrs. Anderson).
Matilda—b. 1824, Wayne Co., Indiana; m. Hugh O'Bryant, 1852, who became the first mayor of Portland, Oregon.
William, Jr.—b. 7 December 1827, Wayne Co., Indiana; d. 23 September 1906, Waitsburg, Washington; DLC No. 332, Douglas Co.; m. Charity Marsh, 13 November 1855, Washington Co., Oregon; she d. 1897, Waitsburg, Washington.
Grandchildren: These two children had been orphaned by 1845 and accompanied the Walters to Oregon. that

year. Their mother was Rebecca (b. 1810, Pa.) Walter who m. Grant Allred.

Joseph Allred—b. 1833, Indiana; DLC No. 240, Douglas Co.; d. California; m. Mary Martin (daughter of John Martin—*see* Roster), 4 September 1853, Polk Co., Oregon.

Eliza Ann Allred.

Watt, Joseph—b. 4 November 1816, Knox Co., Ohio; d. 28 May 1867; DLC No. 4774, Yamhill Co.; cabinetmaker; m. Sarah Elizabeth Craft (*see* Roster), 26 August 1846.

Waymire, Frederick A.—b. 15 March 1807, Montgomery Co., Ohio; d. 28 April 1873, Salem, Oregon; DLC No. 4585, Polk Co.; mechanic; sheriff of Polk Co., 1846; served several years with the territorial and state legislatures, helped to form the Oregon State Constitution; brother to John (*See* Roster).

Waymire, Francis (Cochrane)—b. 19 January 1810, Fayette Co., Ohio; d. 15 October 1878; sister to Mrs. Job McNemee (*see* Roster); m. Frederick, 11 October 1827, Tippecanoe Co., Indiana.

Children:

Elizabeth—b. 18 July 1833, Logansport, Cass Co., Indiana; d. 6 September 1862, Polk Co., Oregon; m. Wm. Williams, 18 April 1852, Polk Co.

Stephen K.—b. 26 March 1836, Cass Co., Indiana; d. 9 November 1879.

Eliza Ann—b. 1 March 1839, Buchanan Co., Missouri; d. 23 May 1862, Hayden Hall, Polk Co., Oregon; m. Thomas Townsend, 21 January 1858, Polk Co., Oregon. Thomas m. 2nd, Minerva Waymire, daughter of John Waymire.

George Washington—b. 5 February 1844, St. Joseph, Missouri; d. 20 September 1858, Polk Co., Oregon.

Jefferson—b. 25 September 1845, Meek Cutoff; d. 15 November 1845, Linnton, Oregon.

Waymire, John—b. December, 1813, Montgomery Co., Ohio; d. 2 August 1891; DLC No. 4129, Polk Co.; built the first wharf in Portland; settled in Dallas, Oregon, to work as a carpenter and merchant; brother to Fred (*see* Roster). John had three marriages.

Waymire, Clarissa H. (Arbo)—b. 11 February 1822, New York; d. 14 September 1869, Dallas, Oregon; m. John, 15 March 1838, Logansport, Indiana.
Children:
Louisa Jane—b. 26 May 1837, Logansport, Indiana; m. Charles Ham, 16 May 1852, Polk Co., Oregon; DLC No. 5223, Polk Co.
Elvira—b. abt 1842, Missouri; m. M.S. Brown, 16 January 1859, Polk Co., Oregon.
Clarissa T. "Mary"—b. 15 December 1844, Missouri.

*Wheeler, Solomon—b. 1814, Smith Co., Virginia; DLC No. 4565, Clackamas Co.

*Wheeler, Melissa Elizabeth (Foster)—b. 1823, Scott Co., Kentucky; d. 1894, Hillsboro, Oregon; daughter of John Foster (*see* Roster); m. Solomon, 9 March 1845, Cass Co., Missouri.

*Wheeler, William—b. 8 May 1826, Ashland Co., Ohio; DLC No. 1133, Clackamas Co.; miller; moved to Douglas Co., 1865; m. Mary Ellen Armpriest, 25 July 1850, Clackamas Co., Oregon. She drowned with 2 children in Umpqua River, August 1876.

*White, Edward Newton—b. 27 April 1828, Hancock Co., Illinois; DLC No. 666, Linn Co.; lived in Prineville (Crook Co.), Oregon, 1885, and engaged in the stock business; m. 1st, Catherine J. Burkhart, 2 July 1848, Linn

Co., Oregon; she d. 1859; m. 2nd, Anna Woodsides, brother to Nancy Hawkins and Samuel Simpson White (*see* Roster).

*White, John S.—b. 5 November 1828, Gibson Co., Tennessee; d. 1 September 1886, Weston, Oregon; DLC No. 607, Washington Co.; m. Elizabeth Lenox, 23 December 1847, Washington Co., Oregon; moved to Umatilla Co., 1861.

White, Nancy (Atherton)—b. 1794, Kentucky; d. 11 April 1864, Oregon; widow of Edwin White (d. 1818).
Children:
See White, Samuel Simpson.
See Hawkins, Nancy White.
See White, Edward Newton.

White, Samuel Simpson—b. 11 December 1811, Butler Co., Indiana; d. 6 January 1901, Portland, Oregon; first Probate Judge in Oregon, appointed by Gov. George Abernethy in 1846; DLC No. 634, Clackamas Co.; settled near Oregon City.

White, Huldah (Jennings)—b. abt 1812, Kentucky; d. 1894; m. Samuel, 6 May 1831, Warren Co., Illinois.
Children:
Edward Milton—b. 1832, Illinois; preceded father in death.
Nancy Jane—b. April, 1834, Iowa; d. 5 December 1859; m. J. C. Ainsworth, 24 April 1851, Clackamas Co., Oregon.
William Linn—b. abt 1839, Iowa; preceded father in death; perhaps the William White of Sauvies Island who m. Lizzie France of Columbia Co., 25 December 1859 on Sauvies Island, Oregon.

*Whitlock, Mitchell—b. 9 February 1822, Howard Co., Missouri; d. 27 January 1898, Marion Co., Oregon; DLC No.

3143, Marion Co.; m. Malvina Engle (*see* Roster), 2 July 1846, Clackamas Co.

Wilcox, Ralph—b. 9 July 1818, East Bloomfield (Ontario Co.), New York; d. 18 April 1877, Portland, Oregon; DLC No. 216, Washington Co.; first teacher and first physician in Portland, a member of the territorial legislature, Washington Co. judge, and land office registrar.

Wilcox, Julia Ann (Fickle)—b. 16 August 1823, Lee Co., Virginia; d. February, 1915, probably Portland, Oregon; m. Ralph, 11 October 1840, Platte Co., Missouri; sister to Mrs. John Jacob Hampton (*see* Roster).
Children:
Francis—b. abt 1844, Missouri.

*Wiley, Richard Evert—b. 23 September 1823, Carthage (Hamilton Co.), Ohio; d. 27 May 1889, Hillsboro, Oregon; m. Jane Baldra, 24 July 1855, Washington Co., Oregon; settled at Hillsboro, Oregon; merchant. Jane was b. 1840, Oregon; d. 1926, Hillsboro.

*Williams, James Edward—b. 6 January 1803, Grainger Co., Tennessee; d. 13 March 1865, Airlie, Polk Co., Oregon; DLC No. 4692, Polk Co.

*Williams, Martha (Wichen)—b. 1807, Virginia; d. 6 August 1881; m. James, 17 October 1825, Knox Co., Tennessee.
Children:
*Jonathan Lafayette—b. 7 March 1826, Grainger Co., Tennessee; d. 24 January 1907, Polk Co., Oregon; DLC No. 4968, Polk Co.; m. Lydia King (*see* Roster), 23 December 1847, Benton Co., Oregon.
*Orlena M.—b. 4 March 1827, Tennessee; d. 24 March 1906, Polk Co., Oregon; m. Isaac Staats, 10 May 1846, Polk Co., Oregon; DLC No. 4710, Polk Co. Isaac also arrived in 1845, via the regular Oregon

Trail. He was b. 23 September 1814, Albany, New York; d. 2 August 1888, Polk Co., Oregon.

*John James—b. 5 January 1830, Grainger Co., Tennessee; d. 31 August 1913, Dallas, Oregon; DLC No. 4673, Polk Co.; m. 1st, Sarah English, 1 June 1852, Polk Co. (she d. 13 November 1861); m. 2nd, Alice Eckersley, 1863, Auburn (she d. 28 June 1876); m. 3rd, Mrs. Annie M. (Larned) Stiles, 22 December 1889 (she d. 27 September 1915); sheriff of Polk Co., 1874.

*P. Wesley—b. 7 July 1832, Jefferson Co., Tennessee; DLC No. 4676, Polk Co.; m. Emma Snelling, Benton Co., Oregon.

*Mary—b. abt 1839, Tennessee; m. Luther M. Doolittle.

*Thomas—b. abt 1841, Tennessee; settled at Independence, Oregon; m. Susan Faulkenberry, 5 September 1862, Polk Co., Oregon.

*Wayne W.—b. 1 March 1845, Jackson Co., Missouri; d. 27 March, 1904, The Dalles, Oregon; m. Virginia A. Tarter, 30 August 1868; settled at Independence, Oregon.

*Malissa Ann—b. Tennessee (probably abt 1834); m. Henry Fuller (*see* Roster), 16 August 1850, Polk Co., Oregon; DLC No. 3773, Polk Co.

*Whitley, Samuel—b. 1789, Virginia; d. 30 September 1868, Jefferson, Marion Co., Oregon; DLC No. 768, Marion Co.

Whitley, Catharine "Kitty"—b. 26 April 1791, Fayette Co., Kentucky, (sister to Alexander and James McNary; *See* Roster).
Children:
Eliza—b. abt 1826, Illinois; m. Lewis C. Richardson, 15 August 1852, Marion Co.; DLC 2695, Linn Co.
Julia—b. abt 1827, Illinois.

John Harvey—b. abt 1828, Morgan Co., Illinois; d. 21 December 1859, Marion Co.; DLC No. 2697, Linn. Co.

Catharine—b. abt 1829, Illinois; m. E.S. Gilkerson.

*Wilson, Amariah—name appearing on the Bancroft immigration list of 1845 and on the assessment roll for Washington Co., Oregon, 1846; no further information.

Wilson, G. Anthony—b. abt 1819, Chariton Co., Missouri; d. 14 February 1849, Hangtown, California.

Wilson, Sarah (Switzler) Logsdon—b. abt 1817, Kentucky; d. 6 April 1852, Multnomah Co., Oregon; daughter of John Switzler (*see* Roster); m. Anthony, 1839, Saline Co., Missouri; after Anthony's death, Sarah m. 3rd, Thomas H. Stoddard, 10 April 1851, Clackamas Co., Oregon.; DLC No. 3994, Clackamas/Multnomah Co.
Children:
Mary Elizabeth Logsdon—b. 17 May 1838, Missouri; m. Wm. Levi Farell, 1853; moved to Texas.
Minerva Catherine Wilson—b. 30 October 1841, Missouri; m. Jesse T. Bowles; DLC No. 3177, Washington Co.
John Greenville Wilson—b. 1842, Missouri; moved to San Francisco.
James Hamilton Wilson—b. 1843, Missouri.

Wilson, William—d. October, 1845, at The Dalles, Oregon, after arrival via the Meek Cutoff.

Wilson, Lucinda (Carter) McWilliams—b. 2 July 1810, Woodford Co., Kentucky; d. 4 November 1879; was first married, 1828, to John McWilliams; she m. William Wilson, 30 August 1834, Boone Co., Missouri; m. 3rd, David Hill, 4 June 1846 (Hillsboro, Oregon, named after him); m. 4th, Wheelock Simmons, 6 December 1850,

Washington Co., Oregon; Lucinda was second wife to William Wilson.
Children:
Mary Helen McWilliams—b. 12 March 1830, Liberty (Clay Co.), Missouri; d. 9 August 1919, Hillsboro, Oregon; daughter to Lucinda Wilson and John McWilliams; m. Michael Moore, 7 October 1847, Washington Co.; DLC No. 558, Washington Co.
Margaret Wilson—b. 1 March 1830, Clay Co., Missouri; d. 27 October 1905, Riddle, Oregon; m. John S. Catching (*see* Roster), 9/10 May 1847; DLC No. 399, Douglas Co.; settled at Riddle.
William L. Wilson—b. 3 May 1832, Clay Co., Missouri; DLC No. 305, Douglas Co.; settled at Cow Creek, Douglas Co., 1853; m. 1st, Hulda N. Mynatt, 24 December 1854, Douglas Co.; m. 2nd, Harriet Haskins, 5 May 1861.
(Also traveling with the Wilson family was Mathias Cooley, orphan. *See* Roster.)

Wooley, Jacob—b. 1796, Sussex Co., New Jersey; d. 26 May 1865, Hillsboro, Oregon; DLC No. 149, Washington Co.

Wooley, Eleanor Rose (Hoover)—b. abt 1795, Pennsylvania; m. Jacob, 12 July 1821, New Lexington, Perry Co., Ohio.
Children:
Henry—b. 28 March 1830, Ohio; d. 5 August 1904, Portland, Oregon; m. Eliza Jane Gibson, 1 January 1856; Washington Co., Oregon.
Edward—b. abt 28 March 1830, Perry Co., Ohio; d. 4 October 1904, Izee, Oregon; m. Sarelia Brown, 28 March 1855, Washington Co., Oregon. Sarelia was b. 1838; d. 1 April 1877, Forest Grove, Oregon.
Rose Ann (Rosanna)—b. 7 August 1832, Athens, Ohio; d. 19 October 1897, Forest Grove, Oregon; m. Henry Buxton, Jr., 28 September 1846, Washington Co.,

Oregon; DLC No. 3340, Washington Co. Henry was b. 8 October 1829, Manitoba, Canada.

Ellen—b. abt 1836, Ohio; d. 7 December 1901, Washington Co., Oregon; m. 1st, Joseph Rafferty, 1 March 1855; m. 2nd, Jerome A. Porter, 1862, Forest Grove, Oregon. Jerome was b. Orleans Co., New York, 5 March 1833.

Zumwalt, Christopher Peter—b. 12 August 1827, Callaway Co., Missouri; d. 6 June 1900, Perrydale, Oregon; DLC No. 2347, Polk Co.; m. Irene Goodrich (1845 pioneer who came to Oregon via the regular route), 3 August 1849, Yamhill Co., Oregon. She was b. 17 March 1831, Ripley Co., Indiana. Christopher came with his guardian, Joseph Hughart (*see* Roster); farmed; a reverend with the United Brethren Church.

THE HERREN DIARY

From *Albany Daily Democrat,* Thursday, January 1, 1891, p. 3:3 and Friday, January 2, 1891, p. 3:3-4.

A Diary of 1845

During the last two or three years there has been a great deal said as to the locality of the "Blue Bucket Mines." This is a place where a train of emigrants coming to Oregon in 1845 is said to have found an abundance of gold, though at the time they did not know what the mineral was. The train of emigrants had arrived at the mouth of the Malheur river where they were met by Stephen Meek, a trapper, and brother to Jo Meek, who claimed to know a shorter route to the Willamette Valley than by The Dalles. He persuaded them to follow his lead and he would lead them direct to the head of the valley by the McKinsey route. After traveling with him some distance they concluded he was a bilk and threatened to hang him. He left them. They became lost, many of their number died and they lost a good deal of stock. It was on the lost trip that they were said to have found gold. The following is an extract from a diary kept by Mr. Herron, father of W.J. Herron, of Salem, and of J.R. Herron, a former sheriff of Linn County. The diary was obtained by Jason Wheeler of this city, from J.R. Herron and copied. Mr. Herron afterwards lost the original. The following were captains in the trains that crossed on this route: Sol Tetherow, Owensby, Sinclair, and McNary. Among those in the trains were Samuel Parker, Mr. Herron, Anderson Cox, Hiram Smead, John Butt, Judge Stewart, Matt Scott, Mr. Terwilliger, Haman Lewis, Henry Marlin (the man who found the gold), Capt. King, H.J. Peterson and Wm. A. Peterson, now of this city. The diary runs from August 23 to September 8, 1845.

August 23rd.

This morning our company was called together, for the purpose of hiring a pilot to conduct us across the bend in Boise River and over the Blue Mountains, down to the Dalles, on the Columbia River. This route will cut off the bend of the road that leads down Burnt River, and is said to be one hundred and fifty (150) miles nearer than the old route. Price agreed on with Mr. Meek to take us through the new route was fifty dollars. So we got up our oxen and started about 9 o'clock, and traveled a northwest course to a beautiful stream of water called Malheur, about twelve miles from where we crossed the river, found plenty of grass and small willows to build a fire to get supper with, so there was no grumbling.

August 24th.

More oxen missing this morning. 11 o'clock before all the wagons were out of camp, traveled about 12 miles, 6 first miles northwest, then changed our course to southwest until we came to same stream of water that we encamped on last night, and found plenty of water and grass and dry willows to make fire with. The route to-day has been dry and uncommonly dusty, and entirely destitute of timber or vegetation of any kind, except wild sage, and it is dying very fast for want of rain; country tolerably level but not fit for cultivation. The Indians stole one horse last night within thirty yards of our encampment.

August 25th.

Started about 8 o'clock and encamped about 4. Traveled over some very rough road to-day, the fords of the creek very rough and rocky, the country very poor and broken, no timber only along the water courses. There are some willows and grass is very good on the low bottoms near the creek. Course to-day generally southwest, distance about ten miles.

August 26th.

Started half past seven. Still keeping up Malheur Creek and crossed it the second time, then we left it and turned into a gap into the Blue Mountains, over some tolerably rough road near our encampment and on the east of it was a boiling spring that afforded water enough where we found first-rate water and grass and willows, and a kind of soft wood called Balm. Distance, eighteen miles.

August 27th.

Late start this morning; nine oxen missing. 11 o'clock before all of the wagons were out of camp, then we moved off a southwest course about ten miles to the head of the same branch that we camped on last night; had some very rough road to-day, passed down one very rocky ravine, the valley of the little stream where we are to-night, and had it very dusty down the branch, found plenty of water and some willows, grass not good, very much dried up, mountains entirely barren, no soil here.

August 28th.

Made an early start this morning. Our pilot told us we had 18 miles to go to grass and water. So we traveled off at a quick pace but found no water, only a small spring that did not afford water enough to drink, so our poor oxen, cattle and horses had to suffer for water another night after a hard day's travel over some of the worst road that they have traveled over yet, for it was uncommonly rocky and hilly. We passed up one mountain to-day that was about three miles high besides several that were from 1/2 to 3/4 of a mile high, and down some that were very near a mile slope. Passed some cedar, though they were small; grass good; course today southwest.
80 miles from Boise River.

August 29th.

This morning we left our dry encampment and traveled about 3/4 of a mile a northwest course, then turning a northeast course one mile, then north 3/4 of a mile, then we turned northwest about 3 miles and passed up a mountain about one mile high; here we changed our course to west about one mile to the top of another mountain, here we discovered water and grass sufficient about 3 1/2 miles off, so we turned a southwest course over some as rocky road as ever I want to travel, for our wagons were off one rock on to another all of the way down the slope of the mountain, which occasioned a mighty jolting and rumbling with old wagons, for both men and cattle were in a hurry to get to water. We found a beautiful little stream of excellent water and plenty of grass, and willows that were dry and some cedar to make a fire with. We passed considerable cedar timber, but it was low and scrubby. We had considerable rain this evening. Distance nine miles.

August 30th.

This morning very wet and rainy; late breakfast. 9 o'clock before we collected our oxen together, 10 o'clock all of the wagons on the roll again. Traveled about 5 miles a west course to the stream that we left the 26th. Here we encamped for there are mountains all around us, and we have the Blue Mountains to climb over again to-morrow that are said to be 25 miles across. Grass very good and plenty of Willows, Alder, and Balm on the mountains. Some cedar but they are small and low; the mountains where we are now are covered with grass; it grows up under the snow in winter and dries up with the heat of summer, but does not rot like it would farther east where it rains through summer, for it seldom ever rains here in the summer. The cattle and horses eat it as well as they would well cured hay. Wild sage growing. Scarce 100 miles from Boise river.

August 31st.

Started about 8 o'clock with the expectation of crossing the mountains to-day. 7 oxen were missing, so we had to leave 5 wagons that did not come up with us until 2 o'clock and would not have overtaken us then if we had not laid by for them, so we traveled only 5 miles to-day and encamped south of a peak of the mountain that is about 2 miles high. We could see it five days before we came to it. There is on its summit a rock that is about one hundred feet high and has on its top some beautiful young pine. Our course to-day was about west over some very steep hills, and some rocks. Grass good and plenty of dry willows and Alder.

September 1st.

Made an early start. 7 o'clock all on the move again, about a southwest course. Soon crossed the little stream called Malheur for the last time I expect that I shall ever see it and unless it was better travelling on its banks than it is, I hope that no other emigrants will ever be gulled as we have been. On leaving this stream we traveled up a hollow or gulch that was I expect as rough a way as ever a wagon traveled. We had to remove some ten thousand stones before we could pass near the head of this ravine. We changed our course to south and turned down a dry hollow about 2 miles to where we found first-rate water. Some took dinner here, and then continued our course south down the branch about 1 mile, then we began to climb the mountains again, passed over some very high ones, until late in the evening we came into a valley and passed through it to a small stream running southwest, and encamped about half past six; found plenty of grass and some dry willow. Distance to-day 15 miles.

September 2nd.

Started about 8 o'clock and traveled about a south course 7 miles to the south branch of Malheur, and waited for one wagon that had the tongue broken out of it. 2 o'clock wagon up with the company. Here we turned a southwest course to a branch of the same stream we left at noon. It had nearly dried up. Grass very good on its banks, and a few willows.

Our road in the forenoon was very good, but in the afternoon the route was very hilly and stone. The mountains still continue covered with grass and some scrubby cedar, but a tree three feet in diameter will not be over twenty-five feet high. The country appears to be getting more level. Distance to-day about 12 miles.

September 3rd.

We started this morning about 8 o'clock, and traveled a southwest course over some very rough mountains and rock roads to another branch of the Malheur that afforded us good water and some grass, though not sufficient, and plenty of dry willows for fire wood, and some small cedar. We passed some pine timber to-day. Weather very warm and dry. There is nothing here to cheer our drooping spirits. We are making slow headway; the country here is so broken and rocky that we cannot get along fast, and we are rather doubtful that our pilot is lost for he has been seven days longer getting to the waters of Jay's river than he told us he would be. Some talk of stoning and others say hang him. I can not tell how the affair will terminate yet, but I will inform you in its proper place; 5 miles to-day southwest and 5 miles west. Total to-day, 10 miles. There is considerable cedar on the mountains here, but it is low and has limbs to the ground.

September 4th.

We started about 8 o'clock and traveled a south course about 4 miles, then turned southwest about 2 miles and passed down a very rocky hill or mountain into the valley of Jay's River, here we turned a west course about 8 miles to a beautiful little rivulet of water but no wood except small willows. Grass is very good. This valley is on the river that we have been looking for the last seven days. I hope the grumbling will cease now as our course appears to be west and the peak at the mouth of Jay's river, near the Columbia, is visible, and our pilot says it is about one hundred miles distance. To-day 14 miles.

September 5th.

We started at 8 o'clock and traveled a southwest course across the valley of Crooked or Jay's river, about 15 miles to a branch of Crooked river, which afforded plenty of grass and some fine dry willows for firewood; the water very bad, hardly fit for use. We passed over some very rich looking soil to-day but no timber. This valley is covered with wild sage. The country looks level as far as we can see to the west. We have been in sight of the Cascade mountains for the last twenty miles. The nights are very cold, days pleasant, looks like autumn had set in.

September 6th.

We started about 7 o'clock and traveled about south 15 miles. Here we came to a lake which caused us to turn to the west about 10 miles trying to get water we traveled until 8 o'clock at night, and encamped without wood, water, fire or supper, or anything to console us, so we laid down and took a good night's sleep, which revived us considerably. 176 miles from Boise river.

September 7th.

We started at 7 o'clock and traveled through a poor sandy valley 14 miles to a small stream of water about ten feet wide and nearly as many feet deep; water good and grass first-rate; no wood only sage. Course to-day west. Distance 15 miles.

September 8th.

We started at 8 o'clock and traveled west about 10 miles over some of the best road that we have had since we passed the Rocky Mountains, but in the evening we had some rocky road for a few miles; here we turned about two degrees north of west for about 5 miles and found no grass and had to encamp in a patch of wild sage, where it was as high as our wagons. About one mile south of where we are we found a little water, enough to cook supper with. The stream of water that we stayed on last night runs out of the side of a mountain through a hole about six feet in diameter; there is water enough within six feet of where it runs out to drown a horse. Passed some plains to-day that were covered. . .

N.B.—Here the diary was torn and mutilated so that I could not proceed with it any farther.

No. of miles traveled, 210. 226 miles from Boise river. 40 miles west of Harney Lake.

—Ben Walker

INDEX

(Roster material not included)

A

Abbot, Pacific Railroad Survey
    Party 82
Adams, Capt. T.M. 8
Agency Plains 60
Agency Valley 29
Alfalfa, Oregon 85
Allen, James 5
Altnow ranch 32
Ant Creek 83
Applegate Trail 12
Applegate, Jesse 138
Ash Hollow, Wyoming 9

B

Bacon, J.M. 116
Bakeoven 103
Bancroft, H.H. 20, 112
Barlow Company 8 - 9
Barlow Road 12, 119
Barlow, Samuel 20 - 21
Barlow, William 9, 18
Bayley, Betsy (Elizabeth) 48
Bayley, Daniel D. 139
Bear Creek 62, 64, 82 - 85, 95,
    115
Belden, H. 115, 119
Bend, Oregon 86, 143
Bendire Range 29
Bennett place 55
Bennett, Lucy Hall 112
Beulah Dam 30
Big Rock Creek 35
Big Sandy River 11
Big Soldier Creek 7
Blue Bucket xv, 32, 81, 84 - 85,
    88, 90 - 91, 93, 95, 97, 99,
    101

Blue Bucket Creek 101
Blue Bucket Train xx
Blue Mountains 13, 15 - 16, 33,
    37, 40, 98, 141
Boise Valley 15
Bolter place 103
Bonneville, Captain xvii, 40
Box Canyon Creek 81
Breese, Eldred M. 57
Broken Top 58
Brown, Captain 4, 20
Bryant, Mrs. 119
Buck Creek 52 - 53, 55, 94
Buck Hollow 104, 107, 109
Buckaroo Springs 28
Buckley, J.W. 84
Bull Mountain 103
Bully Creek 20, 25, 27 - 28
Burnett, Peter H. 3, 16
Burns, Oregon 36
Burnt River 15, 20, 28
Butler, Isaac 101
Butts, Mrs. John (Catherine) 52,
    107, 109, 114 - 115, 119

C

California Trail 11
Camp Creek 53, 55 - 56, 88, 100
Camp Creek Valley 100
Campbell, Robert xvii - xviii
Carter, Fred 86
Cascade Mountains 40, 45, 95,
    101, 104, 117
Castle Rock 21, 29 - 31, 115
Catching, Mr. 115
Cayuse Indians 15
Center family 120
Center, Samuel 81

269

INDEX

INDEX

ADDENDUM TO ROSTER

*Doak, Andrew Jackson—b. 1816, Campbell Co., Tennessee; d. 16 June 1880, Cottage Grove, Lane Co., Oregon; DLC No. 4334, Polk Co.

*Doak, Mary Rebecca (McConnel)—b. 1826, Pike Co., Missouri; d. 29 March 1854, Polk Co., Oregon; m. Andrew, 8 December 1838, Pike Co., Missouri; he m. 2nd, Elizabeth Hale, 16 April 1856, Polk Co., Oregon; m. 3rd, Sarah Jones, 16 June 1864, Lane Co., Oregon; 4th, Catherine Zumwalt, 1871.

Children:

*Josiah Allen—b. 17 February 1840, Pike Co., Missouri; d. 21 April 1907, Bandon, Coos Co., Oregon; m. Ceceilia Isabel Butts, 20 July 1871, Sonoma Co., California. She was b. 21 September 1854, Placerville, El Dorado Co., California; d. 26 October 1936, Marshfield, Coos Co., Oregon.

*Cynthia Jane—b. 10 July 1841, Pike Co., Missouri; d. 30 December 1914, Payette, Canyon Co., Idaho; m. John Angel, 14 or 18 May 1856, Polk Co., Oregon; he was b. 21 April 1830; d. 20 May 1860, Polk Co.; she m. 2nd, Harrison Hale, 28 October 1860, Polk Co.; m. 3rd, Fred Sherman.

*James Thomas—b.1844, Bowling Green, Pike Co., Missouri; d. 31 October 1906, Prineville, Oregon; m.

Malinda J. Briant, 10 September 1863, Lane Co., Oregon.

(Andrew Doak established Doak's Ferry on the west bank of Willamette River, about 6 miles north of Salem. It carried wheat, mail, and passengers. Here the vanished town of Lincoln flourished.)

McNary, Hugh—Nephew To Alexander and James McNary, and "Kitty" Whitley (see Roster); son of Hugh McNary, who was a brother to Alexander, James, and Kitty. A James McNary descendant has stated that the nephew came with these relatives.